*At twenty-two years old, New York City, 1975*

"The Desmond you don't kn[...]
taught me the next level of [...]
true aspects of friendship: tr[...]

"He only knows how to write [...]

"I can describe him in three [...]

"I love myself for writing wit[...]

"The first time we met, we wrot[...]
five minutes—and I'm not b[...]
genius."

"Desmond Child is a game-cha[...]
ducer, and visionary, he has [...]
the global soundscape, addin[...]
ues to light up our musical c[...]

"For more than five decades of [...]
two centuries . . . Desmond C[...]
as the king and queen of pop[...]
lem is trying to figure out wh[...]

"Desmond Child . . . always a [...]

# DESMOND CHILD
## LIVIN' ON A PRAYER
## BIG SONGS BIG LIFE

### WITH DAVID RITZ

### FOREWORD BY PAUL STANLEY

RADIUS BOOK GROUP
NEW YORK

Radius Book Group
A Division of Diversion Publishing Corp.
www.RadiusBookGroup.com

"Midnight Streets" lyrics on page 110 © 1982 by Gypsy Vans Music Company (ASCAP).

"The Truth Comes Out" lyrics on page 121 © 1979 by DESMOBILE MUSIC, INC. / Universal PolyGram International Publishing (ASCAP).

Quote on page 160 from Face the Music: A Life Exposed, by Paul Stanley © 2014 by HarperOne.

"Cuba Libre" lyrics on page 275 © 2023 DESTON ANTHEMS / BMG Gold Songs (ASCAP), Sigersongs (ASCAP).

"Lady Liberty" lyrics on pages 324–25 © 2018 by DESTON ANTHEMS / BMG Gold Songs (ASCAP).

"Mis Cajas De Cartón" lyrics on pages 352–53 and "My Cardboard Boxes" lyrics on pages 354–55 © 2022 by Rodaje Music (BMI).

LA MUSA™ statue on page 353 is a registered trademark™ of Desmond Child dba LA MUSA Elena Casals for the Arts.

For more information, email info@radiusbookgroup.com.

First edition: September 2023
Retail Hardcover ISBN: 9781635768534
eBook ISBN: 9781635768527

Manufactured in the United States of America and Britain
10   9   8   7   6   5   4   3   2

Cover design by Desmond Child and Jorge Rodriguez Real
Interior design by Neuwirth & Associates, Inc.

Radius Book Group and the Radius Book Group colophon are registered trademarks of Radius Book Group, a Division of Diversion Publishing Corp.

For my husband, Curtis,
our sons, Roman and Nyro,
and in memory of
my mother, Elena Casals

*Desmond & Winston, New York City, 1992*

To Winston Simone,
manager of a lifetime

# TABLE OF CONTENTS

"It was Paul Stanley who taught me how to
write stadium anthems the KISS way.
His towering influence is alive in every hit song
I've ever written. There is no Desmond Child
without Paul Stanley."

—DESMOND CHILD

# FOREWORD
## By Paul Stanley

It's 1977. I'm walking down Eighth Street in Greenwich Village when I see flyers on a telephone pole for a group called Desmond Child & Rouge. Their image captivates me: a young man with curly, coiffed blond hair, and three sultry dark-haired urban-styled young women. They're playing an uptown club called Trax. I decide to check them out.

It takes only minutes before I'm blown away. The music speaks to me. The music kills me. Rouge—the three ladies—are sensational. They sing with unabashed joy and sensuality. The backing band lays down flawless grooves. And there's Desmond, front and center. The leader. The front man. The songwriter. The architect.

Des sings with a theatricality more rooted in passion than Broadway.

I think: if Doc Pomus and Laura Nyro had a baby delivered at the Brill Building, his name would be Desmond Child.

I go backstage to meet the man. Turns out we share the same roots and inspirations. We become fast friends. In no time, Des and I are writing together. Our first song, "The Fight," is sung on his group's first album. Our second song, "I Was Made For Lovin' You," becomes KISS's first and only Top 5 song worldwide.

Our friendship is forged in mutual appreciation. Our paths cross often.

Now it's 1984. KISS takes a fledging band called Bon Jovi as our opening act. The group desperately needs a hit. Their manager Doc McGhee asks me to write with them. I agree, but only if I can also produce their album. Doc says no. I say, "Fine, but if you're looking for someone who can cowrite smashes, call this man." I give him Desmond's number. Thank God Doc says no to me and yes to Des who does what I never could have. He solidifies and elevates their writing to a stellar level that becomes a template for decades to come. "Livin' On A Prayer." "Bad Name." Incredible.

With that mega success comes constant requests for him to work his magic with top artists the world over, many of whom have fallen from popular favor. Every time, Des knocks it out of the park.

Ironically, it's sad to see Des sometimes shunned by certain collaborators, where his only crime is reigniting their career. Some go as far as to say, "We don't need Desmond Child." Wrong. They do need him. We all do.

Over the years, he and I go on to write great classics for KISS. On his own, Desmond hits the top of the charts time and again. While some see me as the guy who gives him his big break, the truth is that his meteoric rise is inevitable. Six decades of hits attest to that fact.

In reading his memoir, I learn of the remarkable drama of his life. Some things I already know; many I do not. There's exhilaration, there's darkness, struggle, triumph, heartache—all the elements that constitute a singular and compelling story.

It is my good fortune to continue to connect with this funny, complex and kind shaman. What a joy to watch him pull hit melodies and lyrics out of thin air!

I remain proud—and deeply grateful—to call him a true and loving friend.

# INTRODUCTION
## By David Ritz

JON BON JOVI and Joe Perry had told me about Desmond Child, describing him as a songwriting sorcerer with a magic sauce all his own.

"He's the dude who taught me the true meaning of friendship," said Jon.

So when Des called and said he wanted to discuss doing a book, I was pumped. I'd finally get to meet the sorcerer himself.

He showed up at my home office, sat on the couch, and announced, "No questions are off-limits."

It took less than thirty minutes for his tears to flow. He wore his heart on his sleeve. His story came pouring out—the pain, heartaches, triumphs, transformations.

I was stunned.

I signed on. And off we went, interviewing and writing around the world. Three weeks on a Greek island. Months in Destonia, his Nashville compound. Months in his New York Cole Porter-esque apartment overlooking Central Park. Months in and out of the hottest studios in LA.

Des talks like he writes; Des talks like he sings. His storytelling has a spellbinding rhythm and rhyme. His complexities, contradictions, mental gymnastics, unbridled enthusiasm— they add up to a charisma of astounding singularity.

Ain't no one like Desmond Child.

Ours became more a musical jam than a literary collaboration. His brilliance as a writer emerged in new and surprising ways. His ability to turn a phrase, go deep, employ humor, and, most impressively, bring light to darkness.

In working with others, I've seen how darkness can frighten. But Des not only refused to shy away from the most challenging chapters in his story—he embraced them.

The result is a book of rare courage.

Here's what I did wrong.

Here's what I did right.

This is who I was.

This is who I wanted to be.

This is who I am.

*With David Ritz, Folegandros, Greece, 2016*

PART ONE


FROM CUBA, WITH LOVE
AND CHAOS

# WHAT'S A SONG DOCTOR?

I DON'T LIKE THE TERM. "Song doctor" was something that Gene Simmons said when asked about my contributions to two major KISS hits. In the minds of many rock bands, the doctor comes in to treat the patient—the already composed song—with a couple of vitamin shots. The doctor's role is viewed as minimal. He's not really a writer; he's a fixer. I reject that notion. Of the thousands of songs I've cowritten, I've never simply "fixed" a song. The magic that happens between two or more songwriters is impossible to break down systematically. It's not science; it's art. I may be brought in when a melody or lyric has already been suggested. I may alter that melody. I may continue the storyline or come up with an entirely different narrative. Or start from scratch, which is most often the case. Because I am both a musician and a lyricist, a piano player and a vocalist, a producer and an arranger, I come to a song from many different angles. The same is true with my dozens of collaborators. They bring their strengths as well. That's why my approach is that credit be distributed equally among all participants. Even if someone did nothing but add a few words, change a few notes, or tweak a melody, those additions, changes, or tweaks might be the very thing that sparks the song's success.

But egos are egos, and egos can sometimes undermine the collaborative process and its aftermath. Before you enter the room, the sign may say, "Leave your ego at the door," but when the song is written and you leave the room, your ego is right there waiting for you. When the song becomes a smash, your ego emboldens, especially if you're the bandleader hungry for credibility as a writer. It's easy to forget—or resent the fact—that you didn't write the song alone. I've seen this pattern emerge over and again.

Yet collaboration is at the heart of my songwriting process. I love kicking ideas around. I love working with one or two other composers, men and women whose backgrounds and instincts are different than my own. It's an exhilarating experience that never grows old. No matter what has happened in my life, collaborative songwriting has been a constant.

It's nearly impossible not to become friends with your collaborators.

The experience breeds intimacy. When done best, it's a heart-to-heart exchange. Sometimes, though, it can take a while for hearts to open. Other times, the chemistry is instant.

That was the case when Jon Bon Jovi called to ask me to write with him and his lead guitarist, Richie Sambora.

I didn't know this then, but Jon's plan was that he, Richie, and I would write together and generate some income by composing songs for major artists other than Bon Jovi. Ironically, we got together only months after I was dropped as a writer from Walden Cotillion Music, the publishing arm of Atlantic Records. They didn't think I had written enough hits for them and didn't pick up my third term.

The initial Bon Jovi/Sambora/Child session took place in the dead of winter in a little wooden house on the edge of a New Jersey swamp where Richie still lived with his mom and dad. Nearby was a complex of oil refineries looming over the brown and gray marsh. It was not an idyllic rock 'n' roll setting that day, or maybe it was, as it turned out to be an auspicious beginning of an ongoing collaboration. From the start we adopted a motto, "Dare to suck," meaning no creative idea was out of bounds or subject to scorn.

We worked in a cold laundry-room basement where they had set up a keyboard for me on a rickety Formica dinette table from the fifties. Although Bon Jovi hadn't hit mega-stardom yet, they had a coterie of fans. In fact, through the muddy basement windows I could see the ankles of girls walking around the house in hopes of getting a glance at their young idols. In his early twenties, Jon was the most handsome, and the smartest, of all the hair-band heroes. He was sweet and thoughtful and fixated on fame. His drive was unrelenting. In spite of the fact that I was living in an all-for-one commune, my drive was just as strong.

The session started tentatively. The mood wasn't helped by the buzz of an electric space heater that competed with the gritty hum of white noise emanating from Richie's amp. Jon paced restlessly. To break the ice, I literally pulled a title out of my back pocket, something I had brought along in case things got slow. Instantly, Jon flashed his million-dollar smile, threw in the line "Shot through the heart and you're to blame, darlin'" before the three of us shouted out the title, "You Give Love A Bad Name!"

Jon felt the song was so good that he dropped the plan of shopping it to other artists and decided to cut it with Bon Jovi. Turned out to be Bon Jovi's first Number 1 single. Jon, Richie, and I had formed an inviolable circle of trust.

Yet our productive collaboration almost ended before it started. Their management wanted me to sell my share of the song for $35,000 and remove my name as a cowriter, forever bolstering the idea of Jon and Richie as a self-contained writing team in the tradition of Lennon-McCartney and Jagger-Richards. I was incensed. Bypassing our representatives, I went straight to Jon and laid it on the line.

"Tell them to back off," I said, "or you'll never see me again."

To Jon's everlasting credit, he did the right thing and set it straight. I received a third of the song.

We were back on track a few weeks later in New York City when Jon, Richie, and I borrowed a friend's apartment with an old out-of-tune upright.

It was one of those magical moments when, as Jon said, "Three guys walk in a room with blank pieces of paper and walk out with a song that changes the course of popular music."

Jon wanted to write a working-class anthem. He remembered Bonnie and Joe, two friends from high school who struggled to make ends meet. I could relate. I thought of my own special love story with Maria Vidal when we first started Desmond Child & Rouge.

My first impulse was to suggest, "Johnny used to work on the docks." I was Johnny—Johnny Barrett being my real name—but Jon thought that would be weird because fans would think that he was singing about himself. So we came up with the sound-alike, "Tommy." "Gina works the diner all day" referred to Maria's job as a singing waitress at a joint called Once Upon a Stove, in Manhattan, where, due to her stunning dark looks, her nickname was Gina Velvet, as in Gina Lollobrigida.

Richie added the second "whoa" after "halfway there" that moves upward at the top of the chorus, a "whoa" that would cause generations of Bon Jovi fans to throw their fists up in the air for decades to come. Thus, "Livin' On A Prayer" was born.

After writing with Jon and Richie, I was hanging out with Paul Stanley at his chic East-side apartment. Paul has great style. He was the only guy I knew who zipped around Manhattan in a souped-up, tricked-out black Batmobile sports car.

"Let's go for a ride," he urged.

Racing up the FDR Drive under a full moon with the lights of Brooklyn twinkling across the river, we caught up on our recent activities. As always, KISS was breaking box office records.

"What's new with you, Des?" Paul asked.

I mentioned Bon Jovi, to whom he had recommended me to. Like athletes, rock stars have strong competitive energy. Yet out of pure friendship, Paul was supportive of my new collaboration and wanted to hear what I'd done.

I slipped in a cassette of the final mixes of "Livin' On A Prayer" and "You Give Love A Bad Name." This was before the songs were released.

As the music soared out into the night air, Paul nodded and smiled. His smile spoke volumes. I had the approval of one of my most important mentors.

The Bon Jovi album that featured both songs, *Slippery When Wet,* was released during the summer of 1986 and catapulted the band to the top. The album was Number 1 for eight weeks. Its first two singles—"You Give Love A Bad Name" and "Livin' On A Prayer"—were also number one. On the strength of these two songs, Bon Jovi took its place in history among the world's biggest rock 'n' roll bands.

Suddenly I was the hottest hitmaker in the pop world.

Want a hit? Call Desmond Child. He's the man.

*Mimí, Pinar del Rio, Cuba, 1943*

# DOÑA TRISTEZA

I BECAME A MAN at age five . . . or at least it felt that way.

The scene burns with an intensity that hasn't diminished in six decades. It was 1957 and my mother, at age thirty, was fleeing her husband, the man I was told was my father. I didn't know why we were moving from his dairy farm in Hawthorne, Florida, just outside Gainesville, to Miami. All I knew was that we were roaring down a highway into the heart of darkness. I was seated next to my mother with my little brother Fred, fast asleep in the back seat, when suddenly a huge storm hit—sheets of rain, bolts of lightning, booms of thunder. We had to pull over. We were lost. She hugged the steering wheel and sobbed uncontrollably.

"I can't do this!" she cried to me in Spanish. "I feel so alone."

"Don't cry, Mamá. It will be all right."

But it was never really all right. Even though I managed to calm her down and take charge, I had a terrible sinking feeling. I had to get us to Miami. From now on, my survival . . . our survival . . . were all on me. I had to open the map and show her the way to Miami, where a life of uncertainty awaited. That's one place this story could begin.

But there's a sunnier opening. This one has me escorting my mother into the spotlight. This is where she always longed to stand while I hid in her shadow. Emerging from that shadow has been the challenge of a lifetime.

Whether I like it or not, my mother, though gone from this world for ten years, will still insist on this spotlight. She will find her way into the center of this story and want to make it hers. That's just her way. So let me, with all due respect, introduce to you the one, the only . . . Elena Casals.

A woman of dazzling contradictions, my mother was a combination of Tennessee Williams's Blanche DuBois and Angelica Huston's Lilly Dillon in *The Grifters*. Elena—called Mimí—was Cuban born, Cuban bred, Cuban Cuban Cuban. An extraordinary poet, songwriter, seductress, and con artist, she was a bohemian who wore pants when women weren't wearing pants or, when wearing a dress, would sit with her legs spread open like a man. Her hair was askew, her blue-green eyes burning with passionate ambition. She was beautiful. She was untamable. She was tall and skinny with movie-star charisma that could melt any man. She played with words the way children play with toys. She was a wit. And in so many ways, both fascinating and infuriating, she was out of her mind. Her one hit song, recorded by Cuban crooner Roberto Ledesma, was "Muchisimo," which could be translated as "so very much." There was so very much of Mimí to deal with.

If I tell you that I became a man at age five, let me see if I can figure out when my mother became a woman. That won't be easy, because her history is a scramble of scattered stories, passed down to me by her sisters and brothers.

It begins in Pinar del Rio—a forest of pines by the river—a provincial city three hours west of Havana. That's where Mimí, born January 28, 1927, grew up in a once-noble domicile built after the Spanish American War by Nicolas Martínez Suárez, my mother's maternal grandfather. After his death in 1949 at eighty-nine, their once-prosperous lifestyle degenerated. My mother's parents, Carlos Rodríguez and his wife, Blanca Martínez, lived with their eight children and my grandmother's three spinster sisters, who had inherited the house. My grand-father never made a dime.

Abuelo, as I called him, was a man of intellect and vision. He dreamed of building a bridge from the tip of Cuba to Cancún. Abuela, my grandmother, was proud of her French ancestors. She dreamed of restoring her family's fallen glory. The reclamation of past glory is a major theme in this story. Like my mother and her mother before her, I am driven by aspirational energy. The stigma of falling from affluence to poverty is a pain that remains untreated. My mother spent her life trying to cover up that pain, but the shame never disappeared. It only grew in secret spaces.

Mimí was her father's favorite. She was a wild child and the class clown. When the nuns expelled her for disruptive behavior, my grandfather founded a small school with a progressive agenda. And even they expelled her. Her precociousness endeared her to her dad. She helped him organize his esoteric papers on strange gyroscopic inventions attempting to unravel the secrets of perpetual motion. She embodied the spirit of the modern woman. She would not defer to men. Buying into her father's mad vision, she became the surrogate son his actual sons could never be. She filled her diaries with poems and lyrics. They were both romantics—Abuelo in science and Mimí in art. Even as the winds of fortune blew them in different directions, they would ultimately reunite, the father-daughter bond the major force in my mother's life.

Mimí was forever rewriting her own history, whose climax, she promised me, would be rewards and riches beyond my imagination. That moment was always at hand yet endlessly elusive. I believe she possessed genuine genius. By any measure, she was a narcissist of spectacular proportions who, at the same time, had powerful altruistic impulses. She wanted to both save and conquer the world, and dragged me along with her.

Elena Casals was the woman who gave me life . . . her life. And yet, wildly self-delusional, she deceived me about the identity of my true father for the first eighteen years of my existence.

Meanwhile, back in Cuba . . .

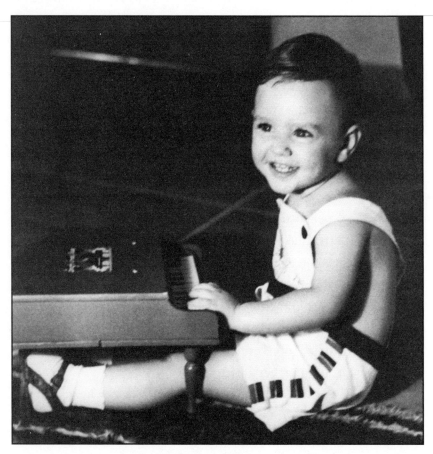

*Edificio FOCSA, Havana, Cuba, 1955*

# VIVA LA REVOLUCIÓN

IRONICALLY, all through the fifties, Cuba enjoyed one of the highest standards of living in Latin America. The country had a prosperous upper class, a healthy middle class, and a poor agrarian class called *campesinos*. When Fulgencio Batista, who had been legitimately elected president of Cuba a decade earlier, took over in 1953, he galvanized power in a US-backed dictatorship that partnered with American mobsters and corporate CEOs.

White upper-class Cubans, historically racist, looked down on him because of his mixed Spanish/Chinese/Afro-Cuban blood. The ruling class, along with intellectual rebels, many of whom, like Castro, were highly educated products of well-to-do families, denounced the deterioration of Cuba's political culture. They saw Batista as a pernicious pimp. Thus, the revolution, realized in 1959, enjoyed broad support among Cuban civil society. In the years before and after, fate swept our family into the vortex of the storm.

My mother arrived in Havana in 1950 to study bookkeeping and typing. She never graduated high school. Unruly behavior was always her downfall. Attention deficit disorder hadn't yet been discovered, but surely she suffered its effects.

In those prerevolution days, Mimí ran with poets and painters. She learned English, wrote her boleros, and befriended the literati. When an engaging young gay man in his early twenties, Jay Jensen, came to Havana with his mother and Tennessee Williams, she attached herself to the trio. She became lifelong friends with Jay, who would later loom large in our life. The four of them sat around Havana cafes where Tennessee, then forty-one, sipped rum and told tales of New York and Hollywood. With the recent release of his *A Streetcar Named Desire* starring Marlon Brando, the playwright was at the zenith of his fame.

Despite the intellectual stimulation Mimí cultivated, she felt like a lost cause. Unlike her younger sister Beba, she lacked confidence when it came to men. She was afraid of becoming a spinster like her elderly aunts in Pinar del Rio. Tall and slender, Mimí did not fit the mold of the buxom and curvy Latin woman. She needed a man to rescue her.

John Barrett, whom she encountered when she was twenty-four in 1951, became that man. They met at the bar at Havana's famed Hotel Nacional. Barrett was a successful petroleum geologist with wide-ranging entrepreneurial interests. An imposing figure, he was a tall and rugged blue-eyed blond *Americano* with big plans for the future. Barrett was Harrison Ford in *Indiana Jones*. Mimí was a beguiling and accomplished composer. One of her boleros, "Doña Tristeza," said it all: "Lady Sorrow." Unrequited love was her favorite theme. Her marriage was born out of a desperate need for bigger and better things than her scrappy life in Pinar del Rio. After a whirlwind romance of little more than a month, John and Mimí married. He whisked her off to the dusty oil fields of Ecuador before a new job took them to the jungles of Venezuela.

Because of his work, Barrett and Mimí moved to remote Lake Maracaibo, far across from a bustling boomtown overrun by World War II European exiles looking to cash in on the oil discoveries. On Wednesdays, while her husband worked, Mimí took a ferry that reached the city's shore. She wandered the town, perusing the shops and taking in a matinee at the only movie house. One afternoon she walked into the empty theater.

*Mimí's wedding to Daddy Barrett, Havana, 1951*

*Mimí and Daddy Barrett, Cuerna Vaca Farm, Hawthorne, Florida, 1954*

A man followed her in and sat next to her. With his slicked-back dark hair and twinkling eyes, he was often mistaken for Errol Flynn. As Mimí watched the film *National Velvet* with Elizabeth Taylor, she felt the heat of his eyes on her. Afterwards, he introduced himself. He was Joe Marfy. Although his Spanish was perfect—he spoke five languages—his heavy accent was foreign. He was a thirty-three-year-old Hungarian businessman with enterprises in several continents. He was a charmer. She accepted his invitation to a sidewalk café where they drank lemon daiquiris. She spoke of her Cuban ancestry, her songs, hopes, and dreams. I do not know whether she spoke of her husband.

They met at the theater every Wednesday for weeks on end. Their dalliances grew longer, their intimacy more intense. Their romance consummated with my conception on her twenty-sixth birthday. Later that same day, Mimí accompanied Marfy to the Maracaibo airport, where he picked up his close friends the Kovacs, Hungarian Jewish Holocaust survivors, and their teenage daughter Valeria.

Out of guilt and fear, Mimí ended the affair without telling Marfy that she was pregnant. One Wednesday, she simply failed to show up at the movie theater—no explanation, no goodbye. Without her phone number or address, Marfy was helpless. Week after week he returned, anxiously pacing in front of the theater. Week after week, no Mimí.

When Mimí told Barrett she was pregnant, he knew the child wasn't his. Because he'd never mentioned his low sperm count, she thought she was fooling him. No fool, Barrett, knowing Mimí was having an affair, quit his job and moved her back to northern Florida, where he bought a dairy farm in Hawthorne called Cuerna Vaca. He turned cold and sullen, began drinking heavily, and wouldn't speak to her for days on end.

I was born John Charles Barrett in Gainesville on October 28, 1953.

Because that was the day of Saint Jude Thaddaeus, patron of desperate causes to whom Mimí had prayed throughout her pregnancy, she called it a miraculous birth.

Mimí was miserable. The dairy farm was out in the sticks. The presence of Barrett's elderly mother, Edith Yates, a severe English woman from Manchester—where she had served as upstairs chambermaid for the Wedgewoods, makers of the famous porcelain—was a source of further pain. Edith's snobbish scorn cut Mimí to the quick, exacerbating her sense of isolation.

My earliest memories are of Mimí writing her boleros on a decrepit out-of-tune upright piano. Listening to her sad songs of vanquished love, I saw tears rolling down her cheeks, wetting the keys beneath her fingers.

*Me and Mimí, Miami Beach, 1954*

# BEBA'S MAMBO

WHILE MY MOTHER HAD FOUND AN ESCAPE from the island, the rest of her family had not. They were stuck, wasting away in the backwaters of Pinar del Rio. My grandfather, the mad scientist, had no means to generate income. My grandmother grieved the loss of her nobility. They had little going for them, save handsome sons and beautiful daughters. The most beautiful was Beba, the fifth of eight, with a sparkling smile and a voluptuous body. Beba was also the most audacious and ambitious. She had the means to flip the script. The old script said, "Nothing will ever change." The new script, "Someday soon everything will change."

It began innocently—or perhaps not. As she walked past an outdoor café dressed in her school uniform, she caught the eye of Jose Pepin Bosch, head of Bacardi rum and one of the wealthiest men in Cuba. At sixteen, Beba was an intoxicating mixture of Ingrid Bergman and Grace Kelly. Bosch called her over and bought her an ice cream. She was flattered. He was smitten. They soon met clandestinely. He began bringing her fancy dresses that she hid in their boxes behind the chamber pot beneath her bed.

In 1952, when Bosch arranged for Beba to meet him at a fancy ball at the local country club, she brought along her little sister Miriam and dressed her up in one of Bosch's party dresses. Beba understood that the only way out of the family's crumbling future was to engage power. Only a powerful man could save them. And since men were her forte, she, by extension, would save her family. All she needed was the right catch.

Those were the thoughts running through her mind when the orchestra paused as the mayor of the city approached the microphone.

"It is my high privilege," he said, "to introduce the twelfth president of Cuba, the honorable Fulgencio Batista."

Batista had already started his alliance with mobsters like Meyer Lansky. He was in the process of consolidating his political base as well as his wealth. Beba caught his immediate attention.

"Who is that stunning beauty?" he asked Bosch. "You must introduce me." A practical businessman, Bosch did Batista's bidding. While the president and Beba danced, he whispered, "Come to Havana."

"Bring me to Havana," she replied.

In the months that followed, Beba and Batista grew closer. Aside from Miriam, neither Beba's family nor Batista's wealthy wife, Marta, had any idea. Marta, in fact, lived a separate life among the Palm Beach and New York elite. Finally, Batista insisted that Beba move to Havana, but it would be on her terms. As a proper young woman about to enter high society, she and her entire family would have to move there as well and be given great favor. Batista agreed and bankrolled the operation. He assured Beba that in due time he would leave Marta. Beba would become his princess of Monaco.

Just like that, my mother's parents and their grown children left Pinar del Rio and relocated to Havana, where my grandfather was appointed president of the Colegio de Comercio, a spectacular transformation from his go-nowhere life. Miriam was awarded a scholarship at the university. Her older brother Carlucho rose in the ranks of the military and studied engineering while the other two brothers, living the fast life, became performers at the Tropicana. The family was given several large apartments in the *Edificio FOCSA,* Havana's toniest address. The exclusive building had separate hidden hallways and elevators for the servants, thus ensuring that residents and the help never brushed shoulders.

Beba made a splash. Her picture appeared in the society columns. She was seen at the Riviera, the Comodoro Yacht Club, and soon became Havana's "It Girl." For her birthday, Batista gave her a shiny new powder-blue Buick to match her eyes. She became a one-woman welcoming committee offering to show the island to American movie stars staying at the Hotel Nacional. Among them, off on a wild binge, was the young Marlon Brando.

My grandparents surely knew that their good fortune was due to Beba.

They certainly had to oppose their daughter's involvement with a married man, but, given the fact that the man ran the country, these objections were best left unsaid. Miriam, who became a radicalized anti-Batista rebel and would soon marry a fiery revolutionary, most probably did object. At the same time, not to be undone by Beba, she went platinum-blond a lá Kim Novak and entered the Miss Cuba beauty pageant. The competition between the sisters was the talk of the town.

The same year the family moved to Havana, 1954, Joe Marfy had not given up his search for my mother. He was still obsessed with Mimí. In fact, he traveled to Havana, hoping to pick up her trail. He went to the Hotel Nacional to have a drink at the same bar where Mimí had met Barrett.

Sipping his Cuba libre, he surveyed the scene. Suddenly at the end of the bar, there she was! That face! Those smiling eyes! It was Mimí. Except it wasn't. It was Beba.

Quickly learning that Beba was Mimí's sister, Marfy questioned her closely. Beba's news shocked him: Mimí had given birth to a boy and was living in Florida. Marfy presumed the child was his. On the spot, he composed an impassioned letter on Hotel Nacional stationery that he asked Beba to mail to Mimí. Loving romantic entanglements, Beba agreed. She enclosed Marfy's letter inside one of her own. Mimí was startled. Marfy had found her! Fate had intervened! Her poetic soul soared. His pleas touched her heart.

"Meet me in Miami Beach," he begged. "Just for a few days. I need to see you. I need to see my son."

Her head reeling with confusion, she nonetheless agreed. At a discreet tropical deco hotel on Collins Avenue, Marfy, Mimí, and six-month-old me were together as a family for the first and only time. During those six days, Marfy convinced Mimí that she had made a mistake in staying in a loveless marriage and should allow him to bring us back to Venezuela, where we would all live happily ever after.

"Tell Barrett the truth," urged Marfy. "Let the truth set us all free." "Give me a month to put my life in order," said my mother. "I will tell him by then."

Exactly thirty days later, Marfy, along with his brother John, arrived at the Hawthorne dairy farm with a U-Haul, ready to move us out.

The encounter was bizarre. For a long while, Mimí and Marfy spoke on the front porch with me playing at their feet. Alas, she had broken her promise and not told Barrett that she was leaving. Then Barrett himself showed up, wanting to know who these strange men were. Rather than answer, Mimí fled inside and locked herself in the bathroom. She refused to come out.

Barrett spoke to her. Marfy spoke to her. Terrified and sobbing, she wouldn't come out. The men didn't know what to do.

They decided to give her time to think and left the house. During a long walk around the farm, Marfy told Barrett the truth about the affair and the fact that he was my father. Barrett had surmised as much. Without rancor, the two men came to a reasonable conclusion: the decision was Mimí's. If her choice was to go off with Marfy, fine; or if she decided to stay with Barrett, so be it.

When they returned, the sun was setting. The clock was ticking. Mimí was still locked in the bathroom. "The fact that she's not leaving with you," said Barrett, "means she's chosen to stay. Don't ever contact us again." Defeated, Marfy and his brother drove the empty U-Haul off into the dark night.

And so, for another seventeen and a half years, the deception continued. Mimí didn't tell me. Barrett didn't tell me. And when, a few years later, I met Marfy in Miami, he didn't tell me. Why the lie?

The reason was Mimí. She lived in fear of being condemned by her father and brothers. To be married to one man while having a child by another was too much shame to bear. Shame kept her from leaving with Marfy, her true love. She'd rather endure life with Barrett than admit to a humiliating transgression. Those were the times.

This seems strange, especially because the family's history was altered—and for years dramatically improved—by Beba's secret affair with Batista. The great tension was between desperation and respectability. The need for respectability is a huge tenet of Cuban life. The need for respectability has been a huge tenet of my life. But desperation is a powerful force, and, though my grandparents may have been shamed by their daughter's dalliance with the dictator, desperation to avoid financial ruin smothered that shame.

Similarly, Mimí stayed with Barrett to maintain her veneer of respectability until desperation cracked that veneer. Before that awful moment, though, Barrett tried his best to forgive her. Because he loved her and was grateful that she had not run off with her lover, he did all he could to make her happy.

*Joe Marfy, Mimí, and me, Cuerna Vaca Farm, Hawthorne, Florida, 1954*

*Joe Marfy and baby Desmond, Cuerna Vaca Farm, 1954*

*Daddy Barrett and Mimí with Joe Marfy, Cuerna Vaca Farm, 1954*

Barrett paid for Mimí's brother Bebo and spinster aunt Laura to come from Cuba to Hawthorne, where Bebo, then sixteen, worked as a farm boy and Laura helped care for me. Barrett also underwrote a trip for Mimí, myself, Laura, and Bebo to Havana, where I was baptized Juan Carlos Nicolás Tadeo Barrett Rodríguez. Barrett stayed behind, tending to the cows and teaching geology courses at the University of Florida. At one point he opened a roadside barbecue stand that went bust.

In 1955, when I was two, Barrett demonstrated even greater devotion to Mimí by moving all of us to Havana and renting an apartment in the storied *Edificio FOCSA*. In the eyes of Mimí's family, I was a blue-eyed blond-haired angel child. Mom dressed me like Little Lord Fauntleroy. I openly embraced this collection of aunts and uncles who, like many Cubans, excelled in theatrical storytelling. They doted over me, and none suspected, nor were ever told, that Barrett was not my biological father.

Though an extremely heavy drinker—he loved his mojitos and pisco sours—Barrett was resourceful and found geological work in Havana. But how to keep Mimí happy? It appeared that moving us into the *Edificio FOCSA* wasn't enough. She got Barrett to underwrite her own beauty shop. Magical thinking seduced her. This would be her big success. After a year, though, the shop went under. The pressure to give away free hairdos to family and friends did her in.

In the winter of that same year, 1955, Mimí met a certain Señor Aguiar in her doctor's office. Aguiar was a physician himself, a noted anesthesiologist. Like my mother, he was married. And like Marfy, Aguiar found Mimí irresistible. I don't know the length of their affair, but I do know that after the beauty shop folded and Mimí became pregnant, poor Barrett had had enough. He bought another dairy farm in Hawthorne and moved us back to Florida. When my brother Fred was born in August of 1956, the infant's dark hair and eyes gave away what was hardly a surprise to Barrett: Mimí's second son, like her first, was not his.

Yet Barrett acted as if he was—and so did Mimí. He indulged her with still another trip to Havana. In 1957, we arrived as one big happy family and reinstalled ourselves in the Edificio FOCSA, to be close to my beloved grandparents, uncles, and aunts. We stayed for several months. I was put into a Catholic school, which was fine with me, until the day Mimí forgot to pick me up. All the parents had collected their children. All the teachers had gone home. I was left alone in front of the school, waiting in vain. I wandered around, crossing the busy streets of downtown Havana. I was traumatized. By mere instinct, I found my way to the *Edificio FOCSA* where I was barely tall enough to reach the elevator button. When I got to our door, it was open, but no one was home. I went to Mimí's powder-blue bedroom and cried myself to sleep on the floor.

It was during this Havana stay that, for the second time, Marfy, in town on business, encountered Beba at the Hotel Nacional bar. It's staggering how, in the story of our family, all roads lead to that one bar.

At this point, Marfy was no longer single. Two years earlier, he had married Valeria Kovacs, the twenty-one-year-old daughter of his Hungarian Jewish friends Mimí had met the day I was conceived. He revealed none of this to Beba. What she revealed to Marfy, though, was that Mimí was presently in Havana and living at the *Edificio FOCSA*. Knowing that, he couldn't stay away. Did he think Mimí might change her mind and leave Barrett for him? Or did he just want to see me, his son? Whatever his reasons, he showed up at the high-rise and was startled when

Mimí stood there holding a six-month-old baby, my brother Fred. At first, he thought Fred was me. But how could that be? I was nearly four. Beba hadn't told Marfy that Mimí had given birth to another boy.

As he entered the apartment, my father saw Barrett in the living room socializing with an oil executive from Venezuela who, by chance, was also a friend of Marfy's. Small world. Awkward moment.

"Joe Marfy," said Barrett. "What the hell are you doing here?"

"Just came by to pay my respects."

Observing this, Mimí, with Fred in her arms, began waltzing around the room as Doris Day's "Que Sera Sera" played on the phonograph. This was her bizarre way of coping or not coping with the arrival of Marfy. She wouldn't stop dancing, nor would she say a word to Marfy, my father, or Barrett, the man she wanted her family to believe was my father.

Much later in our lives, Marfy told me that he saw this occasion as his last chance of winning Mimí back. When she wouldn't stop dancing to look him in the eye, he knew all hope was gone. He started to leave and, in the foyer of the apartment, suffered an anxiety attack that brought him to his knees.

A month later, back in Hawthorne, Mimí was more miserable than ever. She had now twice rejected Marfy's attempt to save her from a loveless marriage. The shame of having two children who were not Barrett's was a secret she could never reveal. The shame of admission was as oppressive as her desolate life on the dairy farm. There were a few respites.

One was the presence of Lee Burnham, a snowbird sculptress from New York who sought the warmth of Florida winters. I believe Lee fell in love with Mimí, who, without reciprocating with romantic passion, did befriend the artist and sat as a model for several works of art. One became known as La Musa, a clay sculpture of a seated woman holding a guitar, her head turned to the side. Looking at it, you can practically hear my mother singing one of her heartbreaking boleros. This fragile artwork miraculously survived many moves and, a lifetime later, was adopted as the symbol of the Latin Songwriters Hall of Fame. In the meantime, the real flesh-and-blood La Musa felt imprisoned by her life in Hawthorne. She kept saying, "I'm suffocating. I can't take it anymore. I can't live with this man."

As it turned out, she couldn't live with any man for long, especially those who tried to love her. I can only speculate that her narcissism kept her from feeling or receiving genuine intimacy. Beyond that, she suffered from bipolarity that encompassed a poetic propensity for fantasy. Mimí's default position was to envision us living in a mansion on Miami Beach. But based on what? Her poetry? Her songs? Her earnings from those sources were nonexistent. These were baseless daydreams. No wonder *The Prince and the Pauper* was my favorite book as a child. I bought into those daydreams.

But that stormy night in 1957 was no daydream. Mimí's decision was final. She was leaving Barrett. She was driving me and my brother into the heart of darkness. Lightning streaked the sky. Thunder boomed. This was real. As she pulled over to the side of the road, my mother was breaking down. At five years of age, I realized that if I weren't in charge, everything would go wrong. As it turned out, everything went wrong anyway.

# GUN RUNNING IN THE EVERGLADES

THE SCENE WAS SURREAL: Mimí took the small settlement money from her divorce and moved us into a new development in Hialeah of identical single-story ranch-style dwellings built against a series of smelly drainage canals leading to the vast and alligator-infested Everglades only a block away. There were rows upon rows of homes with white pebble roofs distinguished only by their pastel colors: mint green, pink, and yellow. The area was barren of landscaping except for squares of sod grass and a smattering of small ficus saplings tied to thin wooden braces.

The surrealism, though, had more to do with the inside of our cookie-cutter house than the outside. We had no real furniture, only mattresses and a Formica-and-chrome dining room set, along with an abundance of other occupants. Sleeping on the hard terrazzo floor were rag-tag bearded Cuban freedom fighters in green fatigues. Machine guns and pistols were scattered everywhere. When I asked Mimí who these men were, she gave a one word answer: *amigos.*

At this moment, Mimí was backing Castro to the hilt. Jay Jensen was also involved. He and Mimí had become close. (Later in life, when Jay became a renowned drama teacher at Miami Beach Senior High School and taught Mickey Rourke and Andy Garcia, he'd jokingly call me his love child.) Jay's family owned a landing strip in the Everglades not far from our little house and, with Mimí's help, conducted an operation that ran guns and soldiers to Cuba to bring down Batista. Which takes us back to Batista's mistress, Mimí's sister, Beba.

In Havana, sensing that Batista, with all his harrowing problems, was about to dump her, Beba married a rich Princeton-educated sugar and tobacco baron. Beba also arranged a marriage for her younger sister Miriam to a famous Cuban movie star. The pope himself annulled the union when Miriam discovered her husband in bed with a man. She continued her university studies, becoming increasingly radicalized. It was at college that she met her future husband Jorge Robreño, called El Mago (the magician), who, like Fidel, graduated law school at the University of Havana, and he became Castro's close comrade. It was Miriam and Mago who recruited the soldiers and secured the guns flown from the Jensen landing strip to a remote location in the La Sierra Maestra mountains on the front lines of battle.

On December 31, 1958, only months after Mimí had left Barrett and we were living in Hialeah, the Cuban city of Santa Clara fell to rebel forces. Batista and his cronies fled Havana. They boarded three planes. Batista ordered his own plane to circle the city three times at such low altitude that people on the street thought it would crash. He never returned, living out his life in exile, first in the Dominican Republic under the protection of Trujillo.

His love for Beba never waned. In fact, he wrote her regularly and even sent for her. In 1973, living in Miami Beach, she was packing her bags to meet him in Marbella, Spain, when the radio announced the news: Batista had dropped dead of a heart attack two days before Castro's assassins were set to kill him.

Batista's legacy was infamous. It was rumored that he had hoarded hundreds of millions of dollars in kickbacks from American gangsters and corporations while looting the national treasury.

After nearly five years of intense guerrilla warfare, Fidel marched into Havana on January 8, 1959. The triumph was complete. From our house in Hialeah, Mimí, Jay Jensen and a party of Cuban sympathizers celebrated. It was a brave new world that, alas, collapsed sooner than any of my family members would ever have imagined.

During that initial postrevolution year, Beba was hit first. Her new husband's sugar and tobacco holdings were confiscated by the state, and, fearing for his life, the poor man fled to Miami and wound up waiting tables and fishing off the causeway bridges.

Meanwhile, Beba's initial mentor, Pepin Bosch, head of Bacardi and heavy financial supporter of Castro, saw the future. It happened during a trip to New York, where he accompanied Fidel for his speech to the UN.

Bosch saw that Castro was a sociopath. He understood that his talk of democracy was window dressing. He further understood that although Batista had been a dictator, Fidel was a tyrant. The second he landed in New York, Bosch contacted his board and made arrangements to pull Bacardi's resources out of Cuba. All that remained were the distilleries with their hundred-year-old oak barrels that Castro seized to create Havana Club, the new state-run rum. Bosch moved Bacardi to Puerto Rico and the Bahamas, maintaining the firm's autonomy and avoiding ruin, his fortune intact . . . but not his country.

Mimí's younger sister Blanquita also got entangled in revolutionary romance. She, her husband Ignacio, and their two children, Lola and Iggy, were living in New York, where Ignancio tended bar in Greenwich Village at the Gondolier, a nightspot frequented by the actor Bob Keeshan, who played TV's Captain Kangaroo. Before Fidel took over, Blanquita, like Mimí, was filled with revolutionary fervor. Urged on by sister Miriam, she took the kids and returned to Havana, where she and a friend from NYU began filming a documentary on Castro. She was also hired to inventory the Napoleonic artifacts at the home of Julio Lobo, a rich member of the old-guard society.

Fidel was sending seized valuables to auction houses in Paris and London, where proceedings were used to replenish the Cuban treasury.

This was when Blanquita met Camilo Cienfuegos, another major figure in the revolution. He was a remarkable man who looked like Jesus. Castro appointed him head of the army, and, like Che Guevara, Cienfuegos quickly became a Fidel superstar. Blanquita fell madly in love with him. Their affair was torrid and short-lived. On October 28, 1959, the very day I turned six and was living with Mimí and Fred in our house by the Everglades, a plane carrying Cienfuegos blew up. Some speculated that Fidel, seeing his comrade's charisma as a potential threat, arranged his death. Either way, Tia Blanquita was devastated.

Love among the revolutionaries was heartbreaking. My aunt Miriam had long suffered Mago's brutality. Rather than remain a battered wife, she left him and began her love affair with El Comandante himself, Fidel Castro.

Her hair fashioned in a platinum bouffant, Miriam was strolling down the street on her way to visit Beba at the Edificio FOCSA when along came Castro's motorcade. Miriam caught his eye, and as she entered the lobby, he told his men to stop. He had to meet her. By the time Fidel and his lieutenants reached the lobby, Miriam was gone. The doorman didn't know her or which apartment she was visiting. Castro was determined. He and his men would knock on every door until the beauty was found. When they finally reached the penthouse, it was Fidel who rang the doorbell. Beba responded.

"Is this where I can find the most beautiful woman in Cuba?" asked Castro, who, at six feet three, towered over her.

Nonplussed and accustomed to dealing with dictators, she coyly answered, "Yes."

Looking beyond her and spotting Miriam, Fidel said, "Not you—*her*." "She's married . . . to El Mago Robreño," said Beba.

Mago was a prominent member of one of two major categories of Fidel's revolutionaries. The first, those closest to him, Camilo Cienfuegos and Che Guevara, fought by his side in the mountains. The second, which included Mago, was the intelligentsia. Two years before the revolution, Batista had closed the university, a hotbed of radical thought. Mago was a prominent student organizer and the son of the editor of El Mundo, the largest Cuban newspaper. He rebelled against his pro-establishment father by joining the revolution. When Fidel triumphed, he rewarded Mago with a high but onerous position: signing the death warrants of thousands of political prisoners that sent them to El Paredon, the infamous firing-squad wall. From that moment on, Mago became an international war criminal.

When Beba told Castro that Miriam was married to Mago, he paused, looked her up and down, and said, "I do not take what is not mine."

His obsession with my aunt, however, didn't end there. He had her followed when she escaped from Mago and wound up in Varadero, a tourist resort on the northern coast. One sunny afternoon she was swimming in the warm water when, out of nowhere, larger than life, Fidel emerged. Thus began their long affair. For months he visited her in a rented seaside shack.

Everything changed when Mago turned on Fidel. His reasons were two: first, Castro's affair with Miriam, and, even more critically, Castro's marginalization of the intelligentsia and scions of wealthy families who had supported him. Fidel had thought nothing of confiscating their homes and businesses. In retaliation, Mago led a seventeen-man coup, poorly planned and abortive. It's hard to keep secrets in Cuba. Mago saved himself only by capitulation: He agreed to immigrate to Spain. With a nod from Castro, he wrote a book condemning the revolution. That allowed him to pose as an anti-Cuban spy in Barcelona. He also ran a money-laundering investment bank, Cumexa, circumventing the American embargo on Cuba. His work as a double agent went on for decades.

Immediately following Mago's arrest, without a shred of evidence, Fidel suspected Miriam's complicity in the coup and unjustly jailed his lover for three tortuous months, where she suffered her first nervous breakdown. Miriam had nothing to do with the coup. In fact, if she had known what Mago was planning, she would have warned Fidel, the man she madly loved. My aunt was never the same. When she finally made her way to Miami, a lost twenty-one-year-old, her spirit was crushed, her life a living hell. There were twenty-eight hospitalizations, where she was raped by staff members and subjected to dozens of electric-shock treatments.

During the sixties, my entire family wound up in Florida, scuffling for whatever work they could find. The great and glamorous Beba was perched on a stool in the bar of the Eden Roc Hotel in Miami Beach. Her place on that stool was secured by handsomely tipping the bartender. With her Grace Kelly sophistication, Beba ran an efficient network of call girls and occasionally made a call herself. During the Jewish High Holidays, she wore a gold necklace holding a Star of David. She remained our First Lady, always impeccably dressed and coiffed.

After the death of Camilo Cienfuegos, Blanquita went back to her marriage. Her husband, Ignacio, never learned of his wife's affair, another famous family secret. He rejoined his wife and children in Cuba, where no one could make a living. Thus, they moved to Miami, where he worked as the maître d' in the Mona Lisa Room in the same Eden Roc Hotel. After work, he filled pink paper ice buckets from the pool cabanas with half-eaten steaks. Aunt Blanquita was transformed from pro-Castro patriot to rabid anti-Communist. I wonder whether her fanaticism was, at least in part, fueled by her suspicion that Castro had assassinated her lover.

Mimí moved in that same direction. It didn't take her long to see that the benevolent savior had become a ruthless dictator. So did her parents, who left Havana and came to live with us in Miami. Exile was a challenge that neither of them overcame. They were deeply troubled and pitifully unmoored.

I gravitated more to Abuela Blanca than Abuelo Carlos. My grandfather was a distant and disillusioned man, spending his days smoking and listening to anti-Castro radio. My grandmother was more emotionally available. Eager to share her faith, she told stories of the saints and their miracles. She also told me tales of her sisters' miraculous pilgrimages to Fatima. On her dresser was a tiny bottle in the shape of the Virgin containing holy water from the grotto of Our Lady of Lourdes—the one thing she had successfully snuck out of Cuba. The minute I caught a cold, Abuela took a drop of that water and painted the sign of the cross on my forehead. I was enraptured by Catholic iconography. Seated on the toilet, I feared that the Virgin Mary might appear while I was going to the bathroom, surely a mortal sin.

I fantasized about becoming a priest—anything to escape the ugliness of day-to-day reality.

Abuela's escape was more than traditional religion. As a girl, she had wanted to study medicine and become a pharmacist. As a female, she was denied that chance while her brothers attended Princeton and Yale. Rather than Catholic school, she had attended the progressive Raja Yoga Academy, cofounded in 1900 by First Lady Ida McKinley, wife of US President William McKinley, and the Theosophical Society. Abuela also adored Rudolf Valentino.

Even though Santeria, the Cuban Yoruba religion associated with Haitian voodoo and its Nigerian origins, was frowned upon by the upper class, Abuela kept hidden offerings. I'd discover them by surprise, crawling under a bed or standing on my tiptoes to sneak a peek at a sacred tray of fruit with a crucifix, rosary, and cigar atop a crystal goblet. These objects were used to cast or block a hex. Abuela believed that the physical and spiritual worlds sit side by side.

Mimí and Abuelo Carlos had been a close-knit partnership since her childhood—he the father inventor-writer, she the daughter editor-organizer. Now in exile, they came up with a plan to lift us out of poverty. They began a company to develop a chemically treated white-glazed reflective coating that, sprayed on roofs in sweltering South Florida homes, would shun the sun, reduce the heat, and cool the interior. I don't know how they funded the grand operation. All I do know is that after their truck was stolen, their business collapsed, and we lost our house by the Everglades.

Ironically, we were saved by the man Mimí had rejected: Joe Marfy, known to me as Uncle Joe. He had left Venezuela and invested in Miami real estate, including a few bug-infested shacks in a shantytown off Biscayne Boulevard. We were allowed to live in one of these shacks. These were terrible times. I was a latchkey kid. When Mimí didn't come home, I had to scrounge for food for my younger brother Fred.

Once in a while, Marfy and his wife, Valeria, would visit us. Or should I say, inspect us. I wasn't sure who these people were, especially because Valeria was bejeweled with diamond rings, gold bracelets, and, despite the Florida heat, a mink stole. Marfy was kind, but Valeria was aloof, walking around speaking Hungarian as she checked for dust. Only as an adult did I learn that Valeria knew that Marfy and Mimí were still secret lovers.

Soon afterward, another left turn: Mimí met an undertaker and descendant of Spanish pirates. After a brief courtship, she married the man and, lickety-split, we moved to Puerto Rico, where, at age seven, I was helping my new stepfather embalm corpses.

*Joe Marfy, Mimí, and Daddy Lopez, Miami, 1960*

*With Mimí, Daddy Lopez, and Fred, Ponce, Puerto Rico, 1961*

# DADDY LOPEZ

THIS FACT ASTOUNDS ME:

In 1961, the same year we were living in Puerto Rico, all three of my fathers were working on that same island: John Barrett had left Florida and joined a Peace Corps training center in Arecibo; due to a regime change, Joe Marfy had lost his business fortune in Venezuela and was regrouping in San Juan; and my new stepdad, Abelardo "Al" Lopez, having gone bankrupt in Miami marketing aluminum T-mops, an idea conceived by Mimí, had moved us to Ponce, a city on Puerto Rico's southern coast, where he ran a funeral home.

When Lopez appeared, I was secretly happy. I knew that Mimí needed a man, and like every boy, I needed a father. But despite that need, circumstances dragged me down. I did all I could to contend with the harrowing reality of living so close to the dead.

The Lopez family had immigrated from Spain to Key West in the 1800s, where they developed an infamous piracy operation that ironically and inevitably transitioned into funeral homes.

Another improbable fact: Joe Marfy attended my mother's second wedding. It seems strange that Mimí would have invited him. Yet the truth is that Marfy would remain on the margins of our life for years to come. There is a wedding party photo of the three of them—sophisticated Marfy and portly Lopez with lovely Mimí in the middle. The impression is that Mimí and Marfy are the ones marrying while Lopez looks on suspiciously, as if to say, "What's going on here? *I'm* the groom."

The bride and groom, along with the bride's two bewildered sons, wound up living in a former colonial mansion masquerading as a funeral home, a formal edifice with imposing Corinthian columns. Most of the interior was devoted to Lopez's work. In one room in the back, brother Fred slept in a cot near Mimí and Lopez. Another cot was set up for me in an oversize bathroom adjacent to the viewing parlor, where, behind enormous heavy gold curtains, corpses lay in their caskets. My head was inches away from the dead.

Mimí thoughtlessly moved me from school to school. First was the Academia Santa Maria where I celebrated my first Holy Communion. I wanted to wear the traditional all-white outfit— I loved the look—but Mimí and Al couldn't afford it. I managed to persuade my mother to buy me a white jacket, tie, shirt, shorts, and socks. They refused to buy me white shoes, but I, a young dandy, carried on until my parents capitulated. At the service, I was surprised to see Joe Marfy along with his wife, Valeria, and their first child Esther.

Because business was bad, my parents pulled me out of the Catholic school and put me in a public school that looked like a cinder block prison. Bullies eager to beat up the gringo. Putrid food. Out-of-control classrooms. A handful of inept teachers. It was hell. When I told Mimí I was never going back, Lopez arranged for me to attend the Episcopalian school across from the funeral home.

After school, Daddy Lopez showed me how to handle the dead. The ordeal of sticking a metal tube into a corpse and sucking out their guts scrambled my brain. The stink of formaldehyde sickened me. The sight of lifeless flesh turning from ghostly blue-gray to unnatural pink gave me nightmares.

On a fine spring day, Daddy Lopez, an affable soul, tried his best to brighten my mood. It was probably a tall tale, but I liked hearing him tell me how during his Navy days he stowed away on Enola Gay, the Boeing bomber that dropped the big one on

Hiroshima. He took me to a mountaintop and spoke of his plans to open a roadside restaurant where all of us would work. I had a sudden vision of being a busboy for the rest of my life. That frightened and infuriated me. My silent retaliation was to imagine him in a coffin, dead as a doornail. That way I'd never have to work at his restaurant, and we could go back to Miami to be with Abuela and my cousins, who continued pouring in from Cuba.

Then came the night we were hit by a tropical storm of biblical proportions. It felt like the end of the world. I was afraid that the monsoon would wash us all away. An ominous feeling filled the house as we ate the dinner Daddy Lopez had prepared. We were all together in our small living space when I saw my stepfather's eyes roll to the back of his head before he collapsed on the ground. Mimí fell into hysterics, unable to do anything. I screamed and, in the torrential rain, ran across the street to the rectory, barefoot and in my underwear, where the priest called an ambulance. It was too late. At age forty-two, Daddy Lopez was dead of a massive heart attack.

Except I wasn't told that. I had spent the night at the rectory, afraid to go back. In the morning, dressed in black, Mimí came to get me. She had already dyed her red shoes black.

"Is he dead?" I asked.

"No," she lied. "But he's very sick."

Later I learned that he had already been embalmed and put in a coffin.

I don't know why, but my mother couldn't ever tell me the simple truth about anything, as if uttering those words would make it all too real.

Due to the fantasy I created when Lopez told me of his restaurant plans, I suffered with guilt. I had envisioned him in the

casket; thus, I had killed him. The students at the Episcopalian
school were made to file past the casket, but I was too unnerved
to enter the viewing parlor. I stood on the street alone. No one
comforted me. When I was told to go inside and tell my stepfather goodbye, I refused. I never looked at Al Lopez again.

Mimí rode in the hearse while Freddy and I rode with "Uncle
Joe Marfy," who, hearing the news, drove down to Ponce from
San Juan to help us out.

The procession stopped at the airport, where, with the casket
in tow, Mimí, my brother Fred, and I flew to Miami with the few
possessions we owned. Before we left, she arranged a fire sale of
all our possessions in the backyard of the funeral home. The
proceeds were paltry.

We arrived in Miami in dire straits. All that kept us from
homelessness was Lopez's Jewish friend Sid, who owned a hotel
next to Wolfie's Delicatessen, a Miami Beach landmark. That
same man had a vacant house in North Miami, where he let us
live rent-free. But fate was not our friend. The kind man died
weeks after we moved in, and, when Mimí couldn't make the
rent, his widow kicked us out in December. A sad Christmas. No
presents. The only tree was the one I fashioned by tying together
branches of an evergreen.

Because Lopez had been in the Navy, a small widow's pension
entitled us to low-income housing in Liberty City. These were
the bare-boned slums. Through Barrett, Marfy, and Lopez,
Mimí had protected us from abject poverty. Now the protection
was gone and, for years to come, we were on our ass. I was overwhelmed by shame, humiliation, and fear.

One of my mother's ways of making money involved the
assemblage of party favors in our home. She assigned me the
task of gluing together thousands of small wooden mallets. After

school, I worked at it for hours. "The faster you do it," she said, "the quicker we get paid." I did it for months. I was nine.

Mimí couldn't hold a job. She worked as an office clerk. She worked at Burger King and brought home unsold soggy Whoppers and stale fish sandwiches. She tried and failed at dozens of menial tasks. Her focus was fleeting. Her only preoccupation was writing poems and songs, where, for a few moments, she beat back her depression. She hung her dreams on that big hit just around the corner.

When she saw I was down, she lifted our spirits by taking me to a cavernous furniture store divided into sections: early American, Danish modern, French provincial. We drifted over to the Art Deco area. I loved the streamlined geometric style with its rounded fronts, chrome hardware, and gleaming glass tops. I was in a Hollywood movie from the thirties that Mimí and I watched on TV. She was Jean Harlow. I was Clark Gable. Unlike the dilapidated plastic-covered crap in our rundown Liberty City slum, here everything was new, everything matched. We sat on the sofa and pretended the furniture was ours.

"What do you think, *mi amor*?" Mimí asked me. "Shall we buy it?"

"Yes!" I screamed. "Can we?"

"*Claro que si!*"

Mimí called over the salesman and confidently ordered the complete living room set—all ten pieces, including a magnificent Art Moderne credenza. God knows where any of this would fit. But that didn't matter.

Insisting that her credit was impeccable, she told him to charge it. She filled out a ten-page form, a lit cigarette dangling from her lips. She handed the salesman the papers, instructing him to deliver the furniture in a week.

The fact that the furniture never arrived didn't stop her from repeating the ritual. Next year we were back, this time seated in the Mediterranean section, where the furniture was constructed with fake wood wormholes.

"Imagine how all this will look in our mansion on Miami Beach," said Mimí with complete confidence.

On the positive side, I loved the spectacular culture of Miami's Cuban-exile community. I say spectacular because, as with most expressions of Cuban emotion, the culture thrived on theatricality. As Mimí's politics shifted, she wrote an epic poem in which Castro is portrayed as a Christ figure who, over time, betrays his ideals and his people. Though she lost all faith in Fidel, she remained a patriot and mourned her sad *guajira* island.

While we were living in the projects, she hosted meetings of the Cuban Songwriters in Exile, an organization she helped establish. I sat on the floor and watched a parade of hyperdramatic poets declaiming the virtues of the Cuban soul. Among those was the magnificent *poetisa* Beba de Cuba, wrapped in the Cuban flag. Her hair was piled in a mile-high frosted beehive, her eyes streaming tears like Tammy Faye. Her poems soared.

Another guest in our home was the immortal Olga Guillot, queen of bolero, Cuba's Judy Garland and Castro's fiercest enemy, a woman so adored by Conrad Hilton that he booked her every time he opened a new hotel around the world. She headlined at the Stork Club as a teenager, where Dean Martin and Jerry Lewis were her opening act. She sang with Edith Piaf in Paris and coached Nat King Cole to sing in Spanish. I called her Tia Olga because she had escaped Cuba with my mother's younger brother Bebo, whom she had met at the Tropicana, where he performed with his celebrated singing group, Los

Bucaneros. For ten years, Bebo was her lover. He often acted as her conductor and helped raise her daughter Olga Maria.

Then came the day I saw Olga's poster in a record store on Calle Ocho, the main artery of Cuban life in Miami. Her dark skin had been lightened to a porcelain glow. They had even turned her brown eyes blue. I was intrigued by the magic of transformational packaging, a concept that stayed with me the rest of my life. Olga Guillot, by the way, released eighty-seven albums during her eighty-seven years. On her last album, she finally sang Mimí's "Doña Tristeza." At least one of my mother's dreams came true.

Lady Sorrow, for all her profound melancholy, could always attract a man. Our lives depended upon it. The fact that one of the men Mimí attracted was a Jesuit priest took me by surprise. I knew him simply as one of her suitors, a man in civilian clothing who came to our house with dinner before slipping into Mimí's bedroom. Fired from an endless succession of low-paying jobs, Mimí had many such men. But after this particular relationship had gone on for several months, she took me aside and told the truth. He was not only a Jesuit priest but principal of El Colégio de Belén, the famous school where Fidel Castro had been educated in Havana and which had been relocated to Miami on Calle Ocho after the revolution.

"This is a godsend," Mimí told me. "He's given you free tuition to his school. The Jesuits are brilliant. This will be great for you."

Hardly.

First off, I had to pretend that my mother's lover, now dressed as a priest, was a stranger. When I passed him in the hallway, I was told never to make eye contact. I hated the charade. When I complained, Mimí's rejoinder was swift: "This man is really helping us. He says you're so smart you're skipping sixth grade and being promoted to seventh. Be grateful, *mi hijo*. I see this as a blessing."

I saw it as a humiliating farce. While I was moved ahead, my classmates had already been held back by two or three years. Most of them were recent Cuban immigrants without English. If I was eleven, they were fifteen, macho soccer jocks with handlebar mustaches and long sideburns. They either ignored or bullied me, a skinny blond *Americano*. Mimí didn't help when she decided that I wasn't displaying enough masculine traits. Her remedy was to take me to a quack for testosterone shots. For all her bohemianism, phallic-centric Cuban machismo was essential to her worldview. The testosterone shots made me hyper and horny.

At the same time, after watching Barbra Streisand's brilliant debut TV special, *My Name is Barbra*, which I loved with all my heart, I took out a Webster's dictionary at the school library and looked up the word "homosexual." The very plainness of the definition, "sexual attraction between people of the same sex," stirred something deep within. But it would be decades before I could come to terms with that stirring.

A year later I watched my second favorite TV special, *Color Me Barbra*, that only increased my devotion to Streisand. I can't explain the correlation between worshipping Barbra and feeling gay, but it was definitely there. In fact, the evidence of my homosexuality was always there.

Who else but a gay preteen would make a beeline to Burdine's elegant department store, where Zsa Zsa Gabor was modeling her own line of clothing? Who else would charm Miss Gabor into allowing him into her dressing room? The scene still blazes inside my head: Zsa Zsa in a nipple-revealing lace bra and slip;

her boobs looking like plastic; her face pink porcelain; her blond bouffant wig coiffed with her trademark heart-shaped bangs; yet her gnarled hands revealing the character of an old witch, liver-spotted and veined.

As she powdered her damp underarms with a pink ostrich-feathered puff, she talked about the meaning of fashion, as though I were a reporter for *Women's Wear Daily.*

"Now, dahling," she said, "you must tell me about yourself."

I was Johnny Barrett. I was a student. My single mom was a songwriter.

"But what is it that you do, dahling? What is it that you love?"

I said I loved watching women get dressed. I spoke the truth. She laughed and air-kissed me on both cheeks.

I haunted the lower lobby of the DuPont Plaza Hotel hoping that, because the Supremes were mascots in this year's Orange Bowl Parade, I might catch a glimpse of Miss Diana Ross herself. And I did! It was her, all alone, smoking a cigarette and pacing back and forth like a caged tigress! She wore a big helmet-shaped flip wig in rusty red. Her dress was a pink-champagne-sequined floor-length sheath with a high slit revealing her right thigh. Her stilettos were glittery silver. Disco mirror-ball earrings dangled like paddleballs.

I reached deep into my reservoir of chutzpah to ask her for an autograph. She looked as though I'd asked to borrow money. Begrudgingly, she accepted my slip of paper, took my pencil, and quickly scrawled her name. When the lead in my pencil broke, she got frustrated and dropped the pencil and the slip of paper on the floor and started walking away. I don't know what I was thinking, maybe because I felt like such a street rat, but I ran ahead of her, and in a grand gesture, tore up her autograph, letting the fragments of paper fall to the floor, which caught her eye as she disappeared into the elevator.

I can't resist adding that later in life, in the tables-have-turned department, I was approached by Miss Ross to produce her. This happened in the nineties at her Malibu beach house, during a party cohosted by KISS's Gene Simmons. "I'm flattered," I casually told the singer, who I secretly idolized since our first encounter, on December 31st, 1965, when I was twelve years old. "But it's probably best for your people to contact my people and see what our schedules look like. Maybe we could have lunch together one of these days and you can tell me what your vision is for your next album." My people never heard from her people . . . I'm still waiting. I would absolutely love to work with her . . . a lifetime dream of mine.

As usual, Mimí still saw survival in terms of men. That's why she took me to the Bacardi building, where, once a month, an art exhibit and cocktail party attracted a high-class crowd. She borrowed money to buy a used red Mustang convertible so we could arrive in style. She dressed me like a young prince, using me to break the ice with men roaming the room. Her affair with the Jesuit priest having collapsed, she was in search of a millionaire. Meanwhile, I was exposed to art and actually did appreciate the paintings and sculpture, even if Mimí never scored.

When she did connect, the relationships were usually brief. There was Edgar, the Colombian pilot, whose bleeding ulcers had him moaning and groaning all night long. There was a gay musician who, with his twin brother, formed a Liberace-like double-piano act. I presumed Mimí acted as his beard, as if he needed one, but he was writing out her lead sheets to present to artists.

*With Diana Ross, Malibu, California, 1994*

*With Lee Burnham's Brazilian walnut bas-relief
of Mimí, Liberty City, Florida, 1962*

And then there was Orlando Ortís Toro, a wealthy and married Puerto Rican businessman who, calling Mimí his assistant, took her on long trips to Guatemala and Nicaragua. Brother Freddy and I were left in the care of my deeply depressed grandfather, who would sit in front of the TV set smoking.

My mother never found a way to break the cycle of poverty. Poverty is soul-crushingly boring, ugly, and dangerous. I needed to escape it but didn't know how. Mimí kept struggling. She replaced the Mustang with a beat-up clunker that wouldn't start. Even if it could, there was no money for gas. It just sat there in front of the house. But just as the broken-down car brought me down, the sight of a work of art—a masterpiece that hung in our living room—raised me up. It was another piece by Lee Burnham, sculpted when we lived on the Hawthorne dairy farm with Barrett—a large two-inch-thick bas-relief in Brazilian walnut depicting Mimí surrounded by three men, each whispering in her ear. The elegantly elongated figures are clad in Greek togas. Seemingly indifferent to her suitor's supplications, Mimí's head is lowered. She appears emotionally shut down, a striking figure, the object of rapt attention to which she's incapable of responding. There's poignancy, even poetry to her inertia. The piece spoke to my soul. The more I lived with it, the more it said about my mother. And then came the day when I came home, and it was gone.

"What happened!" I exclaimed. "Did someone steal it?"

"I had to sell it," she said. "Orlando gave me $1,200."

"Why did you do that? It was art. It was all we had."

"I know," she said sadly, "but right now we need food more than art." I felt gutted.

Mimí was also distraught by her father's failing health. Cancer had attacked his lungs. Abuelo could no longer take me to sell the cachucha peppers, at a few cents each, growing in the back-yard of his tiny wooden house. Similarly, he was too sick to make those humiliating trips to the Freedom Tower in Miami, where he and I had stood for hours in the sweltering heat in a long line of other *refugiados* waiting for our allotment of government-issued spam, cheese that tasted like plastic, and powdered eggs we'd choke on. My grandfather was reduced to the role of beggar.

My mother was determined to save him. Something of a New Age thinker, she also devoured the *National Enquirer*, which wrote about miracle cures. She went as far as to take Abuelo, along with me, to a sawdust tent revival led by a faith healer. We saw a man with crutches approach the makeshift pulpit. After the healer laid hands on the man, the supplicant dropped his crutches and did a little jig. Glory hallelujah! My grandfather joined hands in a circle of the sick surrounding the healer, who, while blessing him, forcefully pushed him back. An attendant caught Abuelo before he hit the ground. We were then led to a table where we were enlisted in a lifetime program of monthly tithing. Naturally we were too poor to pay, but the bills and even a collection agency hounded us for years.

A month after the miracle cure, my grandfather died. I believe his heart was shattered, not only because his grand dreams of building the Bridge to the Americas from Cuba to Cancún never materialized, but because there was no place for him in this new world. His once-proud family had been pushed to the margins of society. In exile, he had lived out his life in silent rage. And Mimí, his favorite, had lost the one man—perhaps the only man—who loved her absolutely.

*Me, Mimí, and Fred, Ponce, Puerto Rico, 1961*

*Me with Violeta Drouet, Niagara Falls, Canada, 1971*

# VIOLETA

FOR YEARS I WROTE unanswered letters to Daddy Barrett, the man I thought was my father. His silence left me forlorn and confused. Why wouldn't he write me back? Was something wrong with me?

After an agonizingly long absence, he finally got in touch. He sent for me and Fred to spend a summer in Ecuador, where he was working as a petroleum geologist. Barrett was growing old. Guilty for all his neglect, he bought me a white wild horse that I named Stingray after my ghetto bicycle back in Miami. I gained the animal's trust by feeding him reams of bananas. Riding was fun except for when Stingray threw me off, resulting in a sprained wrist. It was a lonely time.

Then came the ordeal of having my tonsils removed. The only medical facility near the oil fields where Barrett worked was a small British clinic. An English doctor with a pronounced hairlip spoke to me in a manner I couldn't comprehend. My discomfort was exacerbated by my awkward passage through puberty. I was embarrassed by the hair under my arms and refused to go swimming without wearing a shirt. So after the operation, when I awoke in a hospital gown and realized that the physician and the nurses had seen me naked, I was mortified.

The several summers that Barrett hosted us in Ecuador were both fun and frightening. My supposed father had a light side. After a few drinks, he broke into song and did a high-kick mambo with the flair of Danny Kaye. But if the drinks became too many, he grew sullen and aggressive. He was once so plastered he put me behind the wheel of his jeep and demanded, "You drive!" I had no idea how. But with him shouting slurred instructions, I fought back my terror and somehow managed.

My sexual awakening was confusing. Stingray and I would wander off-road in the dusty desert, where I figured out how to masturbate in the saddle, where no one could see me. I found a stash of Barrett's Playboy magazines in the bathroom cupboard. I did like the glossy photographs of the models' naked skin and pink nipples. But I was hardly aroused. In contrast, when I looked through the medical magazines Barrett kept around the house, I found myself stirred by diagrams of the male anatomy.

As far as body image, my idol was Twiggy, the boyish, reed-thin English model. Hers was the androgynous look I sought to emulate. I was drawn to sexual ambiguity.

It was in Ecuador where I also experienced another major Streisand moment: I saw *Funny Girl* in a dusty movie house with beat-up hard wooden benches and dilapidated chairs. From the peanut gallery, rowdy street urchins threw popcorn, candy wrappers, and an occasional rock at us gringos sitting below. Nothing, though, distracted me from Barbra. As Fanny Brice, she was sublime. I swooned as she sang "Don't Rain On My Parade" from the helm of a tugboat passing the Statue of Liberty. The son of an immigrant, I was moved by that symbol's aspirational attitude.

I must have sensed ambiguity around Barrett's ancestral history, because I once asked him to draw a family tree. He refused, saying, "Why bother?" He also crushed Marfy's offer to send me to school in Spain so I could learn that country's culture. All of this added to my confusion. Why would Marfy make such an offer? And why was Barrett so insistent that I not accept? I now know he was afraid I'd learn that Marfy was my real father. He was probably right. Hungarians, like Cubans, aren't good at keeping secrets.

The highlight of my summers in Ecuador was the presence of the extraordinary Violeta Drouet, who became my surrogate mom. Violeta met my actual mother when Mimí and Barrett lived in Ecuador when they were first married. She was a secretary for British Petroleum in Ancón, close to her home, the small, dusty town of Santa Elena. Elena—my mother's first name—and Violeta became best friends. Then, years later, during my summer visits to Ecuador, Violeta became *my* best friend. She was patient and loving and unconditionally supportive of my talent. A spinster, she lived with her spinster sisters in a house built in the 1800s. She slept in the bed in which she had been born and would die. And most fortunately for me, she played piano. Her loving patience came to fruition when she brought me to the instrument and encouraged me to express myself. The ancient upright grand piano probably hadn't been tuned more than twice in a hundred years; some of the keys were stuck; but none of that mattered. Her encouragement mattered. Her smile. Her sweet method of showing me her effortless technique. The tenderness of her touch. The way she hummed to melodies I invented.

Violeta was a chain-smoker who spoke in a raspy musical Spanish. Her humor belied her tragic life. It had begun hopefully. She adopted an Indian boy, whom she raised righteously. As his sole parent, she put him through college and celebrated his marriage to a beautiful girl. The couple had a boy. Now a grandmother, Violeta bought the young couple a modern printing press that was installed in a storefront on the ground floor of her ancient house. The business thrived. Then tragedy struck:

toxic ink poisoned her son and daughter-in-law, who both died of cancer while still in their twenties.

Violeta at least had her grandson—but not for long. The day of his mother's funeral, the child was kidnapped by his other grandmother. Violeta never saw him again.

Violeta saw me as the child she had lost. I saw her as the calm and dependable mother I had never known. Unlike Mimí, Violeta was not self-absorbed or fueled by crazy fantasies. Hers was not a selfish love. Her heart housed a maternal energy that generated hope. The women I had known growing up—Mimí and her sisters—had led glamorous tragic lives that overshadowed their motherhood. Despite all she had lost, Violeta's love was pure. While my mother played guitar, she never taught me the instrument. Violeta taught me piano. We shared the bench together, our four hands running over those old keys like friends running through a meadow.

She knew I was a collector. As a child, I collected stamps, coins, rocks, minerals, insects, and skulls of everything from mice to cows. Collecting was my way of ordering a world I otherwise couldn't control. Violeta understood this. She indulged me. She led me to a barren paupers' graveyard filled with shallow graves and no headstones. The recent rains had loosened the soil so that actual bones were protruding from the ground. I had no trouble locating a jawless human skull. Violeta joined me in celebrating this wondrous addition to my collection.

In coming back to Ecuador in the summertime, it wasn't so much Daddy Barrett I longed to see. It was Violeta Drouet.

In Miami, I returned home one day to find the skull missing.

"Where is it?" I asked Mimí.

"I threw it out."

"What!"

"I had to. It was bad luck."

"Where'd you put it?"

"In the garbage."

"Someone will find it and think we killed someone."

"Oh, God, I never thought of that."

"You never think of anything!"

I wouldn't talk to my mother for days.

Things calmed down a bit when Mimí came home with good news. She had found work in the music industry. She met a lady lawyer who represented Peer Southern Music Publishing. Maria Luisa Dennis was a Spanish-speaking *gringa* with a glamorous house on Star Island. Her job was to snatch up every Cuban song and songwriter as they arrived in Miami.

Mimí talked Maria Luisa, who had an eye and ear for young, Latin musicians, into hosting wild parties at her home for *descargas*, jam sessions with local musicians and songwriters. Mimí took me along. The décor was Palm Beach chic—rattan furniture with bright tropical fabrics.

Drinking, smoking, and dancing went on through the wee small hours. I fell asleep on the couch only to awake at dawn in a living room strewn with passed-out revelers. Empty glasses, beer bottles, and ashtrays overflowing with cigarette butts. It looked like a battlefield after the battle was lost. Mimí was nowhere to be found. I waited hours until she crawled out of who knows where.

My mother's deal at Peer didn't yield income. She got no advance. All it did was give her bragging rights. It turned into another instance when she had her nose pressed against the glass door of an inaccessible world.

Latin music was one thing. American street music was another. In the open space behind the projects, kids—white, black, and Hispanic—would congregate around the swing sets with their transistor radios blasting R&B, rock 'n' roll, pop ballads, an eclectic mix of genres all on the same station. I wanted to be cool and fit in. That took effort. But appreciating the music coming out of those tiny speakers took no effort at all. That love came naturally.

I bought my first record, Lulu's "To Sir, With Love," and my first album, *Presenting Dionne Warwick*, that included her debut single, "Don't Make Me Over." But being made over was exactly what I wanted. Despite our bond, I wanted to get away from Mimí's difficult life.

I continued to gravitate toward the art form Mimí had mastered. With no formal training herself, she never schooled me technically. In fact, she never schooled me at all. Yet from her example I absorbed the most important lesson of all: great songs are borne of passion. She and I shared musical passion, even as her nightclub-hopping songwriting career and erratic love life diverted attention away from her children.

In February 1964, the Beatles arrived at the Deauville Beach Resort in Miami Beach. A week earlier, they had made their American debut on *Ed Sullivan*, who had agreed that their second appearance, two weeks after their first, would be taped at the Deauville. Thus John, Paul, George, and Ringo flew to Florida to bask in the sunshine and hysteria that awaited them. Mimí and her sisters Beba and Miriam, among the world's most formidable and tenacious women, especially when cultivating celebrities, wangled an invitation to a party for the band that probably wound up in their hotel rooms. Later in life, Mimí hinted that her Beatle was George.

# MAGIC CITY

MIMÍ WROTE A BEGUILING SONG that idealized the beauty and pleasures of Miami and that ignored completely the slums in which we lived. She entered a contest for a new city theme song to replace "Moon Over Miami" and won first prize, given by acclaimed Mayor Robert King High. Unfortunately, the prize was recognition rather than cash. She called the song "Magic City," Miami's longtime moniker.

At thirteen, I saw no magic whatsoever in our neighborhood. I realized I had to make a bold move of my own. The school directly across the street from our grim apartment in *el projecto* was run-down and overcrowded. I wanted something better. Using Aunt Beba's Miami Beach address, I left the Jesuit school, entered Nautilus Junior High, and stepped into a world I had never before known. This was rich city: girls already popping birth control pills, sporting false eyelashes, and wearing micro minis. Boys without licenses driving their parents' Cadillacs. Pot parties at mansions on North Bay Road. Weekend-long acid-dropping trips on sailboats and yachts.

Poor kids like me and my cousin Iggy, Aunt Blanquita's son, who also attended Nautilus Junior High School, had to scrape to get by. We fished for coins out of the fountains at the Fontainebleau, Doral, and Eden Roc Hotels. We worked as cabana and busboys at the same hotels where our uncles and aunts worked as waiters. Outsiders looking in, we felt unwelcome and unworthy.

One major consolation was meeting Susan Dechovitz, my first girlfriend. She was Jewish with a New Age intellectual mother I adored. Her mom, Judy, wore muumuus and beads and dark, exotic eyeliner like Endora from "Bewitched." When I sat at their grand piano making up melodies, Judy was entranced; Susan was bored. At the same time, she allowed me to kiss her and indulge in light petting. Finally, though, she threw me over. Later Susan went on to become a powerful prosecuting attorney, second in command under Janet Reno, who eventually served as President Bill Clinton's attorney general.

Another Jewish girl helped save my soul. Carol Davidson, two years younger than me, had been a child prodigy, a gifted classical pianist. At thirteen, she had the demeanor of a wise and mature woman. Our bond was instant. Decades later, we realized our connection was partially based on the unspoken fact that we were both gay. At the time, though, I simply felt comfortable in her company. She totally got me. She had a calm gravitas that, combined with her sweet disposition, drew me to her. Carol was the youngest of six siblings. Her father distributed industrial sewing machines and her mother had traces of *Mommy Dearest.* Carol liked listening to Janis Ian in her bedroom, which I helped her paint chocolate brown. Her mother, whose sense of interior decor was muted and minimalist, was shocked.

A couple of years after we met, her dad died. Carol went mute. She didn't speak for months. Every day I went to her house and simply held her hand. Being there for Carol, as Carol would always be there for me, helped beat back my insecurities. But only temporarily.

At Nautilus, the stakes were always raised. No one ever wore the same clothes twice. The fair-haired blue-eyed golden boys and girls glistened under the South Florida sun. I had fair hair and blue eyes, but I didn't glisten. I felt totally self-conscious and second-rate.

I followed Toby Manheimer, who was already taking college math courses, into the Southern Student Organizing Committee, a wing of the radical SDS, Students for a Democratic Society. I recruited Carol, bringing her anti-Vietnam War pamphlets that we distributed at school. I now suspect some of that propaganda against the US capitalist industrial complex was surreptitiously sponsored by the Soviets, but at the time the brutal injustice of the war was all that mattered. Beyond protesting, Carol and I ate macrobiotic brown rice and carrots, joined organizations protesting the war, and practiced yoga in Coconut Grove.

I was an outcast and, given my idiosyncratic mannerisms, was bullied by the big boys. When a mean kid in my shop class, Carlos Vega, started throwing wood at me, another kid, a tough guy himself, intervened. He had a tender heart. Mickey Rourke, the future movie star, assumed the role of my protector. I considered it as the irony of ironies that after high school Carlos came out gay. I'd run into him in the clubs, and we became friends.

Another time, Mickey intervened when a second bully, Howard Kasdan, shoved me against the wall and, up in my face, said, "I'm gonna kick your ass." That's when Mickey grabbed him by his shirt collar, snarling, "If you even come at this guy again, I'll kick your fuckin' head in." Years later, when I found out that during that very time Howard's mom was dying of cancer, I felt sad for him.

The following summer, when I was fifteen, Mimí found me part-time work with the great Cuban sculptor Tony Lopez. They had known each other in prerevolution Havana where they'd met in the bohemian circles. As Tony's apprentice, I marveled at his work. He was among the city's leading artists. He sculpted Miami Beach's Holocaust memorial depicting a massive, outreached hand on whose number-tattooed arm nude skeletal figures desperately scramble over one another for survival. It was terrifying. On a lighter note, Tony loved pet roosters. I didn't. They flew around the studio, where they pecked me to distraction. So great was his regard for the animals that he constructed giant fiberglass roosters, painted in whimsical multicolored patterns, that lined Calle Ocho and remain a popular tourist attraction to this day.

That same year, I liked loitering in the lower lobby of Fontainebleau Hotel. It was 1968, and the hippies had arrived. My blond hair was growing long. I longed for adventure. Watching the beautiful people come and go, I dreamed of a life of glamour. I noticed a girl who displayed a strong tomboy vibe. She noticed me. Without speaking, we both felt a kindred spirit. I certainly wasn't out but was secretly in love with a boy in my class, Marco Petit, a six-foot hunk with black curly hair. He was a bass-playing surfer and Christopher Reeve look-alike. His Dominican mom resembled Elizabeth Taylor, and his South Carolinian redneck dad was a dead ringer for Marlon Brando.

The girl in the lower lobby was Lisa Wexler. I was Johnny Barrett. And just like that, we started talking music. She mentioned her favorite, Laura Nyro. Had I heard of her? I hadn't. Lisa said her father was in the music business. What did he do? He was a senior executive at Atlantic Records and staff producer as well. I didn't know what a producer did, but I did know I wanted to be around people in show business. A year younger than me, Lisa came from New York. It was Christmas vacation, and the Wexlers had a house on nearby Allison Island, where she invited me to dinner.

I got to know Lisa's family. Her father, Jerry Wexler, turned out to be the creative force behind Aretha Franklin, whose breakthrough hits—"Respect," "Think," "Chain Of Fools"—were flooding the airwaves.

The Wexlers opened my world. Their dinner table provided a feast of intellectual delicacies. They and their high-spirited friends spoke brilliantly of art and politics. They seemed to know everything about everything. They argued passionately. They loved to laugh. And mostly they loved to talk about not just music but the kind of pop music I was hearing on the radio. They were industry insiders, and, through a chance encounter, I had been whisked inside their exclusive domain.

On any given night, dinner guests included Ahmet Ertegun, Wexler's partner at Atlantic, an urbane Turkish immigrant with an encyclopedic knowledge of cabaret, jazz, and rhythm-and-blues. There was also Jerry's arranger, Arif Mardin, and Tom Dowd, Atlantic's genius engineer who pioneered multitrack recording. Tom often drove me back to the projects and answered my endless questions about the business.

The most meaningful moment came when Lisa dragged me away from the grown-ups' table to her room and played me Laura Nyro's debut record, aptly titled *More Than A New Discovery*. I was transfixed. It wasn't just her voice, and it wasn't just her writing. It was both. Her voice was plaintive, ethereal, beguiling, and soulful. Her songs were hypnotic. I studied her compositions and their unorthodox structure. My study intensified with the release later that year, of her masterpiece, *Eli and the Thirteenth Confession* that contained gems like "Stoned Soul Picnic," "Lonely Women," and "Woman's Blues." Thus began my lifelong infatuation with Laura Nyro, my lady of sorrow, a muse, like Mimí, encased in mysterious beauty. With her long dark hair and sad eyes, she invoked the Virgin Mary, the mother of the god of music.

Because my love for Marco Petit was unrequited, I was forced to settle for friendship. We did everything together. We went to the West Palm Beach rock festival to see Janis Joplin and the Rolling Stones. In the outdoors, we slept on blankets and, though he was with a girl, the close proximity to Marco—his back against mine—drove me insane. We both had down-to-our-waist hippie hair and even began dressing in similar fake velvet pants, wild-colored shirts, and clogs, like Steve Winwood in Traffic. I tripped a couple of times on acid but couldn't keep up with Marco, who lived high.

Marco's girlfriend Toby Davidson deserves a book of her own. She had a creative mind and an astounding body. As far back as junior high, she wore leopard-skinned micro-miniskirts or custom-made tights—one leg emerald-green, the other leg eggplant-purple. Although from a poor family, Toby was resourceful. She worked in a bakery and managed her money in a manner that allowed her to craft her fabulous self-made style.

After Marco broke up with Toby, she and I became an item and, for the first time, I had sex with a girl. It felt great. Everything about Toby was great. She liked feminine boys. She liked Laura Nyro. She liked flea markets and rock music. Our romance didn't last long, but our friendship never died. She wound up modeling for painter Martin Hoffman, who illustrated her in Playboy. For years Toby's nude images on huge canvases were displayed at Hugh Hefner's mansion and clubs. She attended Parsons School of Design and hit it big-time in the cutthroat world of fashion. Bergdorf Goodman sold her own signature line of clothing—Toby Davidson —bankrolled by Ivana Trump. Eventually Toby moved to Kentucky, wrote a book glorifying female jockeys, and married a hulk of a man who transitioned into a beautiful woman.

*Me and Fred with Daddy Barrett, Cuerna Vaca Farm,*
*Hawthorne, Florida, 1958*

*Riding Stingray with Daddy Barrett, Cautivo, Ecuador, 1964*

# FATHER FIGURE

Twelve months had passed since I had seen John Barrett during my most recent summer in Ecuador. It was a sad farewell. He had grown cold, distant, and bitter. He had lost his job at the oil company. Because he was over sixty, it might have been ageism. But I suspect it was his drinking.

Freddy had stayed behind for the school year, and the two of them lived in a tiny, borrowed beach shack provided by the ever-faithful Violeta Drouet. In that very shack, Barrett collapsed in front of my brother, just as Daddy Lopez had collapsed in front of me. Another massive heart attack, another fallen father. The night I learned about Barrett's death I was in Miami with Marco, who held me as I cried in his arms. I hugged him tightly, probably more excited about being comforted by this sexy boy than grieving my father's death.

Poor Barrett. Failure stalked him. Nothing in his life turned out as it should have. He had lost his clout in the petroleum industry. He never found the right woman. Even his kids weren't his own. He died of a wounded soul that, try as he might, could never be healed. At the same time, he was an adventurer who never completely abandoned his sons. At the time of his death, I was still under the illusion that he was my biological father. I felt guilty that I didn't mourn him more than I did. I also felt bewildered. He was a man to whom I was and was not connected. He was a man whom I did and did not know, a man whose tragic demeanor was tempered with occasional ebullience, even as that spirit was ultimately drowned in a sea of booze. His hapless efforts to collate the disparate parts of his life ended in tragedy. I lost a father I never had.

In Miami, the blues got bluer. When Aunt Miriam —former lover of Castro and ex-wife of Mago—took over our house in the projects, Mimí, Freddy and I moved into a shitty rooming house on Normandy Isle. It was dismal. I had to escape.

I was still in junior high when my school friend Evan Shoffran had heard me complain about my daily three-bus ninety-minute trip from the ghetto. With his parents' approval, he invited me to live with his family in Miami Beach. Bingo! That meant I could get to class in just a few minutes. It was a strange house, a big wooden contraption on its last legs. Evan's folks were court reporters, sweet people poor as church mice. We ate boiled peas out of a can and instant powdered mashed potatoes. Evan's older brother Mark partied nonstop. He was deep into pot and Jim Morrison. The walls of his trippy bedroom, where Doors records literally played 24/7, were painted black. I liked it. I was grateful to be away from Mimí.

Except I would never be away from her—not then, not ever.

*Playing Violeta's piano, Santa Elena, Ecuador, 1964*

*With Mimí, Homestead, Florida, 1967*

*New York City, 1976*

PART TWO


THE BIRTH
OF DESMOND CHILD

*Nightchild: Virgil Night and Desmond Child, Miami Beach, 1972*

# NIGHTCHILD

FOUR WOMEN BIRTHED DESMOND CHILD, the man-child who became a musician. The first, of course, was Mimí. The second was Violeta Drouet. The third was Mrs. Marie Louise Mansfield Leeds, my high school voice teacher. And the fourth was a girl my age, Debbie Wall.

Miami Beach Senior High School was hot. We had an award-winning debate team, a choir that sang with the Miami Beach symphony, plus art, drama, orchestra, film and video departments. Competition was fierce. Even the rock 'n' rollers had big chops. Because Laura Nyro's music had me dreaming of becoming a singer-songwriter, I fell in with the rock crowd. My cousin Iggy had a piercing rock star voice and played killer guitar. He began dating my best friend, Carol Davidson, who'd become the pianist for the school choir. I joined the choir led by Sharon McCalister, a young, determined woman whose heavy Streisand makeup, white go-go boots, miniskirt, and tight, low-cut bosom bearing sweaters drove the boys wild. Obsessed with winning the state championship, Sharon pushed us hard, suggesting we take private lessons with her voice teacher, Mrs. Marie Louise Mansfield Leeds.

I couldn't afford those lessons, but Mrs. Leeds took me anyway. She read my hungry heart. She saw how much I loved music and, in lieu of payment, accepted the tropical foliage I'd gathered from the golf course that I passed on my way to her home. Her only requirement was that I'd agree never to smoke, drink, or take drugs. I took the pledge and kept it. She probably saved my life. A Jewish Holocaust survivor, she had once been a celebrated coloratura in the great concert halls of Europe.

Before World War II, her stage name, known throughout Germany, was Marie Louise Mansfield. She had piercing blue eyes and swept-back, strawberry blond hair, and wore large, jewel-encrusted brooches on her stately dresses. She carried herself regally.

Ladies would run up to her in the grocery store and ask, "Are you Margaret Thatcher?" to which she'd reply, "What would Margaret Thatcher be doing in a grocery store?"

We met when she was in her early fifties. The meeting was life-changing. She opened the door to something I had never before known: rigorous study. She infused this study with clear spirituality. When I asked if she believed in heaven, she answered, "You're a drop of water and God is the ocean. Put that drop in the ocean and now *you're* the ocean." Mrs. Leeds was as stern as she was deep. She sat straight up; her spine never touched the back of a chair. She recorded my voice on a reel-to-reel and played it back, over and again, until I was able to self-correct.

I was at her home until day turned to night, so enthralled by her stories that we remained in the dark, neither of us bothering to switch on the lights. She was an art collector with vast knowledge. After World War II, she and her husband scoured Europe for lost paintings. That's how they made their fortunes. On her walls was an El Greco saint and a Turner sunset, and a large, metallic, peacock-colored meteorite she had found in Central Park and carried home was displayed in a glass case. Her cabinet held a dazzling array of Fabergé eggs. Her intellectual range was wide. She knew history, semantics, and politics. She was not above a little gossip. She was the first to tell me that her friend Leonard Bernstein was gay and that I should stay away from him.

*Mrs. Marie Louise Mansfeld Leeds*

*Nightchild, Miami Beach, 1972*

I was content simply to sit at her feet and ingest her philoso-phy rooted in the boundless joy of making precise and immacu-late music. She was all about wisdom, patience, and discipline, and I was her willing devotee. Music was no longer simply music. It was a craft to master.

I met Debbie Wall at Beach High in the tenth grade. Her real name was Debra Wallstein. She had a pale complexion and long, lustrous raven hair.

Her faraway eyes were covered with wire-rimmed glasses rem-iniscent of John Lennon. I viewed her as a combination of John and Yoko. Not surprisingly, when she invited me to the tiny one-bedroom apartment she shared with her poet mother, Faye, I saw that her corner of the small living room that served as her bedroom was plastered with posters of Lennon and Ono. This was 1969, only months after the two had shocked the world by posing nude on the cover of their first album together, *Two Virgins*.

Debbie was a Montreal Jew of caustic wit and daring energy. She was an original songwriter. She was also a budding intellec-tual who introduced me to Herman Hesse, Franz Kafka, and Friedrich Nietzsche. We stayed up all night buzzed out on honey-laced mint-flavored black tea as we analyzed the meaning of life. In the heyday of hippiedom, we concluded that life needed to be explored. Our bond was music. (Debbie's younger first cousin was Corey Hart, the singer who later gained famed in the eighties with "Boy in the Box.")

Musically, we were perfectly matched, our voices a natural blend. Our rapport was not romantic; it was spiritual. We were soulmates, intrigued by each other's quirky artistic sensibilities. More than that, though, we were counterculture-attracted, even counterculture-addicted. In a borrowed classroom, we began an after-school antidrug creative workshop called Awareness II.

(There was no Awareness I, but we thought that Awareness II sounded cooler.) We helped pioneer a green movement, setting up a paper and plastic recycling program at school. We studied John-Roger's Movement of Spiritual Inner Awareness. We read *Autobiography of a Yogi*, ultimately seeking yogis of our own.

After absorbing the works of Meher Baba and Swami Satchidananda, Debbie and I moved into the Maya Family, a legendary commune in Coconut Grove run by a hippie Jewish lawyer who put us to work at his Oak Feed Store, one of the first organic-food outlets in Miami. We loved when our cosmic guide Astrid said things like, "I am invoking the spirits of the Ascended Masters"— and then, suddenly lowering her voice, spoke as though she was one of them. We were acolytes, young, naïve, and hungry for mystical knowledge. In my case, I was also hungry for a family, unlike my own, that was not irreparably fractured.

In keeping with our determination to rearrange our relationship to the universe, Debbie and I also rechristened ourselves. Based on two psychics I had read about, I named her Virgil Night. And based on a character in the Beatles's "Ob-La-Di, Ob-La-Da," she named me Desmond Child. Together, we became Nightchild.

Completely by surprise, at our weekly Sunday darshan, a meal that would feed as many as fifty people, Mimí showed up at the Maya Family wearing hippie beads, sandals, a floor-length muumuu and a long Cher wig. She was with Marfy, who was being a good sport. Mimí wanted in on the Age of Aquarius. If it was good enough for her son, it was good enough for her. In her flower-power getup, she went around introducing herself as my mother. She had to grab the spotlight. I could have died.

The summer before eleventh grade, Virgil Night left for Montreal to visit her dad. After a few weeks, I followed her.

"Don't hitchjack, *mi hijo*," said Mimí in her peculiar patois. But I did. It's crazy, but I stuck out my thumb and, by myself, made it all the way from Florida to Canada, where Virgil's inhospitable father sent me to a youth hostel in an airplane hangar. I thumbed it down to Baltimore and found work as a tomato picker in a garden owned by a born-again cult of Jesus freaks. A heavyset female biker from Boston, Arlene Bolitsky, threw me on the back of her Harley and hauled me down to Meher Baba's retreat in Myrtle Beach, South Carolina. He was famous for coining the phrase "Don't worry, be happy." There, I was allowed to meditate in the small cabin of the recently deceased guru. For hours I reflected on a bronze cast of his holy hands.

Back in Miami, I took to wearing a black cape to school, a nod to the Count Dracula costume I donned every Halloween. Beach High, though, couldn't contain Nightchild. We wanted out. To facilitate our exit, we made a huge shag rug out of multicolored remnants we found in the alleys behind carpet stores. The rug reflected the entire horoscope anchored by a sun in the center. We painstakingly pieced it together on the back of a large old rug we had found in a dumpster, with glue that had us high as kites. We sold the thing for decent money that allowed us to fly the coop.

In the summer, just before our senior year, we quit school and headed up to Boston in search of the city's famous folk scene. It didn't matter that we were dead broke. Nightchild couldn't miss. At a club called the Sword and Stone, we played for ten people. On our way to a commune called Spirit in the Flesh in Warwick, Massachusetts, we hooked up with another hitchhiker, Myriam Valle, who came from a Puerto Rican family in Brooklyn. With her long, straight, dark hair parted down the middle and granny glasses, she looked like Buffy Sainte-Marie. We became fast friends at the commune, where we worked the fields like slaves and slept with fifty strangers in a converted barn dorm that was essentially a firetrap.

After a few weeks, Virgil and I left Spirit in the Flesh but promised to stay in touch with Myriam. We wound up in Woodstock, New York, where Van Morrison was working on *Tupelo Honey*. In 1971, Woodstock was a hippie haven. Our look was goth before goth existed. We covered ourselves in black velvet. I wore a black velvet jacket and knickers with knee-high black leather boots. Virgil wore a Laura Nyro-style floor-length black velvet ball gown. We played at the Joyous Lake, a folk club. Our pay was a cup of coffee and a slice of pie. We were rewarded, however, by the presence of Bernard Stollman and his entourage of New York music-biz hipsters. A lawyer and label owner of ESP-Disk that recorded avant-garde jazz, Stollman was probably more intrigued by our look than our music. He practically adopted us, inviting us to stay and look after his nearby farm, the Acorn Hill House, while he went back to Manhattan. We picked vegetables from the garden and baked our own bread. In the adjacent barn, where Bernard kept goats, my job was to pack and ship loads of ESP-Disk albums that included work by John Coltrane, Ornette Coleman, Sun Ra, and Billie Holiday. The music fascinated us, but the goats didn't. They broke into our room and gnawed on our clothes and song lyrics. (One ESP-Disk album cover featured a photograph of a goat!)

Virgil and I found jobs in an apple orchard in New Paltz. Incompetent pickers, we were soon relegated to a processing plant, where we stood all day at a conveyor belt beside black migrant workers, discarding the bad apples and bagging up the good ones. It was like the episode from "I Love Lucy" when

Lucy and Ethel go crazy trying to wrap chocolates on the assembly line. The migrant workers, who kindly shared their food with us, became our friends, telling us how each year they picked peaches in Georgia before heading north for the apple season.

We sweet-talked our way into the Woodstock recording scene. To break into the business and compete with the artists who were making it—the Carole Kings, James Taylors, and Elton Johns—we needed a demo of our songs. I befriended an engineer at Bearsville Studio, Nick Jamison, where master musician-producer bad boy Todd Rundgren was working on his sonic masterpiece *Something/Anything?* (Todd, by the way, looked at me like I was the janitor.) Nick would let me hang out while Todd was mixing. Because Todd had a no-trespassing policy at the studio, I had to hide to hear his astounding creations. Like Phil Spector, he came up with revolutionary recording techniques. His sense of harmonics was totally original, his sound a pastiche of unexpected key changes and ironic lyrics. To this day, I carry his influence.

Using several of Van Morrison's sidemen, Nightchild recorded four original songs in a converted mobile home behind drummer Dahaud Shaar's home in Woodstock. We used a female violinist, famous for outplaying Jack Benny on his TV show when she was a young child. Colin Tilton, Van's sax man, who played flute on "Moondance," played on our session. Paul Winfield was on bass.

Simply to support us, these stellar musicians worked for free. They called our music great. So, with a reel-to-reel in hand, in November 1971, we made our way to midtown Manhattan to shop our songs and seek a deal.

But something else that happened in New York knocked *me* out, a meeting that altered my self-perception forever.

*With my real father, Joe Marfy, Miami Beach, 1954*

# THE TRUTH COMES OUT

THE HUNGARIAN MYSTERY MAN, Joe Marfy, had learned that I was on the East Coast. He was in New York and wanted to see me. With some reservations—what in the world could *he* want?—I invited him to Bernard Stollman's Riverside Drive apartment, where I was staying.

When Marfy arrived, his demeanor was different. Usually a man of nonchalant charm, he appeared agitated. He paced the room. At times, he gave me intense eye contact; other times he looked into the distance. In his distinct Hungarian accent, he began by saying, "Vell, you turned eighteen years old this past October, didn't you?"

"I did."

"I have something to tell you."

"What?"

"Sit down."

I sat.

"Did you ever vonder vhy I always kept coming to see you?"

"No."

"Because I am your father."

With tears in his eyes, he came over and put his arm around me. I sat there frozen. It was a Luke Skywalker moment. I didn't know what to do, say, or feel.

Marfy proceeded to tell the story of following Mimí into the movie theater in 1953 and the crazy affair that had followed: her disappearance; his unexpected encounter with Beba at the Hotel Nacional in Havana; his trip to Barrett's dairy farm to take Mimí and me away with him—all the details, all the missed cues, all the heartbreaks.

"My marriage to Valeria," he said, "didn't deter my devotion to you. Knowing you are my son, Valeria vas embittered. That's vhy she has always been so aloof. I am sorry for that. I am also sorry that I agreed to Mimí's mandate and continued to hide the truth. But I stand before you today to end all lies. I am finally prepared to take full responsibility as your father, who has alvays loved you."

I was startled. I was speechless. I was confused. I could feel my temples throbbing, my head aching. I worried my brain would crack open from the force of so many thoughts pummeling me at once. Yes, it did make sense. Yes, I did look more like Joe than John. Yes, Marfy had always shown up at critical times for reasons I never understood. And yes, now it was clear. His concern for Mimí and me was genuine. But what was I to make of this incredible revelation? And who was Fred's dad? What was I supposed to feel?

Strangely enough, I felt relieved. Hearing the truth lifted a weight I didn't even know I was carrying. Then came a wave of rage directed at Mimí. I felt diminished. Her pride had deprived me of the father who really wanted me. I was just a side character in the drama of *her* life. Didn't she realize the damage she was doing by pretending that John Barrett was my father and, even worse, reinforcing the lie by naming me after him? Didn't she understand the cruelty of misinforming a child about such critical information? I'd been robbed of a basic human right. I looked back at my childhood as a hoax, a cover-up of the most essential truth. I wanted to get on the phone and scream at my mother until my lungs gave out, wanted to curse her, accuse her, condemn her, denounce her, and then swear I'd never speak to her again.

"I know you feel that vay now," said Joe, "but those feelings vill pass. You understand Mimí's psychological challenges better than anyone. She's a poet, a songstress, a fragile soul."

"She's a liar," I shot back.

"A beautiful liar. A beautiful voman who loves you more than life itself."

"Not more than she loves herself."

"If only she did," said Joe.

My new father began talking about his own life, and, because I now knew that I was his son, I listened intently. I heard how during World War II he had been drafted into the Hungarian army. He was defending Budapest when the Soviets conquered the city in a bloody massacre. During the onslaught, Marfy was shot by sixteen bullets of a Russian machine gun, and if someone had not inadvertently thrown the coat of a Hungarian officer over his body, he would have perished. He miraculously made his way to London, where he was supported by an old friend, a secretly transgender count who would one day become a female world scholar on human sexuality. From there, Marfy went to northern England to work in the coal mines, where he would lay down, and ride a skip deep into a dark, narrow shaft holding only his pick over his chest, which would often break down, often leaving the miners entombed for hours in total darkness not knowing when, if ever, it would start up again.

It took him two years of hard labor to save cnough to make it on board an immigrant ship to Ellis Island in New York Harbor, where he recalled seeing his first glimpse of the Statue of Liberty breaking through a heavy fog and began sobbing uncontrollably because of everything he and the rest of the world had gone through for freedom.

Although he was movie-star handsome, charming, and spoke good English, Marfy struggled to find work in New York. Through Hungarian friends he heard that there were huge opportunities opening up in South America and hopped on the next banana boat to Venezuela. There, beginning with nothing, he started by building oil-rig platforms in the jungles near Lake Maracaibo, his first step in becoming an international business-man. He was an erudite gentleman from humble beginnings who cultivated clients in a multitude of languages, and, later in his life, was knighted by the Sovereign Order of St. John of the Templar Knights Hospitalier: Baron Joseph Marfy. Since the father's title falls on the first son, I would ultimately also be knighted and become Baron Desmond Child de Marfy!

Thus, the upside of this long lie perpetuated by Mimí was that, in the hour it took Joe to tell this story, I'd gone from being no one to someone. It was *The Prince and the Pauper* come to life. Next thing I knew, Joe was urging me to get my high school diploma. He said he'd pay for college. He bought me a Eurorail pass so that during the summer I could visit the continent. Learning that I was dead broke, he gave me and Virgil money to travel back to Miami.

Before leaving New York, she and I went to see Seymour Stein, who ran Sire Records, where he'd eventually sign the Ramones, The Pretenders, and Madonna. We were certain that after hearing our demo he'd give us a deal.

But he didn't. We were down but not out. While in Manhattan, I made a pilgrimage to the home of my muse Laura Nyro, who lived on Riverside Drive. On a rainy day I stood in front of her apartment building for two long hours, hoping to catch a glimpse of her coming or going. She never appeared. If she had, what would I have said? Surely something like, "I love you. I adore you. I want to write like you. I want to be you. Please be my friend."

But the rain never let up, and I left my waiting station shivering and soaked to the skin.

Back to Miami Beach, where the NARM convention (National Association of Recording Merchandisers) was being held; a great chance to sell Nightchild and our songs to the bigwigs. Without tickets, though, how to crash the conference? Easy. Dress up as John and Yoko. I wore the white linen Lennon suit and rimless Lennon glasses. Her jet-black hair down past her shoulders, Virgil wore the long black Yoko dress, a black, floppy hat and big Jackie O sunglasses. Our impression was good enough to fool security. The minute we came to the door, the gatekeepers stood aside and let us make our grand entrance as if we were actually the royal couple. People gasped. Heads turned. Photographers lunged. We made our way through the room until I spotted Clive Davis, head honcho at Columbia Records and the man who'd signed Laura Nyro. Virgil and I took two empty seats at a table next to Clive. I boldly went over to present him with a copy of our demo tape. Up close, Clive saw we were impostors but seemed charmed by our ruse. He graciously accepted our offering.

Two months later, he returned the tape with a note saying thanks but no thanks. Forty years later, he handed me the Clive Davis Legend in Songwriting Award. But in 1972, his rejection convinced Virgil and me to call it quits. Taking Marfy's advice, I enrolled in night school and graduated with my high school class.

My cousin Iggy and I were dead set on winning a contest created by a local radio station. The prize was a brand-new candy-apple Camaro.

Contestants had to create an artwork that illustrated the meaning of Pink Floyd's *Dark Side of the Moon*. Iggy and I studied the record for days. Then lightning struck: the moon was a metaphor for the protagonist's brain. Thus, we made a head out of Styrofoam on which we drew diagrams of the cranial lobes. We stuck in long needles and twisted wires, stuck on a pair of headphones, and placed the head in a plexiglass case that stood upon a custom-made wooden stand. How could we lose?

The big day arrived. Iggy and I went to the station's event, where the entries would be judged. Much to our dismay, the winning entry was hardly brilliant. It was nothing more than a simile of the surface of the moon where the flag of the landing spaceship carried the call letters of the radio station and miniature toy astronauts carried the names of the station's disc jockeys. This taught me a great deal about the music biz. Originality and imagination don't always win the day. Sometimes it's best to go for the kill and simply please the promoters. The best thing about this whole affair was the wild woman I met at the radio station.

At twenty, Lisa Roberts was two years older than me. She liked dressing me up in her disco clothes. She adorned my hair with a black feather boa and my mouth with Revlon cherry-red lipstick. At the time, I was working with Marfy, doing construction on a twenty-three-unit apartment complex he was building on the plot of land off Biscayne Boulevard where he had once let me, Mimí, and Freddy live in a bug-infested shack. The contrast between lifting heavy bricks in a hard hat in the afternoon and wearing David Bowie fuzzy boas at night was exhilarating.

Lisa took me to an Alice Cooper concert at Miami Jai-Alai Fronton Hall, where we both dressed up as Alice clones. She took me to my first gay bar, the Wall on Twenty-Third Street off

Collins Avenue. My discovery of that scene came at a time when I was trying to show Marfy that, like him, I was a real man. Yet I couldn't deny how the boys got my blood boiling. Lisa's intense sexual demands kept me on the straight track—at least for a while.

On the night of her twenty-first birthday, guzzling Southern Comfort out of a bottle Janis Joplin-style, we went disco dancing in platform shoes at the ultragay Warehouse VIII. I drank too much, and, instead of gifting her with a hearty birthday fuck, I fucked up by passing out. Her pleasure denied, she broke up with me the next morning.

Without Lisa, I returned to the gay clubs, but with little luck. This was when the hypermacho buzz cut Tom of Finland look was in. The skinny long-haired hippie look was out. I invariably went home alone and soon returned to my pursuit of girls.

One of those girls was Jill Meadows, on whom I had a crush since junior high. She was tall, flat chested, and chic. In terms of androgyny cool, Jill was the coolest. She wound up as the lead singer for Virgil's post-Nightchild band named the Dairy Queens, before going to New York where she became a fashion model and a follower of Swami Muktananda, founder of Siddha Yoga.

Mimí's next romantic move: marriage to a bland Cuban accountant named Alberto Hernandez. He didn't like me, and I didn't like him. I felt my mother deserved a soulmate whose spirit and wit matched hers, or at least could support her in style. Hernandez was a dud. After a lifetime of disastrous choices and heartbreaks, though, Mimí was ready to settle for whomever she could get. She needed to call herself a married woman. Seeing I had no tolerance of him, Hernandez took my brother Fred under his wing.

Ultimately, Fred followed his lead and studied accounting.

Hernandez didn't like my loud music. One evening, things came to a head when I was in my room playing an electronic keyboard and singing my heart out. A song had just come together.

"Stop it!" Mimí ordered, entering without knocking. "You know Alberto doesn't like noise."

"It isn't noise. It's my new song."

"I don't care."

The heat was building. Rather than argue, I went back to the keyboard and played even louder.

"I said stop!" Mimí screamed. "No matter what you do, you'll never be as great as me."

I was stunned and stopped playing. But something in me clicked and silently said, *"We'll see about that."*

Imagine my joy when I was able to get out of the house. It happened when Marfy sent me to Europe. I flew off to France with Jill. As soon as we hit Paris, I fell for Michel, a seventeen-year-old West Bank bohemian disco boy who looked like Marlene Dietrich. His eyes were highlighted with blue liner, and his straight blond hair fell below his shoulders.

Jill rode the train with me to Geneva, where we saw the sights before parting company. Alone, I arrived in Madrid, where I learned that Marfy, always resourceful, was flush. He lorded over a beautifully appointed apartment in the center of the city. There were four bedrooms, a large living room, a formal dining room with an antique crystal chandelier, a maid's quarters, and a big rustic kitchen, where the walls held my father's collection of African masks that triggered stories of treacherous journeys through the Dark Continent in search of oil leases.

During my stay, Marfy's wife, Valeria, and their three children, each younger than me—Esther, John, and Joey—were also in Madrid. Because I was the product of their dad's illicit affair, my new sister and brothers greeted me reservedly. Esther went to boarding school in Lausanne, Switzerland, while the boys were shipped off to Seven Oaks, an exclusive boarding school in Kent, England, dating back to the reign of Queen Elizabeth I. My stepsiblings were better educated and far more disciplined than me. While Mimí was lenient to the point of neglect, Joe and Valeria were loving yet strict parents. Observing their richly structured family life made me realize how much I had missed.

I left my Hungarian family in Madrid to visit Cuban relatives in Barcelona. I caught up with Mago, Aunt Miriam's former husband, who had survived as Fidel's double agent. The lives of Mago and Miriam, both gifted people, had tragic endings. When the Iron Curtain fell in the eighties, Russian agents, probably ordered by Castro, poisoned Mago to death. My gorgeous Aunt Miriam, a woman of great spirit, never recovered her emotional equilibrium after Castro had betrayed and imprisoned her. In Miami, she got strung out on drugs and wound up in a locked-down room in the psychiatric ward at Jackson Memorial Hospital, where, despite the presence of oxygen, she lit a cigarette. Her bed exploded. The night nurse had wandered off, and only the patients heard her screams. By the time help arrived, she had suffered horrible burns. Only her beautiful face was spared. Mimí and I often visited her in the hospital. In order to clean her fragile body, we watched as she was lowered by straps into vats of silver nitrate. It was a harrowing sight. While she suffered, her children, my cousins Jorgito and Carlito, came to live with us in the slums of Liberty City. After leaving the hospital, Miriam kept smoking, smoking, smoking, until she died of throat cancer at age forty-eight. Another victim of a revolution gone mad.

Before all that, though, my 1973 European sojourn continued from Barcelona to Budapest. I hitched a ride with Mago's friend the Cuban ambassador to Switzerland, whom Mago said laundered money for Castro. We drove to Milan, and from there the Eurorail pass took me to Rome, where I hung out on the Spanish Steps with hordes of other college kids. On to Pompeii, whose closure didn't keep me from sneaking under the fence to inspect the buried city. The sight of a black snake crawling out of an ancient urn still lives inside me.

The Marfy family had gone to Hungary and urged me to join them. I didn't hesitate. First time in my father's homeland. Still under Soviet rule, the city had not recovered from World War II. Life behind the Iron Curtain was dark and gloomy.

While in Budapest, I had a nightmare that my mother was murdered. I woke up in a sweat. At that point, Mimí was trying her luck as a real estate agent, driving old women around in her car to look at homes they would never buy. Now awake, I was sure she was fine. But something told me to call home.

Mimí was *not* fine. Showing a home to a client by the projects, she spotted rival gangs across the street about to do battle. Before she could move, she was shot in the back by a stray bullet, half an inch from her spine. Miraculously, her recovery was quick.

When I returned from Europe, I experienced a miracle of my own. While working as a busboy at the exclusive Surf Club, I enrolled at Miami Dade College. That's where I met a woman who stole my heart. And just like that, darkness turned to light.

*With Lisa Roberts, aka "Lash LaRue," North Miami, 1972*

*Maria Vidal*

# GINA WORKS THE DINER ALL DAY

AT TWENTY, my sexuality still fluctuated in uncertainty. I desired men even as I loved women and their womanly ways. I loved women's voices, women's sense of fashion, women's fragility, and women's strength. Because my mother was a woman of enormous complexity, I was attracted to artistic women who could not be easily understood and who lived life with thunderous passion.

Maria Vidal was a woman of thunderous passion. Like Virgil Night before her, she became the muse who completed all the incomplete fragments of my puzzled psyche. The daughter of a Cuban American Air Force officer, Maria was a stunning beauty with a sensuous body—a perfect body!—a fine singing voice, an original, creative mind, quick wit, poetic sensibility, dazzling smile, and a demanding, dramatic presence that held me spellbound.

We met backstage during a production at Miami Dade Community College, where we also met Diana Grasselli, and the three of us were inseparable. Diana was a Renoir-style beauty with a theatrical flair that kept us laughing in stitches on the floor. After I left Miami for New York University, Maria vowed to join me, and Diana soon followed. NYU awarded me a partial scholarship that was supplemented by Joe Marfy. My schooling was solid—I eventually earned a bachelor's degree in music education—even as my lifestyle grew more fantastical.

As a kid, I watched movie after movie set in New York. It represented the ultimate in urban sophistication. It was always where I wanted to be. It was where I felt I belonged. I could finally be myself. The Brill Building. Broadway. The Village. Warhol. The hustle. The bustle. The city that never sleeps.

From my dorm room I sent Maria love poems, and she, still at Miami Dade, responded with equally passionate love letters. We reunited when I went home to Miami for Christmas break . . . and then things got complicated.

I met Christopher Adler when he was a guest and I a waiter at a chic holiday party at the Surf Club, where the aristocracy, the Du Ponts and Firestones were in attendance. He caught my eye and, apparently, I caught his. He kept asking me for water. Then he asked for my number. A few days later, it was on.

Christopher swept me off my feet. He looked a bit like Omar Sharif—dark-black hair, brown bedroom eyes, large, dramatic nose and vibrant personality. His famous father, Richard Adler, had written the Broadway shows *The Pajama Game* and *Damn Yankees*, and his stepmother was the star English actress Sally Ann Howes. Christopher had talent of his own and would eventually achieve success writing the musical *Jean Seberg* and *Shirley MacLaine on Broadway*. He became another major creative force that stormed through my life. Later we collaborated on a musical about the circus, a project doomed to obscurity.

I never fell in love with Christopher as I had with Maria. He was enchanting and charming, whereas Maria was surely my soulmate. Yet I was smitten. I compartmentalized two entirely different personae. I justified my duplicity in simple terms: I was androgynous. I was David Bowie. I was Mick Jagger. I could go both ways. I could do whatever I wanted. And I wanted it all.

After only a couple of dates, Christopher, with a dramatic flourish, threw me the keys to his Upper East Side apartment that stood empty while he attended graduate school at the University of North Carolina. "Wait for me there," he said.

His New York place was perfect—theater posters on the wall, cool furniture, theatrical lighting, a closet filled with expensive hip clothes that Christopher said I was free to wear. And, man, did I wear them! Check me out in a wine-colored velvet sport coat, silk ascot, and tight black jeans strolling into Reno Sweeney on West Thirteenth Street, the cabaret of cabarets, to see Peter Allen, Ellen Green, Holly Woodlawn, Judith Cohen, Andrea Marcovicci, and Melissa Manchester.

The one time Christopher came to the city, he took me to see his father Richard's Fifth Avenue apartment overlooking Central Park. Cezanne and Matisse paintings on the walls; Picasso ceramics on the mantles and coffee tables; a Modigliani nude above the fireplace. The place emitted the heady fragrance of New York Upper East Side culture. In my secret mind, I set my sights on having such a place of my own.

During that first semester I also found my way into underground culture. After her show at Reno Sweeney called *Airbush*, I met Holly Woodlawn, a transgender actress born Haroldo Santiago Franceschi Rodríguez Danhakl, but brilliantly renamed by Andy Warhol who made her a superstar in his films *Trash* and *Women In Revolt*. Her friend Lou Reed featured her in the first verse of his most famous song, "Walk on the Wild Side." Holly was more than wild. She was brilliant, hysterically funny, and magically unpredictable. She described how she and Lou adhered to an annual ritual of stealing a Christmas tree off the street. After midnight, when the owner was gone, they slowly walked by the pile of tied-up trees, grabbed the bottom of a trunk, pulled out the tree, and calmly walked home.

Holly, whose mother was Puerto Rican, had bright-green eyes like Mimí and took me under her wings. Maybe she saw me as her boy toy. Maybe she saw me as arm candy. For whatever reasons, she dragged me to a John Waters party and took me for several walks on the wild side.

One rainy morning, I happened into the sundries shop at the student center of NYU, where, working behind the counter, stood an African American student wearing denim overalls and no shirt. His Afro was huge and his smile sparkling. I had to get to know him and did. Keith Barrow was the son of Reverend Willie Barrow, a Chicago minister and civil rights leader who had worked with Martin Luther King, Jr. and cofounded Operation PUSH with Jesse Jackson. She was also Barack Obama's godmother.

Keith and I had zero sexual chemistry. When it came to music, though, we clicked. We began writing soul songs that he sang with Patti LaBelle-quality chops. He had a flawless four-octave range and a lethal artillery of original riffs. Hank Cosby, a Stevie Wonder producer, invited Keith to audition for him at Columbia. I came along as Keith's accompanist. Cosby was knocked out, gave Keith a deal, and invited me to rehearsals of Linda Hopkins's Broadway production of *Me and Bessie*. Cosby also encouraged me to play him my original songs and offered helpful critiques. I had a long way to go, but just being in the office of Hank Cosby, a man who was on the phone with Berry Gordy, fed my optimistic spirit.

Keith was out, out, out. It was not in his nature to hide his flamboyance. He once arrived at the Columbia offices in high-heeled diva drag, complete with diamond earrings and a long mink coat. It was as though Aretha herself had arrived. His best friend was Sylvester, another brave gender-bending trailblazer whose falsetto-driven "You Make Me Feel (Mighty Real)" became an enduring anthem of the disco era. Keith recorded one of my songs, "Foolish Hearts," written with Don Paul Yowell, soon to become another major character in my life.

*With Keith Barrow, Media Sound, New York City, 1979*

Keith Barrow's life was tragically short. He was my first close friend to die of AIDS. He was only twenty-nine. His talent was up there with Donny Hathaway's. I was blessed to have known him. He was a miracle of positivity, fun, and love on this too-often loveless planet.

Academically, NYU was great. One of my teachers was Modina Scoville, inventor or the Scoville Method and author of a famous text, *Keyboard Technique.* She wore flower dresses and antique brooches and coiffed her hair like an old maid in a Victorian novel. She taught a singular system, assigning numerals to notes that could be transposed to any key. To this day, that's how most Nashville session musicians read charts. The method helped me develop my piano style influenced by Laura Nyro and Elton John, who, in turn, had been influenced by Leon Russell. Open-voiced haunting chords were the ones I loved most. My extensive vocal training with Professor John Kuhn included German lieder and Italian opera.

I was in a tedious music theory class when I heard the sound of mysterious piano chords floating in through the walls. The chords combined the styling of Laura Nyro and Joni Mitchell. The combination was magical. I had to know who in God's name was able to pull this off. I left the classroom and wandered down the hall until I found the practice room, where the aforementioned Don Paul Yowell was playing. He was a little guy with a sexy vibe. But sex wasn't on my mind . . . for once. Music was. *His* music.

"You don't know it," I said, "but you're going to be my best friend."

*Don Paul Yowell, New York City, 1981*

Don was a brilliant singer-songwriter. His lyrics destroyed me. This is his "Midnight Streets":

*Jesus here we are*
*So small on these midnight streets*
*Particles in a universe of miracles*
*The shuffle of our shoes on this*
*Cobblestone way*
*Shadows and halos*
*Shining round these streetlamps fade*
*Let the morning come*
*Let the morning bring what may*

*Are we all just prisoners*
*Of these hands we're dealt at birth*
*And through the night*
*On these muddy waters*

*Shines the torch of Miss Liberty*
*For what it's worth*
*Are we just sensitive and troubled*
*Or lost in the night*
*Jesus, we're so small on these midnight streets*

Don lived on a cobblestone, midnight street south of Canal in Lower Manhattan where he actually had a view of the Statue of Liberty that inspired his urban torch songs. We developed an Amadeus/Salieri relationship—he, of course, was Mozart and I his envious and adoring colleague.

Beyond the excellent teachers NYU provided, my musical relationships with Keith Barrow and Don Paul Yowell were profound. As an undergraduate, I surrounded myself with young geniuses.

I also began working the Tin Pan Alley circuit. That's how I met Tommy Mottola, who'd one day run Sony Records. At the time he was working out of a tiny cubicle as a song plugger and small-time manager of his one client: Hall & Oates. He heard my songs, said I had talent, and hooked me up at the Chappell Music Workshop, where I woodshedded and wrote with a group of superb African American composers who left an indelible mark on my future sound. Above all else, I sought soul.

Alone at Christopher's, I maintained his apartment immaculately.

Every few days, blasting his cast recordings of Stephen Sondheim's *Company* and *A Little Night Music,* I washed the windows and scrubbed the floors. I also got to know Christopher's friend who lived across the hall, a down-on-her-luck single mom with a toddler. It was she who, some three months after I had been in the apartment, knocked on the door and apologetically said, "Christopher just called. He wants you to clear out."

"As in, moving out of his place?"

"I'm afraid so."

"Did he say why?"

"He really didn't say anything. You just have to leave."

That was Christopher, a man of mysterious ways, who would eventually count Liberace among his lovers.

I wasn't terribly crestfallen, because second semester was starting, and that meant Maria Vidal was arriving. Although the Stonewall Riots had occurred four years before I got to New York and gay liberation was blossoming, I was still far from coming out. I knew my brand-new Hungarian father would never approve. Besides, I had Maria.

I was ecstatic when she moved in with me. Marfy had found me a tiny railroad apartment at 309 East Eighty-First Street, 2FE. Of course, it was smack in the middle of Little Hungary. Because Maria's parents didn't know we were living together, I could never answer the phone for fear they might be calling. The former tenant, an old man, had lain dead for who knows how long before being discovered. It took days to eliminate the stench. The place was also rat-infested, often leaving us in stark terror. We slept in the living room on a foldout couch we rescued from a junk pile and reupholstered ourselves in dark rust-colored velour. The minuscule kitchen area contained the only sink. Wash the dishes and brush your teeth in the same sink.

For a while, life was good. Maria and I were seated at Lincoln Center, where Boz Scaggs was performing his silky "Low Down," when the lights went out—and stayed out for forty-eight hours. The Great New York Blackout of the summer of '77 turned into a two-day party, a scene from *Hair*, everyone romping through the park and generating electric love. Dead-broke in December, I emulated the antics of Holly Woodlawn and Lou Reed, sneaking out in the middle of the night to swipe a fir tree and surprise Maria with the fresh fragrance of Christmas cheer.

Joe Marfy came to visit. Having grown up in the Depression, he could be East European-thrifty. Rather than stay in a hotel, he slept on our metal foldout cot and took us to dinner at Csardas, a Hungarian restaurant where he regaled us with stories of his golden youth in Budapest. One evening when Maria had retired early, he and I had a private chat that shook me to my core.

"I need to tell you about Kati," he said.

"Who's Kati?"

"The love of my life."

"What about Valeria?"

"A different kind of love."

He went on to say that Kati in Budapest was the daughter of his first cousin. He had known her from birth. Shockingly, she was only a year older than me. He was determined to bring her to America. But with the Iron Curtain still in place, Soviet surrogates made leaving Hungary extremely difficult. If I would write her love letters, though, that would establish a relationship that could eventually lead to marriage.

"You want me to marry your mistress?" I asked in total shock.

"It vould only be on paper. It vould allow her to live in the United States, where I vould set her up in an apartment. Once she arrives, your obligation vill be over."

"But I have every intention of marrying Maria."

"And there's no reason vhy you shouldn't—once you marry and divorce Kati."

In retrospect, it amazes me to report that I did, in fact, follow my father's wishes. Much to Maria's dismay, I wrote Kati make-believe love letters that she answered with make-believe love letters of her own. Why did I participate in my father's scheme? I wanted to please him. I also wanted him to keep paying that portion of my college expenses not covered by my scholarship. I also reasoned that these imaginary love letters would lead to nothing. Like everyone else, I was seduced by Marfy's charm. He could talk anyone into anything.

After a few months, I stopped writing because I was trying to persuade Maria into marrying me. She refused, but later said that had I asked her just one more time she would have accepted.

I'm not proud to say that during this time, I had an affair with another woman while I was with Maria. I met her at Trax, a hip music-biz basement club on West Seventy-Second Street. She had a beauty similar to Maria's, with one difference: her eyes were a piercing green. She was a fashion model and later found out she was a close relative to Anne Frank. We dined at my favorite haunts, where many of the waiters actually thought she was Maria.

Why was my moral compass in tatters? Why was I cheating on Maria, the woman of my dreams? Was I trying to become a player in the mode of Joe Marfy? Was I proving my manhood? Denying my gayness?

That denial didn't last long. It ended the moment I focused on a young man I had spotted during a street fair in our neighborhood. My first impression was negative. Stoned out of his mind, he was wearing grungy white shorts, a tight tank top and no shoes. He was dancing by himself and, while his movements were not without grace, he seemed out of control. His dark beard and green eyes were striking. It was those same green eyes that struck me a second time while I was standing with the bar crowd at the maître d' station at Reno Sweeney, applauding cabaret diva Ellen Greene. This time he was beardless, well dressed, and assumed a softer demeanor. This time it was love at second sight. We began talking and quickly learned that we lived on the same block. He was Jewish, younger than me by a few years, effortlessly charming, and eager to share an uptown cab. I couldn't refuse. He invited me up for tea. His small studio apartment was fastidious. He was a fellow Floridian from a wealthy Coral Gables family. He said he was a singer. He asked me to follow him into the stairwell, where, with an echo-chamber effect, he strummed the guitar and sang me "Poetry Man" that took on a definite homoerotic meaning.

This chance meeting was explosive, and I became instantly hooked on him. Maria was waitressing at night, making it easy to steal away across the street to this exciting young man, who

I later found out got off on seducing straight guys. That was his thing. Because I had a girlfriend, I was his perfect conquest. All these confusions didn't matter. I was obsessed with him.

I was busted when, one afternoon after saying I was going to work out, Maria ran to the window to watch me leave, and saw me walking in the opposite direction from the gym. I soon got entangled in my web of lies and finally admitted the truth to Maria, who was crushed and brokenhearted. Maria and I had been together four years before our breakup, during those storybook hungry years where our passion, talent and driving ambition overrode any other distractions, or even the force of nature. But I was growing up and becoming a man and couldn't keep compartmentalizing who I was any longer and living a lie that was tearing me up inside. This complicated my life, not only because of the terrible guilt I felt for betraying the woman I adored, but because that woman was my essential partner in a musical unit we had established together and was taking the city by storm.

*With Maria on NYU graduation day*

*The island sleeps / Our dreams afloat . . . / Awaken as teen angels / Resurrect the dead of night / On Eighty-First Street*

# DESMOND CHILD & ROUGE

My name first emerged in the musical epoch of the seventies through the pop band that I created with Maria and our two best friends, Diana Grasselli, whom we knew from the Miami Dade South Community College, and Myriam Valle, whom Virgil Night and I had met at the Brotherhood of the Spirit commune in Warwick, Massachusetts. We called ourselves Desmond Child & Rouge.

The name was conjured up by Rick Carlock, a comedy writer who claimed to have penned Bette Midler's most notorious one-liners, like "cracking up from lack of shacking up" and the faux-Hawaiian, "Come on I wanna lay ya." One of the members of his troupe, Judith Cohen, was equally notorious for a comment uttered while she and Peter Allen were in the kitchen of Reno Sweeney when a gun-wielding holdup man stormed in to rob the place: "Kill *me!*" she said, before pointing to Peter and adding, "He's the one with talent."

Rick and I were crossing Columbus Avenue by the Museum of Natural History when he said, "Bette has her Harlettes. You'll have your Rouge." Which also had that faux-French Moulin Rouge flare.

I accepted the pronouncement.

Initially the lineup included our close friend from my Miami Beach school days Melanie London, a talented visual artist and comedienne in her own right.

At first, our goal was to shape a musical unit that included sketch comedy between the songs, a singular performance style that would go over in the cabarets and underground clubs. I sang most of the lead vocals, but the women were featured as well. Our material was as original as our campy look.

Even though disco had set in, Desmond Child & Rouge was more pop and rock than most dance music of those times. I had a large inventory of rockish blue-eyed-soul songs. Those songs were rooted in the life I had known—the urban Latin streets of Miami and New York. We were telling stories of that life. We were propelled by seamless dance grooves. We were also before our time. We worshipped at the shrine of sophisticated glamour, but we gave glamour a new countenance. We were living at a time when, on one side, angry punk bands like the Ramones were raging and, on the other, the Bee Gees and ABBA were taking over the airwaves. You were either on the side of Springsteen's hard-rock seriousness or labeled superficial in the mode of Disco-Tex and the Sex-O-Lettes. We were neither, or somewhere in between.

We were a hot ticket in Manhattan. When we headlined the Bottom Line, our performance was broadcast live across three states. The audience stood on their chairs and hollered till their voices turned hoarse. The buzz was so great that our manager told me news that took the top of my head off: We were set to tour with Laura Nyro as her opening act. I burst out in tears. The next week, Rouge and I went to her Carnegie Hall concert to meet her backstage. I brought a bouquet of roses and a heart full of love. When we met face-to-face, I took a deep breath, told her how I admired her and how thrilled we were to be her opening act. Her face went completely blank.

Without her saying so, it was obvious that we were *not* going on tour with her. I apologized and began backing up, as though I were bidding farewell to royalty. I ran down the street to the first phone booth I could find, calling our first manager, cabaret diva Harriet Leider, and screaming, "You lied! Why did you lie?" She confessed the lie, saying she just wanted to encourage us.

Before Desmond Child & Rouge broke through to national recognition, we hustled our wares like people possessed. Seething with hope and brimming with ambition, we stenciled notifications of our club dates on the city streets. We concentrated on midtown, where the national record labels were headquartered. We also plastered our posters on telephone poles and construction sites, not realizing that ad space was controlled by the Irish Mafia. We could have been killed. The leading soldier in our army was Eric Vetro, President for Life of the Desmond Child & Rouge Fan Club. (Eric had been in the NYU choir with me and would go on to become "voice coach to the stars," including Katy Perry, Pink, and Ariana Grande.) Once, the cops caught us putting up posters on Bleecker Street. Everyone scattered but me. There I was, without an ID, holding a dozen posters in my hand. I sat in jail for three hours before Maria sprung me loose.

One of our most devoted fans was photographer Ciro Barbaro. We met through his friend and colleague Gene Bagnato, who brought him to our show. Ciro went crazy for us, and thus began our long creative relationship. He started helping us make fantastical concept photos as artwork for our publicity posters. One of the first ones was a Gulliver's Travels theme, where I had fallen asleep at the piano dressed in a nineteenth-century costume and Rouge were tiny Lilliputians in black cocktail dresses making mischief. Then we did one inspired by the work of Maxfield Parrish, where I was a moonlit dreamer on a rock by the sea and Rouge were mermaid sirens serenading me. Ciro photographed our first album cover on Capitol Records and built a yellow elevator set in his loft for the shoot. He was also at many of our gigs documenting our performances and backstage fun. Thanks to our dear friend Ciro, we have thousands of pictures from those hungry years that capture all the energy and creativity we put into everything we did.

We were shameless in hounding promoters, bookers, and managers. In the pre-social-media age, we traded our mailing lists with other performers and spent every penny on printing and postage. We even managed to get Jackie O's address. We also called our friends, asking them to call twenty more friends to help fill the clubs. Our persistence paid off. If you opened the *Village Voice,* you'd see that we were playing at five different clubs on five different nights. On several occasions we actually played two shows at different clubs on the same night. The club owners bitched, but the places were packed. After playing dives and dyke bars for over a year and opening for everyone from Patti Smith to the New York Dolls, we finally achieved our dream, a booking at Reno Sweeney, where we were discovered by managers Roy Ericson and Matthew Mark, of Starflight Management. By then we had cut out the comedy skits from our show, which meant losing Melanie, and focused on music, music, music.

Fans lined up around the block, screaming for us like we were the Beatles. Rouge had big hair, tight jeans, heavy makeup. I was swathed in red leather. Our band, furiously whipped into shape by guitarist G. E. Smith, was supertight. We traded in synchronized movement. During one incendiary show at the Bottom Line, Maria spontaneously stepped off the stage, walking right onto the tabletops over people's dishes and plates, never losing her footing, creating a sensation. The date was a triumph.

Irwin Robinson, powerful boss of Chappell Music, asked me about my goal. "To be a bigger songwriter than Stevie Wonder," I said. When he broke out laughing, I realized the ridiculousness of my statement and turned red. I knew I had overplayed my hustle. And yet Irwin offered me $75,000 to sign as a writer. I wasn't told about the deal, though, because management turned him down. They were even crazier than me. Maybe they thought they could get more.

Ultimately, they did get us a contract at Capitol Records. Right out of the box, we had a smash debut album, *Desmond Child & Rouge*, a hit single, "Our Love Is Insane," plus an AOR hit, "Westside Pow Wow." (Paul Shaffer, then on *Saturday Night Live* and soon to be David Letterman's band leader, played piano on the record.)

Encouragement did come when our first album, dropped in January 1979, gained momentum. We did signings at record stores where I was upset to see our album in the disco bins. "We're rock," I insisted, "not disco." We did do a national tour, though without our label's full backing. Bob Seger was the king of Capitol and A Taste of Honey the queens. Supposedly we fit in between the two. Like Seger, "Our Love Is Insane" was guitar-heavy, but, like A Taste of Honey, it also appealed to dancers.

Despite the genre confusion, I was tripping out on more than a mild case of grandiosity. At twenty-five, I was certain fortune and fame had come calling. When we headlined at Trax, George Harrison came to see us. Peter Allen sang our praises. The *Village Voice* was ecstatic: "Not since Bette Midler steamed up the Continental Baths with her high camp antics has the city seen anything as scintillating as Desmond Child & Rouge." *New York Magazine* enthused, "Beyond their silky-smooth seductive dance beats, the group displays a strong and delightful musical integrity."

My professional life was soaring, and my personal life was all about the boy with the green eyes. It didn't matter that he was four years my junior, when it came to gay sex he was my teacher. I put all of this into "The Truth Comes Out":

*I confess my innermost secrets to strangers in the dark*
*And my words fly like sparks from my mouth*
*As the truth comes out*

The song appeared on the second Desmond Child & Rouge album, *Runners In The Night*, released the same year as our first, 1979. I thought of it as my ultimate coming-out song, but no one picked up on it.

That second album did more than attempt to clarify my sexual identity. It also marked the end of the group. After reviewer Stephen Holden, at *The Village Voice*, criticized our first record for being superficial pop, I rushed back into the studio to grind out a more credible direction. The record label said our first album didn't go gold because no one understood our eclectic style. This time I was determined that the style would be clear: New York punk-influenced raw artsy rock. We came up with a leaner and meaner sound. We did the whole thing in twenty-eight days—wrote it, produced it, sang it, and mixed it.

Toward the end, when I was frantically trying to complete the record, after working all night, I returned to the apartment at the break of dawn. I didn't see a razor resting on the sink and sliced my finger badly. The wound was deep, but I couldn't stay awake. So I wrapped it tightly, but not tightly enough, because when I woke up some hours later, the bed was covered in blood. I made it to the ER, where nurses stopped the bleeding. The blood symbolized this second album.

That's because raw and raucous didn't really fit into the true aesthetic of our sound, which in retrospect was years ahead our time. This new sparse direction wasn't understood by the LA label, and they completely ignored the record. We got zero promotion. Ironically, Holden, who had labeled our debut release superficial and was now at *Rolling Stone* magazine, bewailed that we had "ripped the paper moon down from the sky" and abandoned the colorful charm of our first album. What the fuck! I was incensed—yet not incensed enough to keep from chasing after the approval of the critical elite.

*Saturday Night Live* was absolutely the most creative and popular show on television at that time. The funny and iconic Gilda Radner, one of the original cast members, loved Desmond Child & Rouge. When she starred in the Mike Nichols-directed Broadway show *Gilda Live,* at the Winter Garden Theatre, she cast Maria, Myriam, and Diana as singers and comic foils. She also secured Desmond Child & Rouge the most prestigious national TV spot of the season: featured musical guests on *Saturday Night Live.* Capitol Records did nothing with this incredible shot for us. They didn't even think to send us some congratulatory flowers.

A month before the show, I threw a big Thanksgiving party. This was held at our manager's elegant brownstone in Brooklyn, where I had landed after "green eyes" had broken up with me, his conquest complete. I was crushed and confused, and the Rouge ladies were angry with me and bickering among themselves. The acrimony was so intense we almost didn't make it on the air. Because we hadn't performed together in months, we were unprepared. The entire *Saturday Night Live* thing was an out-of-body experience. I was there, but I wasn't there.

The year ended with a bust.

And then I nearly broke down.

*Desmond Child & Rouge backstage with Gilda Radner*

*With Jon Landau backstage, Lower Manhattan Ocean Club*

# RUNNERS IN THE NIGHT

THE DEATH OF Desmond Child & Rouge was due to my uncertain sense of self. Jon Landau, the highbrow music critic who'd become Bruce Springsteen's manager, took an interest in me. A champion of my songwriting, but not our singing group, he advised me to go solo. Jon's intellectual acuity reminded me of Jerry Wexler and Ahmet Ertegun, those brainy executives I met as a kid in Miami.

"You don't need Rouge," Landau told me. "You're stronger without them. You can sing, write, and produce. You're a star in your own right."

When Landau hinted that he might even want to manage and produce me, that's all I needed to hear. If Springsteen's man said I was a star, how could I miss? All the hard work and energy we'd put into the group over the past few years had not achieved the success we'd dreamed of–we were exhausted and starting to fight among ourselves. At that point we agreed that the time had come to ask Capitol Records to release us so we could start solo careers.

To secure our early release from Capitol, I had to promise our producer and A&R man Richard Landis that we wouldn't re-form as Desmond Child & Rouge and sign at a competing label, as he said that would be embarrassing for him. I gave my word and kept our promise. Shouldn't have.

My optimism was further fueled when I was cast as the lead in a musical about a circus, ironically the same subject that Christopher Adler and I had tackled for a show of our own. Pat Birch, the choreographer who won a Tony for *Grease*, was directing. The project never progressed beyond the workshop stage, but before its demise I convinced Jon Landau to see me in the role. Jon called it corny, and I was embarrassed. My performance did nothing to raise his appreciation of my talent . . . perhaps even hurt it. At the same time, he reconfirmed his determination to steer my career in the right direction. OK, but then why did Landau suddenly stop returning my calls?

At first, I thought it was just a matter of patience. Jon had a lot going on. After all, Springsteen was bigger than life. So, I waited. And waited. And waited some more. After a year of waiting, it became clear: Jon had probably lost interest in me. Now I understand. Back then I didn't. The rejection stung. And so did the failure of Desmond Child & Rouge. I had no self-confidence, no manager, no record deal, no Maria Vidal, no chance of opening for Bruce.

Thanks to the generosity of Greg Heisler, a *Life* magazine photographer who shot the second Desmond Child & Rouge album cover, I was living at the Oliver Cromwell at Twelve West Seventy-Second Street. Greg was always on the road and let me stay at his apartment, directly across from the famed Dakota, where Yoko and John Lennon lived.

I was still obsessed with "green eyes" who said he had started writing his own songs on his acoustic guitar in the stairwell while studying at Lee Strasberg's Actors Studio. He was also playing me. Given my willingness to please him, I became his toy. Because the sex was so hot—we'd start in the elevator of the Oliver Cromwell and barely make our way to the apartment—I lost my bearings. I got sucked into his pattern of makeup to breakup.

One day he'd say, "We're done."

"Why?" I'd ask.

"You care about me more than I care about you."

"That's cruel."

"That's honest," he'd add. "I'm just not attracted to you in that way. It's over."

He'd leave and I'd fall into a black hole, obsessing about what I had done wrong or why I wasn't good enough. Then a day or two later, he'd call, asking, "Can we talk? Can we meet for coffee?" Then the magic and the nightmare would start all over again.

This back-and-forth physically and emotionally addictive cycle of pleasure and pain pushed my every button and completely undermined my self-esteem . . . till there was nothing left of me. Ultimately, to save myself . . . I had to cut him off.

One positive thing did emerge from my negative experience with him: I came out to Mimí and Marfy. My father had invited me to Madrid for Christmas vacation. One night after dinner, we sat alone drinking white-wine spritzers and eating chunks of sweet Hungarian *beigli*. I spilled out the whole story of leaving Maria for a guy . . . who didn't even want me. I admitted that I thought I was far more gay than bi. I was lost.

My girlfriend, my boyfriend, my label, my managers—they were all gone. My father reacted to the story by telling me a joke. It was his way of commiserating.

"Vell," he said, "this man, he goes to a hooker. Gorgeous hooker. He drops his pants. The hooker points and laughs: 'Who do you think you're going to please vith that?' He answers, 'Myself.' So, there you are—ve have only to please ourselves."

I'm not sure Marfy really understood me. Given his relationship with Kati, he understood secret lives involving the opposite sex, but same-sex attraction was an anathema. At least, that's what my stepmother, Valeria, told me. "Your father is homophobic," she said, "and always will be." The double irony was that the youngest son of Joe and Valeria, my brother Joey, would himself soon come out.

I came out to Mimí during lunch at a health-food restaurant in Coral Gables. She had divorced Alberto Hernandez and married a dashing silver-haired pilot, an Argentine who looked like Cesar Romero. His plane had broken down in Miami and would take a full year to repair. Once it was ready to fly, he was ready to take Mimí to Buenos Aires, where she would attend to her wifely duties. Mimí wasn't about to fly over the Amazon in a small plane. When she refused to leave Miami and her family, he beat her up before skipping out.

It wasn't easy for Mimí to hear me discuss sex. She only half-listened. I could feel her disappointment. For all her artistic liberalism, the macho culture of Cuba mocked queerness in any form.

"You should have married Maria," she said, forgetting that she had always been slightly negative and critical of her. Mimí saw Maria as competition.

Even though she never openly admitted or endorsed my sexual orientation, she never brought it up again. I believe she was secretly happy she no longer had to compete with another woman.

I came out to my parents but still hadn't come out to the world.

What was stopping me?

Insecurity? The undertow of my own innate homophobia undermining me from within? Perhaps an inability to give up the dream, as endorsed by Springsteen star-maker Jon Landau, that I could become a credible solo artist as big as Springsteen or Jackson Brown? I remembered 1976, when Elton John told *Rolling Stone* that he was bi, much less gay, and his career plummeted. Like Luther Vandross, I saw that in the pop culture of the early eighties, open queerness was a no-go.

At the same time, my confidence was shattered, even as my ambition smoldered. I was hell-bent on succeeding, somehow, some way, some day.

Though my affair with a man was inevitable, Maria, though feeling deeply betrayed, was somehow able to forgive me. She knew that as much as I worshipped her, and we were as spiritually and emotionally entwined as any two people could be, I couldn't change that one thing that is so inextricably central to the core of who I am. Around love, loyalty, and understanding of each other, we endure . . . and live forever young as Tommy and Gina.

*Maria and Desmond*

*Paradise Room at Reno Sweeney, New York City*

*Media Sound Studio, New York City*

*Debut-album cover*

*Yanqui, New York City, 1980*

# DAKOTA

A LITTLE BEFORE 11:00 P.M. on December 8, 1980, I was in my apartment at the Oliver Cromwell speaking on the phone with Maria. It was an unusually mild night, and the window was open. Suddenly I heard a blast of five gunshots. They sounded like cannons. Frightened, I hit the floor. Then nothing. Not long afterward, the screams of sirens and the arrival of cop cars. By the time I went downstairs to see for myself, the street was filled with people and the word was out: John Lennon had been shot to death, across the street in the archway of the Dakota.

At the Greek deli on the corner, press from the world over gathered, trying to get the story and figure out what happened. I was numb. It made no sense. Politicians are assassinated. But not pacifist rock stars. Not gentle souls singing of love. Who kills a Beatle? Who kills a poet? Who slays a peacemaker?

It began to drizzle. The sky was crying. A sea of black umbrellas opened up and surrounded the Dakota, once a symbol of the city's vanquished Gilded Age, now a symbol of grief, senseless horror, gnawing pain. I went back to the Oliver Cromwell and sat at the piano and began singing, "Rain falls softly on this bloody street . . . wash away, wash away, wash away our sins tonight . . . why must there be this senseless killing . . . I'm ashamed to be human tonight."

For three days, I joined the throngs as we marched into Central Park, mourning the incomprehensible, celebrating the beauty John gave, grieving the beauty that would forever remain unexpressed. We all stood alone; we all stood together. A community of sadness unlike any I had ever experienced.

While still living at the Oliver Cromwell, and in the aftermath of Jon Landau's rejection, I made a musical move. I started a new alternative-rock band called, "Yanqui," with guitarist John Putnam, Al Scotti on bass, and drummer Mark Kaufman. We rehearsed and recorded, at all hours, up in my apartment. We didn't really have a clear vision, but were emulating, or rather should I say living in the musical shadow of Springsteen and U2, who were dominating the world of rock in the early eighties.

As the band struggled to take form, I also continued to write with and for other artists, like KISS, Ronnie Spector, Michael Bolotin (soon to become Bolton), Billy Squier, Jennifer Rush, and Ellen Foley.

Then, in early June of 1983, through my new manager, Winston Simone, I received a call from megaproducer Jim Steinman, who had just put a hold on my song, "Lovers Again" for his successful artist Bonnie Tyler, who was on a massive roll after her global #1 hit "Total Eclipse Of The Heart." Jim asked me to write a new song to order and said something to the effect of wanting "this song to have to do with 'androgyny,' with verses that sound like Tina Turner; the B section has to sound like The Police, U2, or Hall & Oates; and the chorus has to sound like Bruce Springsteen." So I set out to furiously write the song that would eventually become the cornerstone of "my sound."

On a sweltering afternoon in mid-June, my "Yanqui" bandmates and I played the demo live in my home studio on the twenty-fifth floor of the Oliver Cromwell, where we couldn't have the air conditioner on during takes. We also invited jazz saxophonist, Bob Malach to come and overdub an E Street Band/Clarence Clemons-style soul riff over the intro. Bob had brought his tenor sax, and after a few tries, because the song was in a high key, he almost left to go get his alto sax. But because Bob had already been complaining that the heat made him feel nauseous and started sweating profusely, I was afraid he wouldn't come back. I told him to just roll with it and screech it out the best he could on his tenor sax. After we doubled it, it really had an exciting and urgent sound that brought the track to life.

The next day, Maria and Myriam, of Desmond Child & Rouge, came over with singer Elaine Caswell, and the four of us sang the background vocals. We had to share one headphone set between us, which made us have to keep stopping because we were laughing so hard. With the limited home-studio technology we had, Al and I mixed the song late into the night, and I took the cassette over to Winston in the morning to forward to Jim. Jim got right back to Winston to put it on hold for Bonnie Tyler. And that's how "If You Were A Woman (And I Was A Man)" was born . . . which later became Bon Jovi's epic stadium anthem, "You Give Love A Bad Name," that changed the course of pop music forever and more recently was interpolated into the Number 1 global smash "Kings & Queens," by Ava Max. It's a tale of three hits . . . but that's another story in another chapter in my next book.

While living at the Oliver Cromwell apartments, I regularly heard the thud of heavy boots from the man living a floor above my apartment, Davitt Sigerson, who became a lifelong friend and collaborator—a multitalented artist whose accomplishments ranged from songwriter to producer to record executive to novelist. Being an artist himself, he never complained about the loud sounds and music coming up through the floorboards, and he endeared himself to me by knocking on my door one evening with a single question: "Can I borrow a cup of gay?"

"What?" I asked.

"I started a song called 'Gentlemen Prefer Boys,' and I'm afraid I'm too straight to finish it. Want to write it with me?"

I was in. It was an over-the-top Shirley Bassey-style disco parody about a woman who discovers her man is gay. The lyrics start to reveal various in-queer-manating clues like "lifeguard lipstick on his collar" and "the hungry look in waiters' eyes." Sound familiar?

Eliot Hubbard, cofounder of Reno Sweeney, eventually became head of publicity for Epic Records, working with Cyndi Lauper and Michael Jackson. I met him during the Reno days when, on a tip from scintillating singer David Lasley, Eliot booked us into his club and sent our short-lived career soaring.

Hubbard was a self-made musicologist and a man of singular taste. A trust fund baby—his great-grandfather had cornered the brick market in Boston—he was a sophisticated gentleman with an eye for beauty and an ear for exquisite music. Eliot had a loft in Soho as well as Dove Cottage, an enchanting property surrounded by a glistening pond in Washington, Connecticut, where we'd binge-watch old Bette Davis and Joan Crawford films. In fact, I affectionately called him Uncle Joan. His aesthetic, marrying grandiosity and restraint, had a sweeping influence on me. As time went on, I designed my homes using Eliot's feel for Art Deco and Old Hollywood. His living spaces were like noir movies from the forties. It was through Eliot that I met Ellie Greenwich.

Even at a young age, my goal was to learn from legendary writers.

Author of "Be My Baby," "Da Doo Ron Ron," "Leader of the Pack," "River Deep—Mountain High" and dozens of other classics, Ellie was one of my heroes. She was a Brooklyn Jewish big-boned, chain-smoking, bee-hive hairdo, tough-talking, chick out of the sixties with heavy black eyeliner and dangling rose-colored glass earrings. Ellie was very much like her songs: an innocent. When we met, she was in her early forties and I in my mid-twenties. She was my link to the golden era of first-generation rock 'n' roll. She tearfully told me that she never got over the separation from her songwriting partner and husband, Jeff Barry—and, that every song she ever wrote was for him . . . songs like "Be My Baby," and "(Today I Met) The Boy I'm Gonna Marry."

We wrote in her apartment on Fifty-Seventh Street which, due to agoraphobia, she was afraid to leave. She found levity in telling stories of her childhood when she and girlfriends would sing five-part harmony as the subway roared from Brooklyn to the Brill Building. Together she and I wrote "Jump Start My Heart," a no-holds-barred soul song recorded by Bruce's Big Man, saxist Clarence Clemons. Occasionally I'd tease Ellie out of her apartment. Once we went to a porn shop, the two of us squeezed into a tiny booth as we slipped quarters in the slot to watch a split-beaver peep show performed by a Forty-Second Street honey. We kept dropping quarters onto the slimy floor and laughed our heads off. After the show, we went back to Ellie's place and wrote "Good Things Take Time."

It took me far more time to be an accomplished songwriter than I had ever imagined. That accomplishment was due in a large measure to two mentors who came along at just the right time. The first was Paul Stanley of KISS. Paul was a Desmond Child & Rouge fan. He was the first to appreciate what he called my narrative gift.

"Most songs don't tell stories," he said. "Yours do. Let's write together."

Paul wrote on guitar. As he strummed his acoustic, I studied his hands. His beautifully shaped hands are works of art. He constructs chords and riffs freely, and he's also a great lyricist. Effortlessly, our melodies and words meshed.

It was Paul Stanley who taught me how to write stadium anthems the KISS way. His towering influence is alive in every hit song I've ever written. There is no Desmond Child without Paul Stanley.

He also explained that each band has its own aesthetic. For KISS, that meant the song could never come from the point of view of a victim or loser. It was always about winners. Triumphs. Victories. Positivity. If I came up with a sad vibe, Paul would immediately set me straight. Paul understood the KISS mandate was to make its die-hard fans feel good. His prolific mind created dozens of brilliant titles full of irony, like "Heaven's On Fire."

For all of Paul's dedication to his own band, he demonstrated rare generosity when our first collaboration resulted in a song not for KISS but for Desmond Child & Rouge called "The Fight," based on a riff I had started with guitarist David Landau . . . Jon's brother.

A few weeks later, Paul invited me to a KISS rehearsal at S.I.R. where, during a break, we pulled the heavy black canvas cover off a banged-up grand piano off to the side and wrote "I Was Made For Lovin' You." The song had a strong Motown feel—more on that in a minute—but, although it was a different direction than past KISS smashes, it too became a smash. In fact, "I Was Made For Lovin' You" has become KISS's biggest-selling and most performed global single to date.

The second legendary songwriter I was lucky enough to encounter was introduced to me by Eliot Hubbard: Bob Crewe. Like

Paul Stanley, Bob forever changed my concept of songwriting. Twenty-three years my senior, he as a young man had been both a fashion model and a singer. He formed his own group, the Bob Crewe Generation, and became the creative force behind the Four Seasons, for whom he wrote, along with his cowriter Bob Gaudio, "Big Girls Don't Cry," "Rag Doll," "Walk Like A Man," and Frankie Valli's "Can't Take My Eyes Off You." It was Bob who gave the Four Seasons their signature sound. His sense of production was both pristine and dramatic. His career was illustrious: Berry Gordy brought him in to produce and write for Michael Jackson. He penned hits for Roberta Flack, Lesley Gore, Bobby Darin, Barry Manilow, and Mitch Ryder, and the Detroit Wheels—to mention a few. One of his closest cohorts had been Jerry Wexler, who brought him to Memphis, where Bob cut his first solo album, *Motivation*.

Bob saw me as a willing collaborator and eager student. More important, he was grooming me to become his next big star. We were both gay, both closeted (Bob far more tightly than I), both tenacious workers, both Scorpios. Our relationship remained platonic yet personal. We stayed friends until his death in 2014. Like Eliot Hubbard, Bob's aesthetic was extraordinary. He had flawless taste, eventually becoming a painter of fine art and a sculptor of works of raw, massive beauty.

We worked with Brill Building-like protocol. We met every day at noon at Coq Au Vin, a small restaurant on West Fifty-Sixth Street, where we always split the check. Bob had been taken advantage of so frequently that he adopted a strict policy of going Dutch: fifty-fifty down to the penny. This from a guy who flew his entourage in a private jet to Paris to arrive in time for that morning's fresh croissants.

Bob had left LA for New York, where he lived large in two apartments, one for composing and another his lavish living quarters, where a haunting Victor Thall portrait of Tallulah Bankhead—what could be more gay?—hung in the dining room. We went to his writing studio, where the white walls were bare. There was no furniture except a piano, a hardwood bench and a high leather-upholstered chair with armrests. He couldn't write if he wasn't in that chair. My place was on the bench. He brewed up a pot of black coffee and we went to work. He signed me to his production company, and within a short while we wrote dozens of songs.

"Inspiration is not the point," said Bob. "Perseverance is."

Bob was the one who taught me to drill down. He wrote songs based on titles and lyrics first.

"Get your story straight," he explained, "and go from there. The story is the foundation."

My previous method had been to mumble over a melody for hours at a time and hope for the best. Bob's method was to sculpt the story.

"Why open your mouth if you have nothing to say?" he asked. "It's all about story."

The best example of his storytelling gift is the megahit "Lady Marmalade," which he wrote with Kenny Nolan at the Marmalade Hotel in New York City's Hell's Kitchen, sung by LaBelle and later covered by Christina Aguilera, Lil' Kim, Mya, and Pink. The storytelling is pure Bob Crewe. He paints a gaudy picture of the Creole prostitute awash in black satin sheets while Joe, her beguiled client, surveys the scene with breathless wonder. The narrative is punctuated with a combination of chants ("Go sista, go sista"), catchy alliterations ("Gitchie gitchie ya ya dada") which Bob explained was a Creole street vendor he saw in New Orleans peddling her candies called "Ya-Yas," translated as "get your yayas, Daddy," and a chorus rendered in rhyming French, "*Voulez vous coucher avec moi ce soir?*" ("Do you want to sleep with me tonight?")

Bob's approach to the art of songwriting—methodical while whimsical, reflective while romantic—totally changed my perspective. Before Bob, it was a matter of banging out something. Anything. Mumbling or more like yelping some improvised melodies, hoping they would start magically morphing into words I could stitch together into a lyric. After Bob, it was all about clean rhymes, inner rhymes and alliterations, the nitty-gritty of the craft with an eye toward a cohesive and compelling story. He would say, "Every vertical moment of a song, even the silence between notes, is as critical as the lyrics are, pulled across melody over the chords in time."

A little before meeting Bob, another master entered my life and, with the dissolution of Desmond Child & Rouge, brought me fresh spirit and much needed inspiration. Between her and Bob, I found my footing as an artist.

I met acting coach Sandra Seacat, one of Lee Strasberg's longtime teachers at the Actors Studio. Sandra and her thenboyfriend, my one-time protector Mickey Rourke, became Desmond Child & Rouge fans. A remarkable teacher, Sandra was in line to lead Strasberg's Actors Studio but left after many years because she became uncomfortable with Strasberg's personal method of berating his students to tears to get them to open up before performing a scene. In contrast, Sandra was a nurturer. I was drawn into her circle of disciples that included Jessica Lange, Cicely Tyson, Christopher Reeve, Michelle Pfeiffer, Marlo Thomas, Frances Fisher, Isabella Rossellini, future movie producer Lawrence Bender, and later Harvey Keitel, Ryan Gosling, Gina

Gershon, Laura Dern, and Andrew Garfield. I attended her work-shops, not to act but to glean insights into the nature of creativity. She teaches that your art is the vehicle for your soul's journey.

That's why we're compelled to create art.

"You're a shaman," Sandra would say, "a wounded healer. And by exposing your wounds through your work, you'll do more than heal yourself. You'll heal others." She gave the Method school a deeply spiritual undertone, allowing me to incorporate my fragmented dreams and unresolved pain into song. I did workshops with Sandra where, like my high school teacher Mrs. Leeds, I felt myself in the presence of a master for whom discipline and delight were not mutually exclusive. Discipline and delight in one's craft were two halves of a whole. Sandra's great lesson was that in all creativity, one's soul must be served. No soul, no lasting art. No genuine emotion, no true expression. I looked to Sandra as something of a godsend, a beautiful respite from my ruinous personal life.

Why ruinous?

I kept finding wounded angels determined to damage them-selves or me. At the bitter end of my affair with "green eyes," I happened to be walking up a staircase at NYU when I noticed a young man walking down. He saw me as well. We passed each other, and, on second thought, we both turned around. We were destined to meet.

His name was Michael Cava. A gifted classical pianist and remarkable accompanist, he was a whiz at improvisational motifs that met the needs of dancers of all styles. His sponta-neous compositions had the effortless lilt of Eric Satie or even Chopin. Musically, Michael never repeated himself or failed to thrill the dancers with his spirited melodies. Michael had an Al Pacino look: dark hair, strong, dramatic nose, and large, masculine hands that might have been sculpted by Michelangelo. He was classically beautiful.

Michael was living with Sally Blaine—a friend of mine to this day—and her two young children. Sally was a professor of dance at NYU, a divorcee almost twenty years older than Michael. She was madly in love with him, and so was I.

Michael soon moved from Sally's place to live with me at the Oliver Cromwell. Because he found it difficult to concentrate on work in my apartment, I rented him a studio at the Ansonia Residential Hotel, where he could put the Steinway that Sally had bought him. He was haunted by his past. Anthony, his younger musician teenage brother, had died when a hospital nurse gave him an overdose of insulin. The two boys were as close as twins. His parents reacted bizarrely to their son's death—as though it never happened—and kept Michael away from the funeral and not told where his grave site was. Michael never recovered from the trauma. He also suffered from deep depression and acute paranoia.

Life in fast-paced Manhattan fed his crushing fears, causing him to move to Amherst, Massachusetts, down the street from where Emily Dickinson had lived her reclusive life. Sally remained devoted and found him work as an accompanist to dancers at a college in nearby Northampton.

Though Michael sought the poetic solitude of a small town, he never adjusted. He was incapable, for instance, of keeping his house in order. He couldn't control the chaos of daily living. Garbage piled up, sheets never changed, litter everywhere. His surroundings reflected his mind. Yet the depth and sweetness of his soul kept me coming back. Weekend after weekend I drove four hours from Manhattan to Amherst, where I spent most of the time cleaning up.

Sometimes when I arrived, I found him in a fetal position curled up under his piano. My love for him demanded that I help him. So, I did. And also, I didn't.

To explain that contradiction isn't easy. I want to say that passion brought me to Michael and love moved me to come to his aid. But there's more to it than that. I entered into a vast world of teachers and gurus—some precious, some corrupt. Michael followed me into that world. Part of me—a big part—wanted and needed spiritual instruction. It happened in my thirties, a time when so many of my friends were starting to die of AIDS, and I never felt more lost or vulnerable. That vulnerability led to holy hell.

*With Michael Cava, New York City, 1982*

*Michael Cava (1951–1997)*

*Bob Crewe (1930–2014)*

*Sandra Seacat (1936–2023)*

*Miami Beach, 1972*

# PART THREE

# THE DISCIPLE

*Desmond top row, fourth from right, with Virgil Night (to his right).*
*The Maya Family, Coconut Grove, Florida, 1970*

# GURUS, MENTORS & FRAUDS . . . OH MY!

THEY'RE TEACHERS. They're guides. They inspire and inform. Going all the way back to the seventies, I found myself especially susceptible to gurus, not only because of my peculiar personal history but because of the turbulent times in which I was living.

You could trace my decision to join a guru-led commune to my need for family. My own had been shrouded in mystery and misinformation. I had a false father and a self-obsessed mother, neither of whom had the wherewithal to form a real family. The same was true for nearly all my uncles, aunts, and cousins. I thought back to my high school days when Virgil and I joined the Maya Family, a form of communal life, which didn't last long. Maria and I were family, but one I couldn't sustain. Even Desmond Child & Rouge was an attempt at family. Like my fathers before me, though, I couldn't keep it together. So I kept searching for family.

That family would have to be rooted in spirituality. I couldn't embrace the doctrine of traditional religion, yet I could accept the doctrine of something wildly untraditional: a cult. It pains me to see that word in black and white, pains me to admit that I willingly submitted my life and worldly earnings to so misguided an enterprise. Yet I did. And I did so to escape the shadows of the age of AIDS.

Keith Barrow was the first to fall. A prodigious creative force, Keith passed away in 1983. His mother, Chicago civil rights leader Rev. Willie Barrow, kept his spirit alive; she became a brave force in the gay rights movement. In the dark days of the Reagan eighties, political bravery was in short supply.

My second great friend to pass was Don Paul Yowell, the most talented songwriter of his generation. Because he had played at Reno Sweeney for years, he'd become an unheralded hero to throngs of music professionals and aficionados. His memorial service was packed. It was a sad day, made even sadder by something Don's sister said. She pointed at me and sobbed, "Why didn't you die? Why him and not you?"

I gave no answer. I had none.

Precious friends like Carol Davidson, who had moved to New York to continue her career as a pianist, were worried about me. Knowing about my sexual adventures, Carol repeatedly expressed alarm. She feared for my life.

It's a miracle that I dodged the bullet. It could have easily been me. After a trip to Mexico in 1978, I'd picked up amoebas from either food or water, and, doubling over in pain, was rushed to the hospital and treated with Demerol. It was there that a physician sternly lectured me on the dangers of unprotected sex. A germophobe, I listened attentively. He instructed me on the absolute necessity of safe sex. He spoke with such authority that I didn't dare ignore his admonitions. He saved my life.

Yet I sought another kind of salvation, one that would explain the inexplicable and protect me from what is ultimately unprotectable: myself. I eagerly accepted Sandra Seacat's invitation to meet Swami Muktananda, the renowned founder of Siddah Yoga. With his heavy black eye makeup, Swami's strange look intrigued me. I threw myself into dozens of expensive intensive sessions and met with him personally. I was convinced that he, who claimed to have realized full God consciousness, would lead me to the Truth.

We gathered in a room holding close to a thousand souls, the men and women seated on the floor on separate sides of the central aisle. Famous entertainers like Ellen Burstyn and Roberta Flack were in a VIP section, the circle closest to the guru, that I attempted to enter but was barred. I sat in economy.

Wearing a regal, flowing orange silk garment and trailed by beautiful female attendants in multicolored saris, Muktananda proceeded to the center of the room and sat cross-legged on a golden throne. He gave a short lecture, jokingly quoting pop lyrics before getting serious and saying things like, "Your job is not to battle with the mind, but to witness the mind." Then a long meditation. While our eyes were closed, he went up and down aisles, brushing the heads of his devotees with a fragrant cluster of peacock feathers dipped in shaktipat-inducing sacred oils. He stopped in front of me and held my face, his thumbs on my closed eyelids. Electricity shot through my body. The jolt was terrifying. During the service, we were encouraged to buy fruit to lay at his feet as an offering. When we exited, that same fruit was sitting on a table, to be sold a second time.

Sandra arranged for me to have a private *darshan* with Swami Muktananda. It came at a moment in my life when I felt ready to tell the world that I was gay. I wanted Swami's blessing to be who I am. Instead, he intimated that same-sex activities would damage my vocal cords and hurt my singing career. This was the last thing I wanted to hear. I needed more of an explanation, but when I tried to engage him further, his translator whispered, "Your *darshan* is over." I bowed and left, feeling shut down.

Swami died in 1982, and despite my growing doubts about his wisdom and the rumors that he'd been carrying on with underage girls, I traveled to India, to the same ashram that inspired Elizabeth Gilbert's *Eat, Pray, Love.*

Braving a broken-down bus filled with chickens, I rode five hours outside Bombay to where Swami was freshly buried, sitting in the lotus position and where Gurumayi, the young woman who had been the translator at my *darshan* and who looked like an Indian Audrey Hepburn, had assumed his mantle.

Never a quitter, I was determined to reach the highest levels of Siddha Yoga sagacity. While I was scrubbing the floors, Gurumayi called me to her inner sanctuary to give me Swami's sandals. I accepted this as a great honor, and yet, given my state of confusion—about my career and still-undeclared sexuality— I felt no relief. I threw myself on Swami's grave and asked for answers. None came.

At one point I got word that Michael Cava desperately needed to talk to me. Since there were no phones at the ashram, I had to take that long-ass bus ride back to Bombay. When I reached Michael, he was in the midst of an anxiety attack, insisting I come home. I wish I could have, but I was soon dealing with dysentery that made me too weak to travel. When I finally left India, I was disillusioned yet still seeking salvation. If one guru wasn't working, maybe another would.

That's when I met vocal coach Bill Barber. Bill was two years older than me. He had the aura of a blue-eyed Jesus. He spoke against the tyranny of gurus and religious leaders. That's just what I wanted to hear. He further explained that his mission was to strip away all superficiality so we might identify our fears and blockages and ultimately expunge them. His teaching principles echoed those of *The Power of Now* author, Eckhart Tolle, and slowly his voice lessons evolved into life lessons.

Bill had been a show boy in Vegas who traveled to Broadway to teach singers to drop their excessive vibratos and phrase with polished restraint. He came from an East Texas oil family and had a wealthy aunt in Atlanta who married the head of Pepsi-Cola. Maybe it was family lore, but Bill would often explain that Pepsi was inherently better than Coke because it was made with "all natural ingredients." With all his self-confidence, he maintained the demeanor of to-the-mansion-born. He was soft-spoken with a Southern charm, but as time passed and I surrendered more of myself and my life to him, he became increasingly controlling and occasionally severe.

The commune began as weekend retreats in the woods of upstate New York. Bill then moved us to a rambling solar mansion overlooking the Rudolf Steiner farm in Hawthorne, New York. I left the Oliver Cromwell in Manhattan and officially joined Akwenasa—a Native American term for home. Many of Bill's disciples worked as waiters in restaurants in the Berkshires and the Hudson Valley.

Bill's edicts were bizarre. To the brainwashed, however, bizarre can seem reasonable. For example, Bill considered meditation useless. "One is in true meditation only if one is outside the mind," he proclaimed. "And the only way to be free of the mind is to exist in truth." Truth was everything to Bill, though the term remained mystically ambiguous. He liked to say, "All truth and knowledge is within us." When asked about the truth and knowledge in books, he answered, "There's no need to read books." You'd think that a curious mind like mine would reject such a notion. Yet I didn't. I remained under his spell. In a world where the AIDS epidemic was raging, a cult felt safe.

After two years in woodsy New York, Bill moved us to an original Jeffersonian mansion called Monticola in Howardsville, Virginia, a bucolic spread of forty acres on the James River where I lived for another two years. We cleared twelve of the acres to provide a dramatic view of the great house on the hill.

We painted the house using authentic Monticello white. We farmed the land, and, in my case, I restored and cleaned the fireplaces, in addition to pruning the apple trees, an activity I relished.

Bill was obsessed with the Civil War. He had a thing for Gen. Robert E. Lee. He even hung a Confederate flag from the second-story balcony. He hosted nineteenth-century balls where men arrived in Confederate uniforms and women wore hoop skirts. Electricity was shut down. The only illumination came from real candle chandeliers. Fiddlers provided Dixie dance ditties. One of Bill's fantasies was that our house would turn into a moneymaking museum celebrating the glory of the Old South. That never happened. What did happen was that Bill sat on the porch in impeccable white outfits, reflecting on the apocalyptic future as we, his slaves, worked the plantation.

Inside the mansion, our daily uniforms were khaki trousers, button-down shirts, short-cropped beards, buzz haircuts and brown loafers. Bill was beyond vegan; he was practically a fruitarian. And we ate just what he ate.

Or tried to. I slept in my little captain's bed, ironed my clothes and carefully hung them in the tiny closet space allotted me. Bill was a neat freak and Bill had to be pleased.

It wasn't all bad. I discovered my talent for organizing events. I also edited his writings, designed posters, and did the packaging for the massage-oil company he had us organize, a business that bombed. Nonetheless, my work ethic, always strong, was made even stronger. Maybe because so many of us came out of the gay New York cabaret scene, there was also a lot of hilariously bitchy wisecracking humor. With musicians and singers like Michael Cava and Doug Schneider in residence, playfulness lightened the tense and somber mood.

Once, after getting my first regulation Akwenasa buzz cut I sighed and said, "I'll never be a blond again." Doug shot back with the deadpan comic precision of Ethel Mertz, "You never were." Moreover, I found what I'd been looking for my whole life: a tight and loving family devoted to the greater good and unafraid to live outside the world of mainstream culture. Yet I myself was an outsider yearning to be an insider—a soul comforted by the smooth inner workings of a patriarchal familial system. The paradoxes were overwhelming. I was looking to assert myself as an individual even as I surrendered my individuality. I belonged to a cult outside the workaday world even as I prospered inside that workaday world.

That my prosperity arrived at the same time I slipped into submission to Akwenasa remains a great mystery. Just as the music business was embracing my talent and rewarding me, I was giving those rewards to a guru, Bill Barber, whose approval I required and whose authority I was unable to buck. Bill made me feel that my monetary success was due to him. It was insane.

Certain friends were quick to point out the insanity. Carol Davidson minced no words. She called Akwenasa a fraud. She told me I was being taken in. She repeatedly warned me that this cult was using me like a bank.

"You're sweet and friendly and tenderhearted and in terrible need for an accepting community," she said. "All that's fine. But the community you've chosen is corrupt."

I didn't reject Carol—I'd never reject Carol—but her words didn't register. Bill's brainwashing shielded me from reason. He manipulated us by either showering affection on a member or ignoring that member for days on end. We yearned for his favor and were happy or sad depending upon his acceptance or rejection of us. He also was not above turning us against one another.

We ignored the obvious fact that he lived a double life, using our money to take extravagant trips.

After cowriting "I Was Made For Lovin' You" with KISS's Paul Stanley and Vini Poncia, good money was coming in, but there was a big speed bump. Bass player Gene Simmons hated the song. He thought it smacked of disco and betrayed the signature KISS sound. But because it was a hit, he had to swallow his pride. KISS fans loved it. Compounding Gene's disdain was the fact that after they took off their makeup and sought real rock credibility, many of their devoted followers and fans were put off. And the music critics who had never given them a break pounded them like *they* had been betrayed.

Paul, the most loyal of friends, came to my rescue. As he wrote in his own book, *Face the Music: A Life Exposed*, "When I heard 'I Was Made For Lovin' You' being played back in the studio, I was blown away. Yeah, it wasn't 'Detroit Rock City' or 'Love Gun,' but it was undeniable . . . Was it calculated? Yeah. Was it calculated to succeed? Yes, ultimately it was. But was that a bad thing? It started as a challenge to myself whether I could write in that style instead of meat-and-potatoes rock 'n' roll. It was no different than the challenge I gave myself with 'Hard Luck Woman.' The only difference was the style. No apologies for a hit that people worldwide still want to hear and sing along to."

Despite his bandmate's disdain, Paul insisted that he and I continue to collaborate. Good thing, because it turned out that, with his lead, we struck gold again. Our "Heaven's On Fire" became a rock anthem. This was 1984. Now I had twice come to the aid of Simmons, who had always seen himself leading a self-contained band and resented outside help.

Thus, in discussing their next album with the press, Gene claimed he was putting guards on the door of the studio to keep Desmond Child out. "We're not letting him within a hundred yards of the place," he said contemptuously. The implication was that I was detrimental to the band's integrity. Gene just didn't say it once. He repeated it during a dozen different interviews. I was hurt. I thought—hell, I *knew*—I had helped the band. So why the scorn?

I told Paul that I was crushed and wanted Gene to stop bad-mouthing me. I also wanted an apology. "Let him pick on his enemies," I said, "not the guy putting money in his pocket." Again, Paul took up my cause. Without Paul's intervention, I would never have picked up my phone a week later to hear on my answering machine a four word message: "Hi . . . it's Gene . . . sorry." Click . . .

Apology accepted.

I had signed with Winston Simone, a prominent manager who had been a fan of Desmond Child & Rouge. More WASP than shark, Winston had natural sophistication, exquisite manners, and superb show-business connections. Winston became a devoted friend and my key professional consultant for the next forty years.

Thus, two sides of me were hyperactive at the same time: the hitmaker and the cult member. For all my worldly success, I was still committed to Bill Barber's Akwenasa. It sounds crazy. It was crazy. *I* was crazy. But so were the times. In Reagan's America, I sought refuge in a family that spoke of a world built on conflict-free existence. At the same, living apart from that world, we were insulated. Even better, Bill encouraged us to not watch television, read newspapers, or listen to the radio, and to stay away from our families, who would pull us back into our "old life." That meant I was given permission to break away from Mimí and Marfy.

Another startling fact: I contributed all my earnings to Akwenasa. Looking back, I condemn myself for being such a sucker. But at the time I was convinced it was an act of altruism. I also must admit to a large dose of grandiosity that comes with the idea that the world needs saving and you're the one to do it. All Bill's disciples were jacked up with that high calling.

As I mentioned before, I'd persuaded my former lover Michael Cava to join the cult, thinking that the close-knit community would heal his troubled soul. It did not. Michael and I were no longer lovers, but another man was: David McCracken, a voice student of Bill's and something of a Broadway gypsy— leading-man handsome and affectionate. I actually thought of running away from Akwenasa with him, but Bill caught on and made us break up, enforcing his rule against forming couples.

Bill spoke with absolute certainty. If I had looked hard, I could have easily seen his authoritarian grip. But I wasn't willing to look. Submission was easier than scrutiny. As my songwriting career hit new highs and my income soared, I wound up giving Akwenasa . . . or should I say Bill . . . over a million dollars. Ouch.

Oddly enough, it was my stubborn perfectionism that contributed to the longevity of my stay. When I'm in, I'm in all the way. I was determined to see it through, whatever that meant. I was blind to many things. For example, I somehow accepted the closeted logic of Bill Barber's stance on sexuality. He thought sex was too amorphous to be labeled. He asked questions like, if you masturbate next to a tree, does that make you a tree-sexual? You're not gay. You're not straight. You're not anything. At the moment you engage in sex, you choose whomever you choose. If a man chooses a man, that doesn't make him gay. Or if a woman chooses a man, that doesn't make her straight. It doesn't make you anything. You're just having sex. The big caveat was: you must not engage in sex with anyone if you're doing it out of "need" because need equals fear. Thus, no sex at Akwenasa, except for Bill, who had the freedom to call anyone to his bed.

It troubled me that one of the men he called was David McCracken, who became Bill's boy toy. The two of them even took several trips together. I was devastated. I couldn't help but confront Bill.

"You say no couples, but that's exactly what you and David have become."

"Desmond, you have no idea of the level of consciousness that David and I exist in. You haven't done the work. You're in the place where you can't be 'in relationship' without being consumed by possessive jealousy."

Buying Bill's argument, I decided to double down. Obsessively, I worked on denying myself. I avoided simple pleasures. I sought to exorcise my jealousy. I tried talking myself into being a different person. Yet the relationship between Bill and David pushed all my high school buttons. Social rejection. Not good enough. Not cool enough. I was snuffing myself out.

Even more disturbing was Bill's attitude toward AIDS. He denied its existence.

"There is no such thing," he maintained. "Only those people who do not live in truth can get it."

Wow. I wanted to believe that, but already having witnessed the horrific death of several close friends, I didn't know what to believe. When I brought up the subject of safe sex, Bill shut down the conversation.

Yet for all my confusion, I stayed, comforted by the fact that two of my former lovers—Michael Cava and David McCracken—were there as well. It was a fractured family, but a family, nonetheless.

Despite my devotion to the cult, I snuck out every Wednesday, found a payphone in town, and called Winston to see how my songs were charting. He and I discussed more than my future as a writer. He knew, as did I, that I had the chops to produce. The problem, though, was the glass ceiling. Gay writers were fine. Gay producers were not—especially for the kind of macho bands with whom I was working. Songwriters are equal. But the producer is the boss. And no hetero rocker wants to be dick-slapped into submission by a gay producer. That kind of attitude prevails to this day.

Thus, I was assigned to produce women and gender-bending, trailblazers like Alice Cooper, Joan Jett, Ronnie Spector, and, among others, Cher.

Because I was in great demand, collaborators were willing to come to the commune to work with me. Alice Cooper was one of those. This gave me particular pleasure because, as you remember, Lisa Roberts and I had gone to an Alice Cooper concert, both of us with spider eyes and dressed as Alice. I was a fan. And Alice was a sweetheart.

He came to Charlottesville, Virginia, not far from our cult, where I worked on a rented little keyboard in his hotel room. Fascinating character. He explained that Alice Cooper was originally the name of his band, but when fans started calling him Alice, he embraced it. He was really Vincent Damon Furnier, son of a preacher who was steeped in fire and brimstone. The archetypal character he created was the villain, the antihero of a morality play. For instance, if he cut off the head of a doll, he'd have to face the music—his own head being sliced off by a guillotine falling into a bloody basket.

Our collaboration was surprisingly smooth. He leaned on me for music, and I helped him with lyrics. He came up with intriguing titles—"Bed of Nails," "Poison"—each of which pointed to pain as a consequence of desire.

In contrast to the heavy lyrics, Alice treaded through life rather lightly. He was happy to accept my invitation to dine at the downtown cafeteria in Charlottesville. He grabbed his tray and stood in line with the blue-haired ladies, who were shocked to see him. Alice remained unfazed. He selected gravy-soaked chicken fried steak and lemon icebox pie. He invited me to Scottsdale, where he lived with his beautiful wife, Sheryl. He told me stories of his golfing buddies, George Burns and Milton Berle.

"Uncle Miltie's big dick was legendary," said Alice. "Once, after a round of golf, Milton, George, and I were in the locker room when a man, boasting of his own endowment challenged Milton. At the time, we were all fully clothed. The man wanted to bet a hundred dollars. Milton was reluctant. But George wise-cracked, 'Pull out half and take his money.'"

When it came time to record the album, Alice and I went to Bearsville Sound Studio in Woodstock, owned by Albert Grossman, Bob Dylan's one-time manager. I pushed Alice hard, remembering how back in Miami Mrs. Leeds had pushed me. Vocalists need prodding. The prodding paid off. I got Steven Tyler and Jon Bon Jovi to sing with Alice and Joe Perry to play guitar. Joan Jett let Alice help finish a song that she and I had started, "House Of Fire." We named the album *Trash*, after the Andy Warhol movie that starred my friend Holly Woodlawn.

There was an attempt by A&R man Bob Pfeifer—resentful that I had excluded him from the writing sessions, which was against Sony record company rules of A&R guys—to cut me out of the mixing process. I was outraged. I'd created a Phil Spector-like wall of sound that, without my participation, would collapse. Thankfully, I threw enough of a fit that the powers-that-be—namely Alice's mercurial manager, Shep Gordon—reversed Pfeifer's decision. The result was a monster hit. *Trash* sold more than four million copies and rejuvenated Alice's career. It was his biggest-selling album of all time.

Other people came to visit me in Virginia, including the fabled Diane Warren, one of the most successful songwriters of the modern era whose hundreds of hits include Toni Braxton's "Un-Break My Heart" and Aerosmith's "I Don't Want To Miss A Thing." I first became aware of her when I heard John Waite singing her song, "Don't Lose Any Sleep." I was obsessed with the song that was produced by Rick Nowels, who, coinciden-tally, had married Maria Vidal. Rick gave me Diane's number.

My calls remained unanswered until Bon Jovi's "You Give Love A Bad Name" hit Number 1. Then she called me back.

"Welcome to the Number 1 club," said Diane, calling from Los Angeles.

When I finally met Diane, I discovered that her idiosyncrasies matched or surpassed mine. So did her drive to write hit songs. She works at it night and day. Her devotion to her craft is beyond obsessive. All of this is to my liking. Diane is funny and fast and naughty and nice. For years, she worked in a little room in a Los Angeles office building that no one was allowed to disturb. No cleaning, no organizing. For Diane to write on her small keyboard, nothing can change. Earthquakes have erupted, knocking over tapes, and scattering files. No matter, the mess must remain. Diane does not suffer change, not to mention fools.

Yet despite her mania to compose in one single space, she jumped on a plane and flew to Virginia, where we became instant sister-brother.

Psychologically, our relationship was complex. It had elements of my relationship with Mimí. Like my mother, Diane is a composer with highly competitive instincts. Also like my mother, those instincts impacted me. The collaboration/competitive paradox went on for years and essentially defined our highly creative dynamic. Diane significantly helped me, yet at times hurt me. The hurt would never last. Just as I always forgave Mimí, I always forgave Diane.

During our collaboration, Diane was coming off hits—Laura Branigan's "Solitaire" and DeBarge's "Rhythm Of The Night." Our mission was to write for Bon Jovi. We worked at a guest cottage at Akwenasa. That's where we noticed a Nina Simone album someone had left on the coffee table. We decided to borrow the title, *Wild Is The Wind*. (Titles can't be copyrighted.)

We started fooling around with ideas but decided it would be smart to head up to Jersey and finish the song with Jon and Richie, thus guaranteeing its inclusion on their next album.

The trip was both stressful and successful. The stress came with Jon's reluctance to write with Diane, whom he considered too pop for his rocker's sensibility. I convinced him otherwise, but it didn't help when Diane spilled coffee on Jon's expensive guest towel. And while I found her quirky personality endearing, Jon found it annoying. Nonetheless, with the help of Jon and Richie, we completed the song, "Wild Is The Wind" that was recorded on their megaplatinum album *New Jersey*. During the production, I flew to Vancouver, where, in the studio of producer Bruce Fairbairn, I tweaked lyrics with Jon by day and tagged along with the band by night. Two more songs I wrote with Jon and Richie climbed the charts: "Bad Medicine," hit Number 1 and "Born To Be My Baby" Number 3.

I was flying high.

A star in the world of pop music.

A star in the world of spiritual discipleship.

But when would those two worlds collide?

Turn the page.

*"Bad Medicine" writing session with Jon and Richie,
Rumson, New Jersey, 1988*

*Songwriting with Richie Sambora and Jon Bon Jovi, A&M Studios, Hollywood, 1992. And again, in 2007 in Pacific Palisades, Los Angeles.*

*The Birdhouse, Nashville, 2012*

*With Steven Tyler, Avatar Studios, New York City, 1997*

# DUDE LOOKS LIKE A LADY

As my hits written with Bon Jovi put me on the map, Aerosmith's eccentric A&R guy, John Kalodner, came calling. In his signature nasal tone, he said, "Hey, Des, you have to write me a hit with the assholes," his term of endearment for Aerosmith. Kalodner was looking to bring the group, once huge in the seventies, into the eighties. He figured Steven Tyler and Joe Perry could use my help. I suspected that Bon Jovi wasn't too thrilled. Because the two bands shared the same producer, Bruce Fairbairn, sibling rivalry was in the air.

Additionally, Steven and Joe, proud men, weren't looking for an outside writer imposed upon them. They'd told me that they'd never done it before.

In Steven's autobiography he described our first session. He viewed me as some Cuban with a mustache, although I've never had a mustache. He compared me to Juan Valdez, from the Colombian coffee commercial of the 1970s. He wrote that by the time I arrived, the song was basically written, and I merely added a few little words here and there. In Joe Perry's autobiography, he said I came up with the title, "Dude Looks Like A Lady." Both versions are wrong.

I came to an airplane-size hangar where the band rehearsed. There were rows upon rows of dozens of guitars—everything from glitter gold to faux tiger skin. There was a mountain of Marshall amps and the trademark mic adorned by an assortment of long, colorful scarves. Off in a corner were Steven Tyler and Joe Perry. Tyler, a born people pleaser, was friendly and welcoming. Perry was not. He viewed me as an intruder.

Steven and Joe had been working on a track loop based on a backward guitar riff that sounded like a blues harmonica.

173

"We've come up with this riff," said Steven, "but not much more."

"Sing it for me," I urged.

"Cruisin' for the ladies."

"It's bad," I said point-blank.

Hoping to break the ice, I jokingly added, "It's kind of cheesy. Sounds like a bad Van Halen song . . ."

Joe Perry looked at me with crossed arms, with his head tilted back and how-dare-you eyes.

"I had started with another line," Steven said sheepishly. "Came from being at a bar with our roadies and seeing this sexy blond on a stool. We were having fun figuring out who was gonna hit on her first. When she turned around, though, she was a he. It was Vince Neil of Mötley Crüe. So I said, 'That dude looks like a lady.'"

"That's a smash hit title!" I exclaimed.

"But we don't know what that means," said Joe.

"I know what that means," I said.

"We don't want to insult the gay community," Joe added.

"From the beginning of time," I said, "people have loved men dressed as women. Look at Uncle Miltie in his Carmen Miranda getup."

In kicking off the verses, I suggested, "'Cruised into a bar on the shore'"—fresh from Bon Jovi, I had the Jersey Shore in mind—"'Her picture graced the grime on the door.'"

"I hate that line," said Tyler.

"Why?" I asked.

"That's not rock."

Steven couldn't hear the word "graced" in a rock song.

"When you sing it," I said, "you'll make it rock."

Next, I wrote a strip club line about throwing some cash down on the stage.

"I'm not singing that," said Steven, who instead jumped in with, "She's a long-lost love at first bite."

But, to me that line killed the story. Now the singer actually knew the "lady" with whom he'd once had an affair long ago. Where's the surprise?

"No, man," said Steven. "It sounds cool."

I suspect he'd previously come up with the line and had finally found somewhere to put it.

I also had a problem with his next line: "Baby, maybe you're wrong, but you know it's all right . . . that's right."

Not only did it sound condemning, but it switched from third to first person—hardly the Bob Crewe gold standard of songwriting.

Even with Steven's contradictory lines, "Dude Looks Like A Lady" shot to the top, giving the group new life. The song was sung by a dude who *did* look like a lady. That's the irony that pulled people in. Steven was singing about himself. (When it was used in the film *Mrs. Doubtfire* for Robin Williams's famous broom dance, they started with the second verse—"So never judge a book by its cover/Or who you gonna love by your lover"—lyrics that anticipated the transgender movement by thirty years.)

Years after the publication of Steven's memoir, I reminded him of the true sequence of events surrounding the song's composition. He didn't argue. All he said was "I like your story better than mine."

The story got even better when my manager, Winston, was told by their manager, Tim Collins, that initially Steven didn't want to work with me because he'd heard I was gay. "What difference does that make?" Steven was asked. He provocatively answered, "I'm afraid I'll fall in love with Desmond. And if I fall in love with Desmond, then I won't be in love with Joe—and that'll ruin Aerosmith."

The next day, Steven showed up at our second writing session, but Joe did not. It was just me and Steven in this cavernous warehouse, all alone.

Steven was ready to write. He told me the story of his life. He wanted a song for his new wife, Teresa, who saved him from drugs. The story was fascinating, but Steven's big liver lips fascinated me even more. That's why I suggested we write the title "Angel." In repeating the word "angel" over and again, he'd have to contort those lips in a manner that would evoke Mick Jagger singing "Angie." It worked. "Angel" was their next hit.

My sessions with Steven and Joe were as lighthearted as they were serious. At times they got testy. When the three of us were writing "What It Takes," Steven grew frustrated looking for a lyric.

"I wish Diane Warren was here," Steven sniped, knowing how to push my buttons.

Furious, I shot back with "If that's what you think, then call fucking Diane."

I got up and walked outside to my rental car. He ran after me and apologized. When the song was finished, Steven said, "That's one of the best things we've ever written. Now we get to live forever . . . in this song." That was Steven—snarly one minute, endearing the next—not to mention funny. He, Joe, and I wrote another winner for the *Pump* album: "F.I.N.E." (acronym for Fucked Up, Insecure, Neurotic and Emotional).

Another thrill: I got to work with one of the icons of the golden age of rock 'n' roll, the ageless Ronnie Spector. It turned out that the first song I'd written with Diane Warren and Paul Stanley, "Love On A Rooftop," became a hot commodity. Clive Davis loved it. So did mogul Charles Koppelman, who wanted it for Ronnie. My manager, Winston, said fine, as long as Desmond is the producer.

I enthusiastically stepped into the role and Ronnie Spector became the first artist I ever produced. I loved producing "Rooftop," a hit that followed Ronnie's smash duet with Eddie Money, "Take Me Home Tonight." Standing next to her in the vocal booth, I insisted that she was singing her iconic "whoas" wrong. Defiantly, she turned to me and snapped, "Don't try to teach *me* how to sing a 'whoa.' I invented them." As the original Ronette, she was right. I backed way off.

Another blockbuster collaboration: Diane Warren, Michael Bolton, and me. We wrote several songs together that Michael recorded in the late eighties. One of those, "Love Cuts Deep," was about the brokenhearted futility of romance. After my string of unsuccessful relationships with men, from Marco Petit to Christopher Adler to Michael Cava to David McCraken, I was emotionally desolate. I couldn't help but view love through the prism of pain. Mimí's love came with all sorts of crazy baggage. The same was true of both my faux-father, John Barrett, and my real father, Joe Marfy. They were troubled men dealing with worlds of unresolved conflict. I stuffed all those feelings into song.

My reputation as a producer was growing. Jennifer Rush, who had written and sung her stunning original version of, "The Power Of Love" that was played at the wedding of Prince Charles and Princess Diana, summoned me to the studio. Jennifer was a brash Jewish chick from Queens, a twenty-four-carat New York character who was tortured that Celine Dion's version of her song, and not hers, had become the worldwide smash. In a rare instance, I produced a song that was not my own, "I Come Undone," which hit for Jennifer in Europe.

There was also the gutsy Bonnie Tyler. I slipped in as the substitute for her usual producer, Jim Steinman, who was off in hell working with Meat Loaf. Bonnie was a kick. She loved to drink, dressed to the nines, and had an infectiously cackling laugh that broke up the studio. I wanted to produce her whole album but was budgeted for only three songs. I took the three-song budget and, borrowing from Peter to pay Paul, cut a full ten-song album. When I delivered it, the Columbia Record exec said he heard no hits. I pointed to "The Best," a song I had begged its writer, Holly Knight, to let me produce first on Bonnie. Columbia never promoted it. But when Tina Turner covered it a year later, Capitol Records promoted it into the biggest song in the world.

I also adored the enigmatic Joan Jett. I found her incredibly attractive, meticulously groomed, deadly honest and seductively masculine. I fell in love with the boy who lives inside her.

When I played Jon Bon Jovi the song that Joan and I wrote—"I Hate Myself For Loving You," another Desmond Child oxymoronic title—his only comment was, "Fuck you," and he walked away. I think he liked it.

There was also the irrepressible Cher, who, when I entered her life, was getting ready to reinvent herself as a dramatic film actress and rock star. No big movies, no big songs, no worldwide tours . . . yet. In 1987, she was signed to Geffen Records by John Kalodner, who brought me in to produce. Using every weapon in my arsenal, I called on all of my collaborators to jump on Team Cher. Jon Bon Jovi, Richie Sambora (later Cher's lover), and I wrote "We All Sleep Alone," which became a hit for her off her eponymous Cher album that also included "Main Man," a song I had written and recorded on Desmond Child & Rouge's first album. Diane Warren and I wrote "Give Our Love A Fighting Chance" and "Perfection," and with Michael Bolton I wrote "Working Girl."

Two years later, when it came time for Cher's next album, *Heart Of Stone,* I contributed four songs. These two albums hit at the same time as her acting career exploded, following her Academy-Award-winning performance in *Moonstruck*. At this particular moment her image graced the cover of a thousand magazines.

Through her rock resurgence, she had reclaimed her divine diva status and could do no wrong. But when she was in the studio with me, she would become withdrawn for reasons she chose not to share. I wasn't about to pry, but neither was I about to compromise my producer's obligation to help bring out her best. The pressure was intense. With maniacally driven A&R man John Kalodner breathing down my neck, I was up against a hard deadline.

Cher was reluctant to leave her Malibu beach house. I finally coaxed her into giving me a studio date in Santa Monica. She arrived three days late. Despite her tardiness, I was elated. She would be mine for the next five hours. Except she wasn't. She hung out in the lounge and expressed no interest in singing. To make matters worse, a film crew showed up for an interview. I told them she couldn't. She told them she would. And, of course, she did. Once the camera was rolling, her mood lifted, and she became the world's warmest openhearted best friend. Now it was time to get her to sing. She resisted. I insisted.

I guess my pushiness overwhelmed her reluctance. I forced her to stand at the mic and give it her all.

In order to keep her at the mic, I set up a special tea set next to her with her favorite tea blends and organic honey so she wouldn't wander off, to be whisked away by her waiting limo. Somehow, I prevailed. The result was a series of brilliant performances. The huge hit off the album was Diane Warren's "If I Could Turn Back Time." I was there when Diane, literally on her hands and knees, approached Cher and begged her to sing the song. Cher was indifferent at first but ultimately was persuaded . . . thank God. At the recording date, produced by Diane and Guy Roche, I arranged the background vocals and sang them with Maria Vidal and Robin Beck. The hit video featured a battalion of rowdy sailors cheering Cher on as she straddled a giant phallic-shaped cannon.

I was grateful that despite—or because of—our struggle, Cher sang my songs, "Just Like Jesse James," "Emotional Fire," "Does Anybody Really Fall In Love Anymore" and "Love On A Rooftop" with deep passion.

Though our relationship never flourished, we were cool. On more than one occasion, Cher has told our dear mutual friend Joanna Staudinger, "Send Desmond my love—but you keep most of it."

*With Cher, London, 1991*

*With Jon Bon Jovi, Cher, and Steven Tyler,*
*Meadowlands Arena, New Jersey, 1990*

*With Joe Perry and Steven Tyler, Four Palms, Miami Beach, 1996*

*Tallinn, Estonia, 1988*

# THE EVIL EMPIRE

THE PARADOX WAS CONFOUNDING. The Akwenasa code was all about stifling emotional expression. Even though there were lots of laughs, underneath it all, fear and a deep coldness permeated the commune. You'd think that I, a young gay Latino man yearning for sensuous warmth, would rebel. You'd also think that I, a songwriter whose hits were rife with over-the-top emotions, would see the absurdity of my living situation. Yet I stayed. I continued to take orders and tolerate the intolerable. It was weird.

What, if anything, would break the spell?

In the fall of 1988, the same year President Ronald Reagan went to a Moscow summit with Soviet leader Mikhail Gorbachev, glasnost, the policy that supposedly granted new freedom to Russian citizens, had been launched. Person-to-person interaction was encouraged between American and Soviet artists. Music Speaks Louder Than Words, an exchange program that resulted in an album of a dozen songs, brought to Moscow American pop composers to collaborate with Russian writers. I was part of the group that included Mike Stoller (of Leiber and Stoller fame), Barry Mann (of Mann and Weil), Diane Warren, Michael Bolton, Cyndi Lauper, Billy Steinberg, Holly Knight, Franne Golde, and Brenda Russell.

We stayed at the Rossija Hotel, a massive fortress with three thousand rooms. Despite glasnost, I felt imprisoned. At the end of every hallway sat a matronly female guard behind a wooden desk. Behind her stood a soldier, rifle in hand. I know our rooms were wired, because if someone mentioned, even in a whisper, that they needed a comb, five minutes later there was a knock on the door with a functionary holding a comb.

During the day we joined a group of talented Russian writers eager to jam. Some had guitars, others played piano, and within minutes we were freely exchanging musical ideas. It was beautiful and enlightening.

I was assigned a female translator named Olga and made friends with Lonya, a singer who looked like Jim Morrison. Vladimir Matetsky—called Bad Vlad—became another member of our clique. Everyone loved telling me, "You give Vlad a bad name." We grew close in no time. Lonya often snuck into my room, where he spent the night on the floor next to my bed. Like me, he was eager for real friendship and willing to risk severe punishment just to stay with me. Lonya led us through the back streets of Moscow. There is a photograph of me in a long gray glen-plaid overcoat, black cashmere scarf and dark woolen cap. I'm standing in a nineteenth-century cobblestone passageway, the golden leaves of autumn at my feet, puffy pink clouds adrift in a blue sky above my head. When I look at it, I see a desperately lonely thirty-five-year-old man.

Lonya helped assuage that loneliness. A man of faith, he took me to his favorite Russian Orthodox Church, and, as he pointed out the elaborate iconography—bronzed and tiled portraits of bearded patriarchs and blessed saints—he stopped to pray before each altar. His eyes sparkled and his soul smiled. I could feel his joy.

Olga brought me further joy when she hosted a secret dinner party for me in her apartment on the grim outskirts of town. The building was a typical Soviet blockhouse, gray and depressing. The festivities had to be done on the sly, since translators were forbidden from socializing with foreign visitors.

Thus, she had to draw the blinds and light candles. The hush-hush ambience made it even more special and dangerous.

She laid out a spread of Russian delicacies. It was an evening when she, Lonya, Vladimir, and I vowed that our friendship would not end on the fifth and final day of the program. When that day came, snow fell gently on their faces as tears fell from our eyes. I can still see my new friends running along the train platform and waving goodbye.

The train from Moscow to St. Petersburg was memorable for several remarkable scenes. The first was our KGB minder hitting on Diane Warren. The ferocity of Diane's refusal took all the air out of his Soviet machismo. The second scene unfolded in the middle of the night. Wearing pajamas and earplugs, I was in my sleeping compartment when a shrieking howl woke me out of my dreams. I stuck my head out of the cabin door and saw a barefoot Cyndi Lauper in the galley, chugging down a bottle of vodka and singing the blues. The third scene was a cinematic portrait: When morning broke, I walked to the dining car and caught a glimpse of gorgeous and sultry Brenda Russell. She wore a pillbox hat and pensively stared out the window, where a vast sea of snow sparkled in the morning sun. Smoke from her cigarette formed spiraling curlicues. Brenda smiled at me and sweetly said "Good morning." All seemed right with the world.

That rightness came to a dramatic end on our bus tour of Estonia, an unlikely time to experience an extraordinary epiphany. The female guide was pointing out monuments when she suddenly went off script. In an impassioned plea, she railed against the Soviet Union's brainwashing propaganda: "You have no idea what we have to endure. We have no freedom. We're not allowed to think for ourselves. This is a living hell. Please help us. You've got to help us. We want to be free. We want democracy. Tell the world. You are artists. People will listen to you."

As she spoke her shocking testimony, Diane Warren and Michael Bolton were sitting behind me. Because they were giggling over some silly joke, I'm not sure they even heard what she said. That infuriated me. Here, at great risk to herself, this woman was pouring her heart out about the "evil empire" that had entrapped her country, and my colleagues were laughing. I took it seriously because I related so intensely. I saw Akwenasa as the Soviet Union. I saw Bill Barber as a dictator. For the first time, I clearly saw myself imprisoned in the same way that the tour guide was imprisoned. The difference, of course, was that she had no choice, and I did. Her spontaneous and powerful testimony opened my blinded eyes. I suddenly saw the real truth. I had given myself over to a mind-control cult. I had been brainwashed, or more accurately, allowed myself to be brainwashed. The guide's brave rant against the totalitarian state awoke me from a deep sleep. I had given up my own individual vision and dreams. I couldn't make any independent decisions without adhering to Bill Barber's edicts. What could be more deadening or dehumanizing? At that moment, I knew I could no longer tolerate Akwenasa, not for another day, not for another minute. I realized I felt closer to Olga and Lonya than to the people with whom I had shared everything I had over the past four years.

Something had to give.

From Estonia, we took a ferry across the Baltic to Finland, where I met Tuomo Railo, a handsome twenty-one-year-old ballet dancer whom I encountered at a Helsinki department store. I took him back to my hotel room where it was straight to bed. Feeling especially free because of my decision to quit the cult, I was frantic for love. Tuomo moved with such freedom and grace, highkicking and fashioning pirouettes as we walked down Helsinki's windswept streets. I felt as though we were in a

Hollywood musical movie. As the days and nights passed, one lovely romantic moment folding into another, I promised that I would see him again, and soon.

When the plane landed in New York, I went straight to the Akwenasa crash pad at Columbus and West Eighty-Fifth Street. I was shocked to see Bill Barber there. Oh well, this was as good a time as any to face him.

I showed Bill all the pictures from my trip and explained how I was experiencing new and powerful feelings. He reacted indifferently. Trying to find a gracious way out, I then suggested that perhaps it was time to take everything he had taught me and apply it to the real world. He didn't argue. He merely smiled warmly and reassured me everything would be all right, and that this was something we should all "look at together" as a community.

I traveled back to Virginia and nervously made my way to the Jeffersonian mansion that had been my home for the past two years. The sky was overcast with a winter storm on the horizon. I entered the big house that I had entered so many times before. This time, though, I entered with considerable trepidation. A community meeting was called. All the members were asked to solemnly gather in Bill's massive master bedroom, where we sat in a circle on the floor. Bill asked each of them to respond to my decision to leave. Their responses were ugly. Accusations flew. I was a narcissist. I was a traitor. I was a fool. I was a hypocrite. I was a quitter. Bill saved the most biting critique for last when he looked at me with his cold Jesus eyes and said, "Desmond, you are the most selfish human being I have ever known. And I suggest you leave right now."

I could have said, "This is a cult. Not only is it a cult, it's a Confederate cult. And not only is it a Confederate cult, it's a cult run by a manipulative closet queen who has brainwashed all of you. Follow me and find your own freedom!" I could have accused them of being Branch Davidian-style nuts. I could have ranted and raved about the hundreds of thousands of dollars I'd given this tinhorn messiah.

Instead, I said nothing. What would be the point? No one had put a gun to my head. I had joined Akwenasa of my own free will. Finally free of the cult, I could claim ownership of my own mind and talent. It would take me a while to lose the jargon of Akwenasa truth-talk, but there was no going back. I was out of the cult cocoon. In fact, I was thrown out. In the middle of the stormy night, I had to hurriedly gather my things and drive to the airport, where I waited till daylight for the next flight to New York. I never saw Bill Barber again.

Now that my brain was halfway clear, I was no longer thinking about this stifling cult. I was thinking about Tuomo, emotionally trading one for the other.

I wanted to get away from the East Coast. The farther from Bill Barber, the better. I never wanted to run into him again, which I feared for many years to come. That's why I headed out to Los Angeles, where I moved into the Oakwood apartments above Warner Bros. studios in Burbank, where undoubtedly every future rock and porn star landed when they first hit Los Angeles. By mid-December, I was settled in and eager to head to Europe, where I arranged for Tuomo to fly from Finland to Spain.

I hadn't seen my father in a while. For the past four years, I had been missing at the Marfy table. His invitation to spend Christmas in Madrid with my Hungarian family was most welcome. At last—the return of the prodigal son. It gave me a chance to be with Valeria and Joe's youngest son, Joey, who, much to my delight, came out to me. Dad now had two gay sons and I had a gay brother. Those facts made me feel less lonely. My complex surrounding illegitimacy softened. Joey was a loving sibling. He was twenty-one and I was thirty-five, but the age gap hardly mattered. We went clubbing together and formed a deep and abiding bond. Like our father, Joey was also a superb raconteur. He had charm and smarts, and, although no one could compete with Marfy's propensity to suck all the oxygen out of the room, Joey came close.

It was also good to see my sister Esther and brother John. I actually saw less of my father than I would have liked—mainly because he was busy running off for secret phone conversations with Kati, his young mistress in Budapest. Marfy's manipulations never stopped. I overheard him suggesting that Kati attend nursing school. That way, he reasoned, he'd have someone to care for him in his old age. Which was exactly what happened.

I was excited because finally someone was coming to care for me.

When Tuomo arrived, I booked us a room at the Madrid Ritz. At the family home, Tuomo and Marfy got along splendidly. Marfy was relieved that I had left the cult. He and Tuomo bonded over the common Hungarian-Finnish lineage dating back to the ancient Huns. After charming my father, Tuomo charmed Valeria. Always the gallant gentleman, Tuomo invited her to dance virtually every dance in the grand ballroom of the Ritz during a New Year's Eve gala. I'm sure being in Tuomo's arms thrilled my stepmom nearly as much as it did me.

In early 1988, I sent Tuomo a ticket for Los Angeles. What I had hoped would be a long-lasting love affair started to evaporate quickly, after a few weeks, as reality set in. Tuomo was lost in LA. Until then, he had been living with his parents. He was a mama's boy who had never traveled away. He also couldn't drive, and I suddenly found myself being his chauffeur, trying to keep him from getting bored.

In Helsinki, he was a lead dancer in a major ballet company. In LA, he knew no one. The culture shock was overwhelming. On a personal level, I started to realize that what I had been calling love was infatuation. The age and cultural differences were too wide to bridge. It just wasn't going to work.

Tuomo flew home, where his career blossomed. He married a fellow dancer, and together they've lived a wonderful life. He remains in my heart as someone who helped me transition out of a terrible situation and made me feel lovable again.

I was still starved for affection. My breakup with Akwenasa was fresh.

I had, after all, left my family of four years. I was yearning for someone to love me, as the old song says, body and soul. I made that connection not in LA, where I envisioned my future, but back in New York. On the Upper West Side, in a restaurant behind the Beacon Theatre, I met a man—*the* man—who transformed my life.

*Helsinki, Finland, 1988*

*Portrait by George Hurrell, Hollywood, 1989*

*Desmond and Curtis, Casa Paloma, Santa Monica, California, 1990*

PART FOUR

THE BOY FROM MISSOURI

*With Richie Sambora and Alice Cooper, the Village Recorder,*
*Los Angeles, 1989*

# LOVE IN A LIMO

ONCE OUT OF THE COMMUNE, I could work 24/7. And I did, throwing myself into my career like a madman. All I wanted was hit songs. My thinking was simple: success can erase all mistakes. For so long, my focus was inward; now all my energy was outward.

Alice Cooper was still on my radar. I flew to New York to talk to him about future collaborations. We dined at Coastal, a hip restaurant in back of the Beacon Theatre at Seventy-Fourth Street and Amsterdam. Alice was always lovely to me. Our collaboration led to a good gig: I was named music supervisor of the Wes Craven movie *Shocker*, in which Shep Gordon got Megadeth to cover Alice's classic hit "No More Mr. Nice Guy."

Since *Trash* had been a stunning comeback for Alice, I presumed we'd soon be working on the follow-up. I envisioned an Ozzy Osbourne-meets-Nine Inch Nails direction, a dark piece of modernity moving away from the pop rock we'd done before. But his A&R guy, Bob Pfeifer, wasn't having it. Bob managed to convince the label that Alice no longer needed me. Instead, Pfeifer installed himself as the main cowriter and brought in another more accommodating UK producer, Peter Collins. The resulting record, *Hey Stoopid*, didn't really work, and Alice, along with Pfeifer, were soon gone from Epic Records.

Yet Alice and I remained close and would often dine together. That night at Coastal, though, there was more on my mind than music. My mind was on the maître d', a strikingly handsome, soft-spoken, and gracious gentleman. He looked like Brad Pitt if Brad were a bit better-looking. I didn't catch his name, but I believe I did catch his eye. I returned some weeks later with my assistant Michael Anthony, a wonderful friend who'd helped facilitate my move to LA. The restaurant was about to close, and I asked the maître d' if we could be seated and, by chance, would he like to join us. Yes!

His name was Curtis Shaw, who, when not managing Coastal, was studying acting with famed teacher William Esper. He had an agent who regularly sent him out on auditions. Working several jobs at once, he was also self-sufficient. He was sharp without being opinionated and curious without being naïve. He'd been brought up in a liberal-minded and modest mid-Missouri home. Like me, Curtis had graduated college with a major in music education. His mom, Mary Ann, having been raised in a fundamentalist church, was a high school English teacher, and his father was a professor at the University of Missouri. Curtis had a sweet disposition, calm and reassuring. He was a good listener, an essential quality for anyone interacting with a compulsive talker like me. Beyond his intelligence and sensitivity, he exuded a tenderness that touched my heart.

In April of 1989, I told Curtis I was running off to Miami to find an apartment for Mimí but would be back in a week. Would he then accompany me to Queens, where one of the Rouge ladies, Myriam Valle, was celebrating her birthday? He agreed.

Flying to Miami, I reflected on how I had inherited Mimí's conviction that one day . . . songs would bring untold wealth. With money pouring in, her thinking was no longer so crazy. I was able to get her a deluxe apartment facing the ocean. From her perspective, though, it was her musical genes, manifest in me, that deserved the credit. My hits were as much her triumphs as mine. She continued to contend that if only she had more exposure and better contacts, she would soar. Listening to her lovelorn music, I didn't disagree. But listening to her ongoing fantasies about the millions she would soon make brought me back to the sadness of my childhood. Mimí was still lost in magical thinking.

I left her and returned to New York, where I planned my first date with Curtis. I decided to go all out. I went for my white-knight-in-shining-armor look. Dressed in white jeans, white sneakers and a white sweatshirt, I arrived at Curtis's St. Mark's Place apartment in a white limousine. He candidly let me know that ever since he saw me that first night with Alice Cooper, without knowing who I was, he had felt a strong surge of energy. That's all I needed to hear.

"Excuse me, sir, but do people ever make love back here?" I asked the driver.

"It's your living room," he replied.

And with that, I pressed the button that raised the darkened panel behind the driver's head.

We instantly jumped on each other, and it was more than passionate lovemaking. It felt like real love, spiritual love, more love than I had ever given or received from anyone. It was a love that felt permanent. It was a love that had to be housed and protected, which was why I bought Curtis a miniature crystal castle and said, "Someday, I will give you a real castle."

In various forms, those castles did appear, but it took a while. Other events unfolded first. Curtis had been cast in a production of the musical *42nd Street* at the Tulane Summer Lyric Theater in New Orleans. I promised to attend. Before that, I took Curtis to meet Mimí during the same time he'd slowly been introducing his mother to the idea he had a close male friend with whom he was growing ever closer. One morning she awoke with the realization that her son was gay. When she asked Curtis point blank, he answered honestly. The second of four boys, he had described himself as "the daughter my mother always wanted." The emotional fallout was heavy, but Curtis's loving mom experienced a remarkable transformation of attitude.

Over the years, she came to accept her son's homosexuality not as a choice but his true nature. The Missouri Curtis, where he had hidden that nature, and the New York Curtis, where he had not, were finally reconciled.

The first domicile that Curtis and I shared was not a castle. It was the top floor of a duplex on La Jolla in West Hollywood. Below us lived Tomi and Evelyn, two delightful elderly Hawaiian Mormon ladies. I rented a tiny studio a few blocks away, which was where, of all people, David Lee Roth showed up.

Years earlier, before I had songs on the chart, Winston had proposed that I write with Roth. "Why in the world would David Lee Roth want to write with Desmond Child?" his manager asked arrogantly. But hits always turn heads, and a few years later David Lee, hungry for a hit, came calling. He showed up with a cassette tape of burlesque stripper music, saying this was his new direction. While the song played, two actual strippers burst into my closet-size office, big-breasted gals adorned in fedoras, raincoats, and stilettos. They dropped the raincoats— nothing underneath!—and started writhing and humping each other before breaking into a sequence of synchronized split beavers. When the song ended and their act was over, they said, "Call us if you need any more . . . inspiration."

Always the showman and infamous prankster, Roth relished creating unforgettable moments. Yet that day we never wrote a note.

A few months later, I was invited to write with Van Halen, who had been on the outs with Roth for years. Minutes after I met Eddie and the boys, who should show up but Roth himself, talking about me like I was his long-lost friend. I suppose David Lee had heard about the session and wanted in. Eddie wanted him out. The result was much confusion, an incoherent dialogue between the two former bandmates, and no music making. Torn between two rockers, neither David Lee Roth nor Eddie Van Halen ever contacted me again.

The lure of big stars is a magnetic force of no small energy. A prime example is my idol Barbra Streisand. While working in Miami with Diane Warren, I got an urgent call from John Kalodner at Geffen Records.

"This is on the QT," he said, "but Barbra's not happy at Columbia. She's feeling misunderstood and neglected. David Geffen wants to take care of her and asked me to find her a hit. Do you have anything?"

I had to think fast. To get Streisand to record one of my songs was the answer to a lifelong prayer. Yet I had to be honest. "I really don't have anything that would suit her," I said.

"Can you write something, quick?"

"OK! I'm here at my mom's place in Miami Beach with Diane Warren now. We'll get right on it."

Maybe someone tipped them off, but not five minutes later, the phone rang again. On the line were Columbia Records president Tommy Mottola and his number-two man, Donny Ienner.

"We need a song for Streisand," said Ienner, "and we need it right now. What do you got?"

Not mentioning anything about the Kalodner call, I said, "I happen to be here with Diane Warren. We'll have something by the end of the day."

"Great. Soon as you're finished, get on a plane to LA. We're setting up a meeting with Streisand. You'll play it for her personally."

"Holy shit," said Diane. "We're in the middle of a tug-of-war for Barbra Streisand."

On the spot, Diane and I knocked out a killer anthem, "One Look In Your Eyes" that we sang to Ienner over the phone.

"Great," he said. "We're going with that. Now get here."

I took a scrap of notebook paper with the lyrics, stuck it in my back pocket, and, dressed in my lucky white linen suit, flew to LA, where a limo whisked me straight to Barbra's enclave on Carolwood Drive in Beverly Hills. When I arrived, I was ushered into a den where everything was cream and white: the walls, the carpet, the grand piano. Four men in dark suits, white shirts, and black ties—Mottola, Ienner, Barbra's executive music supervisor, Jay Landers, and her longtime manager Marty Erlichman—sat on the couch like a row of penguins. What I didn't know was that Mottola and Ienner had only met Barbra for the first time earlier that day. The small talk was awkward. My heart beat madly as I waited to meet the world's greatest star of all time.

The moment arrived. Barbra made her appearance in a long white cashmere sweater-dress. Together, she and I looked like the white-on-white cover of *Guilty*, her epic, hit album with Barry Gibb. Barbra sat on the plush beige carpet leaning back and looking off in the distance.

"Desmond wrote 'Livin' On A Prayer' with Bon Jovi," said Ienner. "One of the biggest songs of all time."

"What's a Bon Jovi?" she asked. "Maybe my son Jason heard of it? I only listen to Sinatra and Tony Bennett. So . . . play it."

I was both superexcited and anxious—superexcited to be in the company of the great Streisand and her collection of power moguls, and anxious because I'd just written the song with Diane and barely knew the chords. I soldiered on, though, singing the lyrics from that piece of scrap paper and relying on memory to get me through the melody. I did a decent job. *I'm singing for Barbra Streisand. What the fuck!*

When I was through, Barbra came over to the piano and whispered something in my ear. I was hoping to hear her say, "I love it!" Instead, she asked, "Can you type?"

"Well . . . with two fingers," I started to answer hesitantly. Why did it matter if I typed?

"I can't read your handwriting," she said in her New York twang. "I have to have the lyrics typed out."

"I can do that," I assured her.

"But what if I get up in the middle of the night and wanna hear it?" she asked in a fast Brooklynese right out of *Funny Girl.* "There's nothing for me to hear."

"Barbra . . ." Ienner tried to break in and reassure her.

"I'm always getting up in the middle of the night," she went on.

"That's when I like to listen to music. But now there's nothing for me to listen to."

"No worries," said Ienner. "We'll send Desmond to a studio right now to lay down a piano vocal you can listen to whenever you like. You'll have the tape within two hours, I promise."

"Make sure I do," Barbra insisted. "Because if I get up in the middle of the night and there's nothing to listen to, I won't be happy."

"We want to make you happy, Barbra," said Mottola. "Everyone wants to make you happy." Barbra rolled her eyes and shot me a little smile.

Happily, I ran over to A&M Studios, where I banged out a rough demo. A messenger rushed the tape back to Barbra, with typed lyrics. The rest was silence; she never recorded the song. Maybe it was too rock or too pop. It wasn't written in the harmonically sophisticated style of Stephen Sondheim, Michel Legrand, Henry Mancini, or Marvin Hamlisch, but there's more to the story . . .

Of course, John Kalodner heard the song and immediately cut it with Cher.

Desmond and Diane strike again!

*Diane and Desmond, Hollywood, 1991*

# DISCIPLINE

AT THE START OF THE NINETIES, the writing was on the wall: The hard rock bands with whom I'd written megahits—Bon Jovi and Aerosmith—were suddenly considered global stadium-packing legacy acts like The Rolling Stones, Bruce Springsteen, and U2. But from one day to the next, MTV switched to an unrelenting nonstop Nirvana-crazed format. The Seattle sound was transforming American music, and an invasion of indie shoegaze grunge bands signed straight from their parents' garage were in. Iconic corporate touring and merch-driven rock bands that could deliver huge and loyal audiences were out. My chief *consigliere,* Winston Simone, was warning me that if I continued pursuing business as usual, I'd be through.

In the meantime, Curtis and I had moved from our modest West Hollywood walk-up into the former Russian consulate from the twenties—a magnificent Spanish Revival mansion in Santa Monica that we named Casa Paloma. Restoring it to its former glory and adding interior-décor touches of my own, we overspent like crazy. But it was worth it. As our designer, Laura Clayton Baker, said, "The house evoked nostalgic memories of Desmond's great-grandfather's house in Cuba and of the majestic Mediterranean estates on Miami Beach where he had grown up." The details were extraordinary: soaring high-ceiling beams hand-painted with a Russian flower/leaf pattern. Santa Monica visual artist Carole Free recreated the original Tree of Life spiral design over the massive tile Batchelder fireplace; vintage moss-green velvet camelback sofas; a Collard and Collard grand piano from 1837; a Tiki room complete with tiger-print, zebra, and leopard-skin rugs; a deco bar; bird-of-paradise trees; a black-and-white portrait of me by George Hurrell, the great photographer of the golden age of Hollywood; an enormous master bathroom of green, white, and yellow tile taken piece by piece from the Getty Ranch House in Malibu and stored for twenty years by the Santa Monica Heritage Museum; an interior courtyard; a lush garden; an outdoor fireplace; a stenciled ceiling in the formal dining room that still bore the marks of champagne corks past.

Imagine the glamorous dinners once held here! The showplace I'd been seeing in my dreams—a showplace casting the shadows and lights of a vintage Ingrid Bergman film—had come to life.

In addition to welcoming show-business luminaries to our home, we also sheltered old friends. With Curtis's generous support, I invited my former lover, the immensely talented Michael Cava, to live with us. Michael was suffering emotionally. Because he had followed me into Akwenasa, I felt responsible for his well-being. His stay at Casa Paloma was difficult. We took him to various cult-survivor meetings and found him therapists, but nothing could assuage his crippling paranoia. I recorded and released a CD of his exquisite music, *Michael Cava Piano Solos*. Ultimately, he left Los Angeles for Seattle, where, with choreographer and dancer, Rip Parker, he was able to build a beautiful life and creative partnership, creating moving and alluring dance works at the University of Washington, including the soul-gripping *Songs In the Dark*. It was Rip who lovingly cared for Michael during his last days, and he died of AIDS at age forty-six. For all of us who adored him, Michael's spirit remains, his improvisational genius a rare and enduring gift.

I faced a crossroads in my career. Grunge was happening. Nirvana was omnipresent. You couldn't get away from "Smells Like Teen Spirit." Its MTV video crushed every band I was working with. The hard-rock anthems I had been writing were becoming commercially irrelevant. Given the music biz's changing landscape, I decided the smart move wasn't to keep writing for soon-to-be-out-of-fashion bands, but to write hits for myself. Why not do the thing I'd always dreamed of doing, the very thing I'd tried to do—and came damn close to realizing—with Desmond Child & Rouge? Become a star in my own right. Become George Michael . . . become Sting . . . become Bono. My singing voice was strong. My stage presentation was dynamic. My songwriting was legendary. As a solo artist, why couldn't *I* become legendary? Why did *I* have to lurk behind the curtain and watch someone else take the bow? Those dark years at Akwenasa hadn't dampened my desire for glory and fame. Now was the time to go for it.

And so I did.

But before I did, in the summer of 1989 I went to a mega rock festival in Moscow headlined by Bon Jovi, Mötley Crüe, Skid Row, Scorpions, and Ozzy Osbourne. Before the show started, I heard Doc McGhee, manager of both Bon Jovi and Mötley Crüe, adamantly insist that none of the groups use pyrotechnics during their sets.

To everyone's shock, Bon Jovi's set was augmented with huge pyrotechnics. Backstage in the wings, the other bands were fighting-mad. A saloon brawl broke out when Mötley Crüe's Tommy Lee punched Doc McGhee in the face. You never want to let a testosterone-heavy band of fiercely competitive egomaniacal rock gods believe they've been duped. Mötley Crüe fired Doc on the spot. "Go manage Alvin and the Chipmunks," said Tommy.

Earlier that morning at breakfast, I was with Richie Sambora when Tommy Lee walked by with his wife, Heather Locklear. The gaze between Heather and Richie was like lightning. You knew a thunderous storm was imminent. At the time, Richie was with the beautiful keyboardist Jennifer Blakeman.

Jennifer told me how the story ended:

"Sometime after Moscow," she said, "I was driving down Sunset Strip, listening to Howard Stern. Howard said, 'I hear Heather Locklear's in town at the Plaza. Let's have some fun. Let's call her.' Heather answers the phone, and, in a sleepy voice, says, 'Hello? Who's this?' 'It's Howard Stern, Heather. Who's lying next to you right now?' She hesitated before saying . . . 'Richie [pause] Sambora.' At the precise moment I learn that my boyfriend is in bed with another woman, I look up and see a huge billboard advertising *Melrose Place,* Heather's current number-one TV show. Plastered across the billboard was a twenty-foot-long picture of Heather that simply said 'Bitch.'"

While still in Moscow, I reunited with my Russian friends Olga, Lonya, and Vladamir Matetsky, and promised I would bring them to LA.

After Russia, Curtis flew to Budapest where he met the Marfy brood. Good will and loving acceptance all around. From there Curtis and I took a romantic tour of Europe: the hydrofoil to Vienna, a drive through the Alps, the Hotel Danieli in Venice, a weekend in Paris. We were accompanied by my personal assistant Michael Anthony, his boyfriend, Tom Massman, and one of my New York minders from Winston's office, Stacey Dutton. Feeling especially grateful to be surrounded by such sweet souls, I footed the bill. This Bob Crewe-style two-week "only the best" jaunt cost some $150,000.

Once settled back in America, I flew Olga, Lonya, and Vladimir to LA. and put them up in a hotel. When I took them to a Santa Monica supermarket, they were so startled by the abundance they broke down in tears. We went to the Grand Canyon, where Lonya got a little lost, and then to Las Vegas, where they all got *very* lost. The culture shock was too much.

Lonya called the city demonic. He freaked out. So, I had to send them back. Our friendship nonetheless survived. After all, it was that initial experience in Moscow that gave me the guts to quit Akwenasa. I owed my Russian friends my life.

Back in LA, I secured a contract for my solo record with not just any record company, but one I considered prestigious: Elektra, run by the imperious mogul Bob Krasnow. My label-mates included Tracy Chapman, 10,000 Maniacs, The Cars, Anita Baker, and Michael Stipe, all *Rolling Stone*-worthy artists. In fact, while I made the record, *Rolling Stone* ran a feature on me, anticipating my breakthrough as a solo artist.

While cutting the record, Curtis and I hosted one of our more fabulous parties at Casa Paloma. Bob Krasnow, who saw himself as a world-class chef, volunteered to prepare pasta with his pal, impresario George Greif. At the time, Krasnow saw me as his next bright star. I saw Krasnow as a tough guy with classy taste in music. He was symbolic of the men who had made their fortune in the music biz back in the profit-crazy eighties. His Manhattan apartment was bizarre: to reach his living room with its Jackson Pollocks and Mark Rothkos, you walked, in blue surgical booties, across a granite slab over a stream of running water and river rocks. No matter, Krasnow was my mentor, and I was determined to bond with him.

Curtis and I pulled out all the stops for the dinner party and invited, among others, Jon Bon Jovi and his wife Dorothea;

writers Barry Mann and Cynthia Weil; Diane Warren; Allee Willis; my good friend, Jyl Klein; record executive Seymour Stein, whose date was singer Tommy Page; Maria Vidal and her husband, Rick Nowels; and photographer George Hurrell whom I introduced to Bob Krasnow. As a result, Krasnow hired Hurrell for the cover shot of Natalie Cole's *Unforgettable* album. It was Hurrell's last portrait before his death a year later, in 1992.

Krasnow and Greif came over early that afternoon to work their magic. The results were spectacular: pasta al dente, a divine tomato sauce, a salad splashed with the finest olive oil known to mankind, a wine of rare vintage and noble character.

At eight p.m., we were seated in our formal, candlelit dining room. The talk was lively, the writers, producers, artists, and execs getting on famously. The gossip was as delicious as the food. Just before the dessert of roasted pears covered in espresso mascarpone cream, we heard loud banging at the door. Who could it be?

I went to answer, and before I had time to react, standing before me were two menacing street characters in Elvis gold, aviator shades, diamond-encrusted chains, white basketball sweat suits, and Milli Vanilli dreads.

"Oh, that's for me, it's my guys!" exclaimed Krasnow, jumping up from the table and slapping them both high fives. With that, he led them back through the kitchen into the maid's room, where they most likely did a coke deal. I know that because when Krasnow returned to the table he was sniffing and rubbing his nose, his eyes on fire. Our guests were somewhat horrified but said nothing and looked at me. I was upset. Here I was, a ghetto rat, trying to put on a fancy dinner party, when the ghetto caught up with me. Yet I held my tongue. After all, Bob was the key to my next stop: Rock Star.

That never happened. The album I wrote and produced was deeply flawed. In this case it was probably a mistake to produce my own record. People kept saying, "Who knows how to produce records better than you?" In truth, I lacked the objectivity to hear myself clearly and make decisions about what material to include. More critically, I still hadn't learned the lesson of the second Desmond Child & Rouge record: *Don't take yourself so seriously.*

Oh, Lord, did I take myself seriously! Every song had to be a work of high art; a soaring anthem designed to make the angels weep. I pulled out all the stops. I cowrote with Burt Bacharach. I wrote with Diane Warren. I wrote three new original songs of my own. I collaborated with Richie Sambora. Joan Jett sang backgrounds. I duetted with Maria Vidal.

On what I hoped would be the breakout single—"Love On A Rooftop"—Elektra underwrote a melodramatic video. I play the part of a straight long-haired go-for-broke brooding rock star engaging, in and out of bed, with a gorgeous female model, as I sing my heart out atop a New York skyscraper.

Looking to please everyone—the executives at the label, the radio stations, the fans, the critics—I ultimately pleased no one. After two years of intensive work, the record was released in 1991 to little fanfare in spite of enthusiastic endorsements of musicians like Paul Stanley, who called it a masterpiece.

I called the album *Discipline*, with its sexual implication. The word also described my working method. I was disciplined, yes, but had I looked deeply into my soul and revealed who I really was? No. In fact, I still hadn't publicly identified as gay. During my *Rolling Stone* interview, I avoided the subject.

Amazing when I think back: I had lived a gay life for well over a decade; I was living with a gay man; I was immersed in gay culture; I was gay, gay, gay, but I nonetheless demurred. I wanted nothing to get in the way of stardom. I had lost myself again. This whole project could be seen as a fucked-up form of conversion therapy. That shit never works.

Before the record disappeared, there was, at least, a promotional trip to London. Bringing along Curtis, whom I introduced as my assistant, we stayed at the Draycott Hotel in Chelsea, where Marfy made a visit. Always glad to see my dad, I was surprised by the presence of the six-foot-five, twenty-two-year-old man accompanying him.

"Meet your brother Paul," said Marfy.

"My brother?"

"Vell, he looks like you, doesn't he?"

He did appear to be a taller version of me. He had stringy blond hair, green eyes, and a distinguished demeanor. In a most correct British accent, he told me he was a singer-songwriter. Why, I asked my father, had he never even mentioned Paul?

What followed was another startling Marfy story: Years ago, he was driving through Switzerland, where he picked up Charlotte, a beautiful young hitchhiker. For a few days, they made love in a remote chalet. She became pregnant. But because she came from a wealthy and prominent Swiss family, she didn't need money and, in fact, didn't want Marfy's involvement in their son's life. She moved to London where Paul was born and raised. She and Marfy stayed in touch. Occasionally he visited his son but never felt obliged to tell me about Paul's existence. Now that we were all in London, he thought it was time to introduce us . . . that maybe I could help guide him in music.

I was shocked by the presence of a new brother, but Marfy was always shocking. Somehow, though, those shocks were mitigated by my father's unruffled presentation. He always announced astounding news—that he had a mistress in Budapest, that he had an English son with a Swiss woman—with a beguiling smile and a wink.

I liked my new brother. I was secretly happy I wasn't the only bastard in the Marfy family. Paul was a cool character, and I was glad that he and Dad attended the publicity party for *Discipline*. The highlight came when Lulu joined me in song—the same Lulu who had recorded the first single, "To Sir, With Love," that I had ever bought. We harmonized as if we had been duet partners for years. During the party that followed, I noticed that the Oscar-winning actor Gary Oldman, a regular Draycott denizen, had wandered into the room and sat himself at the grand piano in the corner. For the next ninety minutes, he played a polished cocktail jazz, never once bringing attention to himself. It was a beautiful touch to a magical evening.

The beauty of discovering my new baby brothers came at a terrible price. Joey, whom I loved deeply, died of AIDS on January 15, 1991, the night that Desert Storm was launched. He was twenty-four. He had been a student at William & Mary, where he was studying languages and planned to become a diplomat. He had those skills—intelligence, charm, and compassion. His decline was horrific. He had developed Kaposi's sarcoma that for two agonizing years disfigured him terribly. His mother, Valeria, moved to Virginia to nurse him the last year of his life. I joined our family at his deathbed.

After Joey died, Valeria was diagnosed with breast cancer. She divorced Marfy, who as a result was finally free to marry Kati and bring her to America. Amazingly, Valeria forgave Marfy. The death of her son convinced her that everyone must be forgiven.

"The pain of Joey's passing taught me that forgiveness was the only path forward," said Valeria. "I had no energy for revenge or scorn. Joe Marfy was a charmer and a scoundrel. But I refused to spend the rest of my life trapped in bitterness. I let all that go."

A few years later, my brother Paul died at twenty-five. He had fallen asleep with a lit cigarette in his grandfather's home in Geneva and was consumed by a blazing fire. If only Marfy hadn't waited so long to introduce us! I wanted to know and love Paul in greater depth—and help him in his career—but never had the chance.

In comparison to these losses, the death of my solo career could hardly be called tragic. I had not found fame as a singer but later learned what might well have been a gift. Fame is a tricky business model. Your self-esteem is your stock fluctuating on the judgments and whims of others. What goes up always goes down.

*Rehearsing "Obsession" with Burt Bacharach and Maria
at Casa Paloma, Santa Monica, 1991*

*With Brooke Shields, New York City, 1992*

# CHRISTMAS IN MY SOUL

I WASN'T ABOUT TO STAY DOWN. I was already a known songwriter and producer and was determined to double my hustle. Thus, I hustled my way to Nashville, where Curtis and I rented a log cabin atop a hill outside the city.

As rock 'n' roll died and shoegazing grunge took over the air waves, I heard a song sung by Garth Brooks that he had cowritten with Victoria Shaw called "The River." I thought, This is Bon Jovi with a twang. There's a place for me in Nashville.

It takes more than luck to get a cut. It takes strategy.

I made a point to meet Victoria Shaw, a smart, fast-talking New York Jewish girl, very much like the kind I went to high school with at Beach High. Not only did we hit it off, we wrote a song recorded by Garth Brooks and Trisha Yearwood. I like to think that was the song that brought them together. It was the title cut of Trisha's *Where Your Road Leads* album. Not long afterward, they left their spouses and ultimately married. The lyrics said, "I believe in miracles, I believe in signs, I believe that mountains move one prayer at a time." Prayer was always a lucky word for me.

Next, I set my sights on Wynonna Judd, the Adele of her time. She invited me to her home two weeks after she had given birth to her first child, Elijah. I had been with her for an hour when Ashley Judd appeared. Ashley had left a movie set to be with her sister.

"What the hell are you doing?" asked Ashley furiously.

"Writing a song," said Wynonna.

"You booked a writing session?"

"Yes."

215

"When I moved mountains to get off work to be here with you!" she screamed, and broke into tears.

I, who hadn't even been introduced to Ashley, shrank into my seat and quickly made my exit. I was clearly in the wrong place at the wrong time.

Undaunted, I plotted my next move. I was crazy about Wynonna's big hit "Only Love" and saw it was cowritten by Marcus Hummon, husband of soon-to-be CNN hero Becca Stevens, who led a small Episcopal church on the Vanderbilt University campus in Nashville that Curtis wanted us to attend. All of a sudden, I started going to church religiously, where Marcus sang during Communion. Within no time, I talked him into writing a song with me for Wynonna.

With her infant in mind, we came up with "The Future In My Arms." We drove to Leiper's Fork, where Wynonna lived on a rambling ranch surrounded by rolling green pastures. It had been raining for days. The sky was dark and threatening. We went into her family room, where she was nursing her baby boy. As we played the song, the clouds broke and a luminous beam of golden light illuminated the red-haired Madonna and child. She wept. It was a goose-bump moment. And Marcus and I knew we had scored.

But not so fast. Her longtime producer Tony Brown told me what happened next. He wrote a lush chart that she loved. They carefully went over the lyrics. They discussed her phrasing. She was ready. The studio lights were dimmed. She went into the vocal booth, closed her eyes, and began to sing. She sang like an angel. And then, without warning, she stopped. She pulled off her headphones and broke into tears, running out without explanation.

When I heard the story, I called her the next day.

"Oh, Desmond," she said, "I'm so sorry, but every time I walk into church, the whole congregation turns around and stares at me. I know it's because I had my baby without being married."

I said, "No, they turn around and look at you because YOU'RE WYNONNA JUDD!"

I'm still waiting for her to cut it.

Never give up on a song.

Brooke Shields wanted a singing career and had the pipes to pull it off.

With Winston's help, RCA gave her a deal and hired me as her songwriter and producer. I was pumped. Beyond her classic beauty, Brooke is a hoot.

I invited her and her controlling momager, Teri, who, like Mimí, dominated her child's life, to Eliot Hubbard's enchanted Dove Cottage in Connecticut. Brooke, Eliot, and I took long walks in the moonlight. By the side of the road, decrepit tombstones and crypts were scattered about an old rural cemetery. When the headlights of passing cars shone on us, we assumed the disposition of the dead, walking like zombies, our stiffened arms stretched before us.

We also had fun in the city. One evening, Brooke, Teri, and I were dining at the Café del'Arte in midtown Manhattan. Teri had her back against the side of our booth and grew increasingly annoyed as a diner in the adjacent booth was tapping the top of the banquette with her red-polished fingernails. The tapping drove Teri to distraction. Without warning, she took action. She pivoted her head and proceeded to kiss the tapping fingers. The possessor of those fingers emitted a shocked "My God!" When she jumped up from the table, we saw it was Florence Henderson. Teri was shocked. So was Florence. Turned out that they knew each other, and there were big hugs and laughs. Brooke and I kept our heads down, looking to get lost in our minestrone.

My friendship with Brooke endured. As much as I respected her musical talent, Brooke was hysterically funny. I saw her as a true comedienne.

"I know Teri likes putting you in dramatic art movies, but I see you doing comedy with your own sitcom," I said.

A few years later she brilliantly reinvented herself in *Suddenly Susan*.

Eliot Hubbard also arranged my next big Streisand moment by inviting me to her opening night at the MGM Grand Garden Arena in Vegas. Tickets were $1,000 each. On the plane in from LA, I'd been reading an unauthorized Barbra bio, junky but fascinating. I decided to go first-class all the way. I had a limo waiting for me at the Vegas airport. Pulling away from the curb, I happened to notice Jason Gould, Barbra's son, waiting in a long line for a cab. Not sure what came over me, but I put down the window and yelled, "Jason, get in!" Although we were complete strangers, he jumped right in. Within a few minutes, it was as though we were lifelong friends. The banter was wonderful until I noticed my tell-all Barbra bio sticking out of my carry-on. Fortunately, I was able to push it out of Jason's view.

The concert was worth the grand—and then some. The stage was designed to resemble her living room: white furniture, complete with an antique tea set and vase of exquisite flowers. I was smitten. That night she sang only to me. Dear Barbra, when will we ever meet again? When will you ever sing one of my songs?

A lot less fun were two intense recording dates with Michael Bolton, who was, at that point, selling more records than God.

On the first date, I was producing "How Can We Be Lovers" for his *Soul Provider* album, a song he, Diane Warren, and I had written. We had worked days with dozens of musicians filling twenty-four tracks. Michael was on his way to the studio to start laying down his vocals when my engineer inadvertently erased all eighteen of the twenty-four tracks as we were overdubbing a cymbal crash at the modulation of the song. We had nothing. Michael was not a patient man. I knew he'd flip out, so I immediately ordered all the studio engineers on hand to help lift up the recording board as one would lift up the hood of a car.

"What's wrong?" asked Michael when he arrived.

I lied. "Trouble with the board."

"Let's just move to another studio."

"It'll be fixed in no time. Just hang out in the lounge and I'll come get you."

I kept stalling until I finally said, "It's late. Let them work on this thing and we'll knock out the vocal tomorrow morning."

Reluctantly, Michael went home—which was when I swung into action. I had my assistant call all the musicians back to the studio that very night. We worked nonstop for twelve straight hours, rerecording every note. When Michael showed up the next morning, I hadn't gotten a wink of sleep, and was in the same clothes.

"Everything okay?" he asked.

"Everything's perfect," I answered.

None the wiser, he went on and recorded "How Can We Be Lovers" that shot up the *Billboard* Hot 100 to Number 3.

The next date with him, some years later, didn't have a happy ending.

Michael was set to sing another song that he, Diane Warren, and I had written, "In The Arms Of Love." Bolton had decided to cut a Streisand-style orchestral album, employing producer David Foster and arranger Jeremy Lubbock, the biggest names in the pop field. He invited Diane and me to the session. As he ran down "In The Arms Of Love," Diane and I looked at each other. He had inadvertently changed the melody, we thought for the worse.

"Tell him," Diane told me.

"*You* tell him," I told Diane.

"You're braver," she argued.

Her flattery got me going. During the break, Michael was alone in the lounge when I approached him gently.

"You sound fantastic," I said, "but try and remember the original melody that you first came up with."

"Nobody tells me how to sing!" he snapped.

I tried to calm him down, but fury got the best of him. He lost it. He kicked open the door so that everyone—Foster, Lubbock, Diane, and the entire sixty-piece orchestra—could hear him screaming at me at the top of his lungs.

"*Who the fuck are you to come in here and tell me what to do?*"

Shocked, everyone stood still. I felt like a bucket of ice water had been poured over my head. I walked out and didn't speak to Michael for ten years.

I appreciated RATT, the heavy metal superband that had been big in the mid-eighties. In the nineties, they were looking to change their sound and hired me to produce *Detonator*, their fifth album. I cowrote ten of the eleven songs and gave them a glam-rock feel I felt confident would reignite their popularity. "Lovin' You's A Dirty Job (And I'm The Man To Do It)" was the single. RATT fans ate it up. The album was great but released at a time when hard rock band sales had started to slip.

Rod Stewart called. He invited me to his mansion on Mulholland Drive.

Instead of being ushered into the house I was taken to a huge remote studio trailer parked right in front of the grand entrance.

We were supposed to be writing together, but Rod was in the control room with his engineer, to whom he whispered something I couldn't hear. Speaking on behalf of my rock star "cowriter," the engineer matter-of-factly said, "Play something." I started noodling on the piano. Melodies flowed, but, thirty minutes later, I looked up to see that Rod was gone.

A few months later, Diane Warren and I had written a song perfect for Rod's scratchy, soulful voice. Hard to believe, but this time he came to my house. Like a prince, he sat in one of the retro boomerang-shaped leopard-skin chairs at Casa Paloma. He looked right at home. I mistakenly cued up the demo tape that Diane and I had recorded at a moment when Diane said, "Fuckin' Rod Stewart would be an asshole not to cut this song." We tried to laugh it off, but Rod remained stone-faced. Nonetheless, he listened to the song and went crazy for it. He said he wanted to cut it that very night!

I spent the next four hours planning the session. I booked all of his favorite musicians. I got the studio, the engineer, the assistant engineer, and ordered the catering. All systems were go. But then, just as I was leaving for the studio, his manager sent a message. Session canceled. No explanation given. No explanation needed. The rock star had changed his mind.

I could live without Rod, but I could not live without Laura Nyro.

That's why my heart started pounding when I got the call of calls: Laura Nyro was reaching out. Years earlier in New York, I had waited for hours in the rain just to get a glimpse of her leaving her Upper West Side apartment, praying that one day this woman might be my friend. Then there was the humiliating encounter backstage at Carnegie Hall when I'd thanked her for agreeing to let Desmond Child & Rouge open for her—only to learn that our then-manager had invented the story to look like she was delivering for us. Now in Los Angeles, I read that Laura was playing McCabe's, an intimate venue that was nearby, and naturally I went. After her inspired show, I sent back my card. By the time I arrived home, there was a message on my answering machine. It was Laura. She wanted to meet me. I sat on my bed and wept. I'd been waiting for this call for twenty-five years.

Laura came to dinner at Casa Paloma. It was a beautiful occasion. I invited Maria Vidal and Diana Grasselli. The three of us harmonized backgrounds as Laura sang songs from her *Gonna Take A Miracle* album with LaBelle. She couldn't have been sweeter. Ciro Barbaro, who'd photographed Desmond Child & Rouge during our early days, was a charming and hilarious addition to the evening. I had Laura sign my piano. Over the years, other artists would do the same, but no signature—or artist—has ever meant as much.

Our friendship grew. I came to know Laura as a proud feminist, heroic, and frail, whimsical and profound. I loved her delicate demeanor. I loved her idiosyncrasies. I loved everything about her. When she invited me to her estate in Danbury, Connecticut, I came running. I expected to be ushered into the living room and see her seated at a long concert grand piano. Instead, I was shown to a section of her property where a prefab boxcar-shaped cabin had been set over a Japanese pond with gurgling running water underneath. Because she was out of money, she'd been forced to rent out the big house. Seeing I was a bit shocked, she assured me she was fine.

"If you listen carefully," said Laura, "you'll hear the stream running just below us. The sound of water is all I need."

Knowing she liked ice cream, I arrived with five pints of different flavors of Häagen-Dazs. She served me a salad of iceberg lettuce and Wishbone dressing, followed by pasta with store-bought tomato sauce. She introduced me to her son Gil, who slept in a small alcove. She explained that Gil was the child she had with Prince Harindra Singh, whom she had met during her time in India with Sri Swami Satchidananda, founder of Integral Yoga. We compared notes on our many gurus. We admitted that we were both blessed and disillusioned. Laura also introduced me to her life partner, the painter Maria Desiderio. And then, in poignant detail, Laura explained how the coldhearted music business had robbed her blind.

Before I left, I told her how she had transformed my life. I felt incredibly grateful for this priceless opportunity to look Laura in the eye and say, "You are a genius, a musical angel, a channel of healing love."

We hugged and said goodbye.

I was later honored when she asked me to open for her at the Oak Room of Manhattan's fabled Algonquin Hotel, where Dorothy Parker once held court and the great Andrea Marcovicci sang for a quarter century. It was to be one of Laura's last performances.

Not long after, Columbia Records failed to renew her contract. I was infuriated. I called executive Donny Ienner and said that dropping Laura Nyro was like dropping Bob Dylan. How could they? He feebly replied that he simply had too many acts and had to "clean house." The rejection devastated Laura. Her end came quickly.

Laura Nyro died of ovarian cancer at age forty-nine. Her ashes were buried under a large oak tree on the same property where we had dined in her cabin. For her memorial concert at the Beacon Theatre, I sang her ethereal and erotic ballad "The Man Who Sends Me Home." Then Rouge joined me on stage to perform her immortal "Christmas In My Soul."

Laura's soul is alive in mine.

I tried to keep that spirit alive on the land she once owned. My intention was to buy it from her estate and form a retreat for women artists in her memory. At the last minute, I was outbid by $25,000 and not even given a chance to counter. In an attempt to start a Laura Nyro foundation and museum, I asked the help of her first manager, David Geffen. But Geffen was still hurt about something that had happened twenty-eight years earlier: Laura had refused to leave Columbia for Geffen's new label, Asylum, because of her loyalty and attachment to Clive Davis, who signed her there. Clive told me that Geffen offered him a partnership at Asylum. Davis refused, later labeling that decision one of his biggest regrets. Instead, Geffen signed Joni Mitchell, whose fame eclipsed Laura's. My call unnerved Geffen who, enraged, hung up on me.

Laura left half her estate to Maria Desiderio and half to her son Gil.

When two years later Maria died, also of ovarian cancer, things got complicated. The woman caring for Maria, inherited Maria's half of the estate and told the Rock & Roll Hall of Fame, when Laura was posthumously inducted, that Gil had been dis-inherited and thus was not invited to the ceremony. I reached out to Jann Wenner, head of the Hall, and also appealed to Bette Midler, who was inducting Laura, to set the record straight. Justice prevailed. Gil was called to the stage to accept the honor in his mother's name.

May her name and music never be forgotten.

*With Laura Nyro, Santa Monica, 1993*

PART FIVE

LA VIDA LOCA

*Desmond and Curtis, Laguna Beach, 1993*

# THE EARTH SHOOK

AND FREAKED US OUT. The Northridge earthquake, on January 14, 1994, was a signal: *It's been fun, but now it's time to run. Get out of LA while the getting's good.* Easier said than done. We were leaving precious friends and memories behind.

Sandra Seacat, the acting and spiritual teacher who, unlike so many of my other gurus, stayed in my life as a creative force, came to live with us in Casa Paloma. On any given day, Laura Dern and Isabella Rossellini would be hanging out in our kitchen with Sandra. Our Santa Monica life was good, but the rumbling ground beneath us, the wildfires spreading over the parched landscape, the Rodney King riots, and the madness of the O. J. Simpson trial convinced us it was time to move on.

Five years into my relationship with Curtis, I remained faithful. This was a new phenomenon. I had neither lived nor even witnessed a monogamous relationship in my family. Mimí was wild. My aunts were wild. Marfy was wild. I cite their wildness only to re-explain that domestic context from which I emerged. Wildness was all I knew, and wildness took me a long time to unlearn. The blessing is that the powerful bond between Curtis and myself gave me the hope of faithfulness. But the question remained: could I tame my wildness and attain what I had been long searching for—a relationship built on trust?

Family was on my mind when I made the decision to move back to Miami, where I had not lived since my first years of college, twenty-three years before. Now in the mid-nineties, I was a forty-two-year-old songwriter with money pouring in from an ever-growing catalog of hits. With the unrealized launch of my career as a solo singer, I felt the need for a different kind of renewal.

Thoughts of Miami were never far from my mind. And, of course, thoughts of Miami led to thoughts of Cuba. And thoughts of Cuba led to thoughts of what Mimí had always seen as her family's fallen nobility.

Well, what if I reconnected to my roots? What if I returned home a nobleman in the field of pop music? What if I took all the pain of my impoverished childhood and rewrote the story? Where I was once nobody going nowhere, I could now be somebody going somewhere. Instead of a poor kid living in the projects, I could be a king living in a castle.

And then there was music, the Latin music I had heard as I grew inside my mother's womb. Before Lulu, before Janis Joplin and Dionne Warwick, and even before the divine Laura Nyro, Mimí was my music. Mimí wrote, sang and hustled songs while I was still learning to walk. Mimí had a heart full of music. For all her insanity, the sanest part of my mother was married to melody. I missed those melodies that had raised me on the streets and beaches of Miami. I wanted to go home.

But because the home I returned to as a successful adult had to overwhelm the home I had known as a bewildered child, I felt compelled to outdo even the wonders of Casa Paloma. I wanted more than a mansion—I wanted a compound. I found the perfect spot, an enclave in Miami Beach directly across the water from Allison Island, where, as a kid, I had visited the Wexler family and been introduced to the world of intellectual affluence. The Wexlers had taste, money, and brilliant ideas. Now I had money; through men like Eliot Hubbard and Bob Crewe, I had developed taste; and the success of my songs seemed to say that I had brilliant ideas.

The heart of the compound was a spacious waterfront home with lavish 1930s Spanish Revival charm—carved coral limestone Deco entryway, Mediterranean tile, lush interior courtyards, spiral staircases, a pool, guest quarters, stunning views of the city and the sea. What made the house even more special was that the receipts of its sale would go to a foundation researching a cure for AIDS, the disease that killed its former owner.

The property also included a carriage house that housed my studio, named the Gentlemen's Club, where we were among the first to install the Pro Tools technology of recording history, a digital audio workstation that revolutionized the industry. We bought an additional structure for production and a mansion around the corner for Mimí, fulfilling her dream of living in grand luxury on Miami Beach. A building across the street held offices for me and chief of staff Brian Coleman, plus our own accounting department. We then lined the street with elegant royal palm trees. Thus, my name for the complex: Four Palms.

I kept pushing, pushing, pushing. I zipped from one building to another on a golf cart. The regulation dress code for my hardworking staff of twelve was black jeans, black T-shirts, and black work boots. Subconsciously, I might have been reacting to Akwanesa, where wearing black was forbidden.

For whatever was wrong with Barber's community, it did teach me to organize and run an enterprise of workers. Maybe I was looking to form my own cult in reverse. Any way you look at it, it was a busy beehive buzzing with creativity. Naively, I thought Mimí might settle down to a quieter lifestyle.

Sadly, though, Four Palms marked the beginning of her emotional decline. Her affair with one of the gardeners didn't come as a shock. That was Mimí's longtime pattern. I also wasn't surprised that, behind my back, she was giving the money I gave her to some of her down-and-out siblings, enabling them and further adding to our dizzying family dysfunction. Neither was I completely surprised when Mimí would crash into one of the many writers' workshops I conducted, playing her songs, cornering producer friends, and, even at age seventy, trying to promote her career. When she wanted something, she knew how to put on the charm.

All that was business as usual. Unusual, though, was the way my mother kept repeating herself and, at times, struggled with memory. I detected the start of dementia. That detection, however, was uncertain. After all, my mother had always been volatile, her behavior unpredictable. Maybe this was just more of the same. Maybe her idiosyncrasies were simply more pronounced. But deep down I knew.

I also knew that my job in Miami was to push my music to a higher level, artistically and commercially. That's why I was especially excited by the chance to work with Chynna Phillips, daughter of the Mamas & the Papas' John and Michelle Phillips. Chynna had been one of the three members of Wilson Phillips— the other two were daughters of Beach Boy Brian Wilson—a group whose debut album sold eight million copies. In 1994, when Chynna had left the trio to break out on her own, my manager Winston Simone put us together.

I loved our collaboration. Chynna was gorgeous, funny, and filled with joy. She and I wrote three songs, and I produced four on her debut (and only) album, *Naked and Sacred*. There was great anticipation. The suits were sure they had a blockbuster. Unfortunately, they booked Chynna on *Saturday Night Live* before she had a chance to test out the material in clubs, but that would have meant tour support. She was underrehearsed, underprepared, as I was when Desmond Child & Rouge performed on the show. She was another victim of typical music industry overconfidence: executives who think a singer can just walk on a show and kill it. Her single sank, and the album never recovered.

Later that same year, Jon Bon Jovi was on the treadmill, and I was on the bike. While we were working out at his New Jersey home, warming up for a writing session, a Bush song was blasting from the speakers. I kept hearing the words, "Kiss the rain, kiss the rain."

"What a great title!" I said. "I wish I had thought of it. Kiss the rain."

Jon looked at me sideways and wisecracked, "It's 'Glycerine,' you asshole."

"Wow, so we have a title. Let's write the song."

"Nah," he said. "That's a chick title. Save it for someone else."

I did that. I had set my sights on collaborating with Eric Bazilian, from the Hooters, who had solely written Joan Osborne's mammoth hit "One Of Us." So when Miles Copeland, the man who managed the Police, invited me to a songwriters' camp in France that Eric was attending, I jumped at the chance. I jumped even higher when I learned that Carole King, one of my all-time idols, would also be there. Like Ellie Greenwich and Cynthia Weil, Carole is also a quintessential Brill Building songwriting diva.

My plan was that Eric and I would write "Kiss The Rain" for Billie Myers, a singer from England with a huge voice and serious style. I knew she'd kill it. Because Doug Morris of Universal Music had recently given me my own label imprint, Deston (a fusion of Desmond and Winston), I saw Billie as our first artist.

I arrived at Copeland's estate, Château de Marouatte, southwest of Paris, called the Castle, an actual medieval fortress, complete with moat. But before I could get together with Eric Bazilian, Miles put another plan in action: He had me and Eric writing with Alannah Myles, a Canadian who, after her monster global hit "Black Velvet," couldn't get arrested. Ms. Myles showed up looking like a storybook villainess: dark-gray cape with flowing cowl in the back, blood-red lips, hair dyed shiny jet-black, skin ashen-white. She was scary. And demanding.

"Give me a song like 'Black Velvet.'" Eric and I played a few ideas.

"Not 'Black Velvet' enough!"

A few more ideas.

"It needs to feel more like 'Black Velvet'!"

We took a different approach.

"No, no, no! I'm not feeling that 'Black Velvet' vibe."

I lost it. "Alannah, you cannot keep saying 'Black Velvet,'" I said. "You're like someone who's lost in a house of mirrors. Everywhere you look, you see yourself in that damn 'Black Velvet' video."

Her head turned around like *The Exorcist*. Then she became Norma Desmond, tilting her head back and clawing her chest. With unapologetic arrogance, she said, "How dare you! *Youuuuuu* do not know *meeeeeee. Youuuuuu* do not know my fans."

And with that, she stormed out, slamming the door behind her. Eric and I, who had not said a word to each other yet, poked our heads out the door and watched as she swooped across the stone courtyard in the pouring rain, her cape blowing behind her. The two of us fell on the floor howling with laughter until our stomachs ached.

Meanwhile, with Alannah gone, Eric and I wrote almost all of "Kiss The Rain" in less than thirty minutes. I suggested we leave the second verse for Billie Myers to write. Just as we were making plans to fly to London and record Billie, Alannah knocked on the wooden door and curtly said, "I'm ready to work." Miles had made her march back.

Given my first impression of her, it didn't take long for me to come up with the hook "I'm bad for you, and that's good," one of those "You Give Love A Bad Name" paradoxes that seemed to suit Alannah's Cruella de Vil demeanor. She turned out to be a good sport, recording and releasing "Bad 4 You" in Canada, where it became a big hit.

The next day. Miles set up a session with Carole King and myself. I was thrilled—less so when I arrived to find this Charles Manson stand-in sitting at the keyboard. I realized that we'd been booked in with one of Miles's new writers, an unknown. I commandeered the second keyboard. So when Carole walked in, there was only a chair for her to sit in. The session was beyond awkward. Manson and Carole kept giving each other secret winks and hand signals. Having learned at least one good lesson at Akwenasa—don't withhold, confront—I asked Carole if she and I could step outside.

"What's going on?" I asked her. "I waited my whole life to write with you."

She burst into tears. "I just didn't want you to know that I'm really not a lyricist. And with two good piano players, there's nothing for me to do."

"We'll put you on a piano," I said. "We'll work it out."

We hugged and went back inside. Not five minutes went by when Manson man was called away on an emergency. Back in the US, his brother had been in a car wreck. He ran out, leaving us alone. We finished the song, and a few months later Carole came to Four Palms to work with me on the demo. Afterward, we sat on my dock watching the dolphins swim by as the sun set turned the tropical sky flamingo-pink. Her war stories were heartbreaking.

Both Carole and Eric Bazilian stayed in my life.

The following week, after our writing sessions at the Castle, Eric and I flew to the UK and met up with Billie Myers at the Halcyon Hotel, where Eric set up a mobile studio in the basement. She wrote the second verse and sang a brilliant lead vocal. If you solo her track, you can hear the sound of the up-and-down police sirens whizzing by. "Kiss The Rain" was a smash. At least Deston Records had one solid hit, though the label, given my professional and personal distractions, didn't last long.

A few months later, I met up with Eric in Dublin, where we went to write with Jon Bon Jovi, and I saw that, of all people, Carole King was starring in Neil Simon's *Brighton Beach Memoirs*. We went to the play and afterward invited Carole to hang out with us. She, Eric, Jon, and I went to a nightclub owned by U2, where we ran into prim-and-proper Martha Stewart throwing back shots and cursing like a sailor. A bizarre Irish night among the stars.

Aerosmith turned up in Florida. Steven Tyler and Joe Perry were headquartered at the Marlin Hotel in Miami Beach and invited me down to Joe Galdo's studio, located on a lower floor, where we wrote two killer songs, "Hole In My Soul" and "Ain't That A Bitch." Their A&R guru John Kalodner insisted that Glen Ballard produce, the same Ballard who had struck multi-platinum with Alanis Morissette's *Jagged Little Pill*.

This all was happening when Steven, always on edge, was searching for a new sound. They had spent months programming the album on Glen's Synclavier system, holed up at the Marlin Hotel in South Beach. Joe seemed increasingly frustrated with the slow-moving process of layering multiple tracks commandeered by Glen . . . something a real band like Aerosmith had never done.

When I dropped by, unannounced, at the drum overdub session at Criteria Recording Studios to see what was happening, I noticed that the two tunes I'd written with Joe and Steven were not listed on the production board. I spoke up and asked them why.

Put on the spot, they all looked around at each other as Ballard, who's one of the nicest people I've ever met, stepped up and said, "Sorry, man . . . they're going in a different direction."

I couldn't help but say, "The Rolling Stones haven't changed their direction in thirty years."

The remark hit home. No one said a word. Steven always saw Aerosmith as the American Stones, so it wasn't long after my comment that Ballard left the project and there was peace in the valley. The more traditional Aerosmith album, aptly titled *Nine Lives*, included my two songs.

In the midnineties I had heard a demo version of a song called "MMMBop," by a three-brother boy band called Hanson. I liked their sound, and, seeing they had covered songs by the Jackson 5 as well as the Coasters, I understood their roots in pop harmony. Their demo had been strong enough to attract a major label. Steve Greenberg at Mercury Records asked me to write with them. The boys—Isaac, 15, Taylor, 12, and Zac, 9—were from Tulsa but living in LA with their family. I flew out for the session in their rented house in the West Hollywood hills. In this pre-GPS era, I got lost and called Diane Warren, who lived in the neighborhood, for directions. When she asked me whom I was looking for, I told her I was going to write with Hanson. She hadn't heard of them.

What had they done? I said I'd heard a demo I liked. I also told her that the drummer was nine years old.

"Desmond," said Diane, "you've reached your lowest low. You're writing with a nine-year-old?"

She nonetheless gave me directions and I arrived on time. The boys were blond, long-haired, blue-eyed, all-American stars, shy but affable. Their dad looked like the father on *The Brady Bunch*. Mom looked like Mary of Peter, Paul and Mary. She wore a long, flowered hippie dress and diligently tried to keep the other siblings who were not in the band from disturbing us. The household vibe brought to mind a religious cult, which, of course, was nothing new for me. I felt comfortable.

Zac was on drums, Isaac and Taylor on guitar and keys, and a keyboard was set up for me. In a couple of hours, we worked out what became one of my favorite songs. I suggested the title, "Weird," because that was the big teen word of the time. Everything and everyone was weird. Weird also applied to my sexuality. "We've lived in the shadows, but doesn't everyone?" the lyrics said. "Isn't it strange how we all feel a little bit weird sometimes?"

Neither Mom nor Dad nor any of the three Hansons objected to the story. In fact, they thought it fit their family's outsider identity. Released as a single, "Weird," with Taylor's yearning lead vocal, was a hit. Gus Van Sant directed a video in which the boys, observing that weird assortment of human beings who inhabit New York City, perform on a subway platform, singing for their supper as they're suddenly submerged underwater and start swimming in the subway car. The album, *Middle of Nowhere*, came out of nowhere and sold more than ten million copies worldwide.

After its triumph, Diane Warren called me and asked for their number.

"So much for my lowest low," I said. "I guess you want to welcome them to the Number 1 club."

A sweet coda: a lifetime later, not having seen them since we wrote the song, Hanson was the keynote artist at an ASCAP Expo. I surprised them onstage in the middle of the song "Weird" and told the story about how I had written "Weird" about being gay. The boys didn't look shocked.

Being a good sport, Taylor said, "I knew that."

Taylor's brother Zac shouted out, "That's why everyone thinks you're gay!"

Another boy band, another international phenomenon, impacted my life indirectly. I was unfamiliar with their records and never worked with them. One of its former members, though, had an earth-shattering impact on my career.

*With Hanson, ASCAP Expo, Hollywood, 2018*

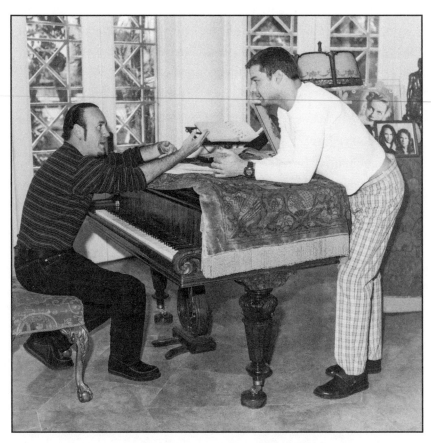

*With Ricky Martin, Four Palms, Miami Beach, 1999*

# THE CUP OF LIFE

MIAMI ENERGY IS LARGELY Latin energy driven by Latin music. Miami reconnected me to my Cuban roots. I went salsa dancing at Debbie Ohanian's Starfish, and, on separate nights, I took Steven Tyler and Jon Bon Jovi to Centro Vasco Restaurant. It was there I heard Albita, who, along with her band, had just pulled off a harrowing escape from her native Cuba. Annie Lennox-like, she stepped out in a tailored man's suit and slicked-back hair, projecting a seductive androgyny. I loved her outsized personality and gutsy chops. She was signed by Gloria Estefan's husband, Emilio, who, in an attempt to mainstream her, coaxed her into cocktail dresses and spike heels, but she was scorching-hot all the same.

Hot Latin music got all over me. I'd forgotten how much I loved the syncopated flavor of those dance grooves that went back to the island of my origins. It felt free, sensual, and optimistic.

Had it not been for these three people I might have missed the conga line of history. Richard Jay-Alexander, the son of Cubans, directed Ricky Martin in the Broadway show *Les Misérables*; Debbie Ohanian, our mutual close friend who discovered and encouraged Richard to cast Ricky as Marius; Carleen Simone, wife of my manager Winston, had seen Ricky singing on *General Hospital*. They all raved and went on and on about this young Puerto Rican star I should work with. He already had a huge hit in Spanish—"Maria"—cowritten by Draco Rosa and K. C. Porter, who, before Ricky ascended to the role, had been the lead singer of Menudo, the eighties boy band sensation. I watched an aerial video clip of Ricky in Buenos Aires, where officials closed down the city and hundreds of thousands of people poured into the streets to watch him perform live on an outdoor stage. It was insane. I had to work with him.

Winston arranged a meeting. I later learned from Ricky's mercurial manager, Angelo Medina, that Emilio Estefan, the formidable "Godfather of Latin Music," tried to get them to turn Ricky's limo around during his six-block drive to Four Palms. Emilio saw me as a rocker and understandably argued against my expertise in Latin music. Fortunately, destiny intervened, and Ricky showed up.

In person, Ricky was like the blazing sun. All energy and heat. Also Puerto Rican, Draco was scruffy, and if he had been wearing a red beret you'd think you were looking at the young Che Guevara. A soulful antiestablishment intellectual, his uniqueness was striking, with tattoos on his fingers and a Bible in his hand. After Ricky had aged out of Menudo and went solo pop, Draco had led the avant-garde soul band Maggie's Dream with Lenny Kravitz. When Draco and Ricky rejoined forces, Ricky brought the charm and Draco brought the art.

Auditioning to be Ricky's producer, I played them a song recorded by the Hooters, "Private Emotion," that was perfect for Ricky. They agreed.

They also agreed that Draco and I should start writing original songs.

A month later, we were lunching in Beverly Hills with one of my comanagers, David Simoné, an Englishman who knew soccer. He explained the significance of an anthem for the World Cup. Such a song could go worldwide. Draco and I took careful note, and on the plane back to Miami, singing back and forth to each other while beating on the tray tables, wrote "The Cup Of Life" or "La Copa De La Vida." It was a chant—"Go, go, go . . .

*ale, ale, ale*"; it was an exhortation—"Push it along, gotta be strong, don't ever stop, right to the top"—it was a confirmation—"The cup of life, this is the one"; and a celebration—"Tonight's the night, we're gonna celebrate." Above all, the song exploded with an irresistible pulse. I was able to translate what I had learned with KISS and Bon Jovi: take a fist-in-the-air anthem and give it a Latin spin. We cooked up a stew of percussion and horns that radio hadn't heard since Gloria Estefan broke the cultural barriers with her crossover hits "Dr. Beat" and "Conga."

"The Cup Of Life" was selected as the 1998 World Cup theme where Ricky sang it at the Stade de France on July 12 to over a billion viewers in 200 countries.

Thank God France won the game that day. Not only did "The Cup Of Life" shoot to Number 1 in that country, it became Number 1 in twenty-two other nations. The press was calling it *the* global moment for Latin music.

Next, we needed a smash single for Ricky's debut English-language album. Draco and I were fascinated with the idea of Ricky as the Latin Elvis. But why stop there? Sinatra had died the year before, and his records were all over the airwaves. Ricky had his own version of that sexy Sinatra swag. Angelo Medina, Ricky's manager, was urging us to write what he termed a Spanglish anthem that no one would forget. With all that in mind, Draco and I cooked up a Rat Pack/James Bond horn-heavy Latin dance charmer and called it "Livin' La Vida Loca." It was cited by the *Wall Street Journal* as the first one hundred percent digitally produced song to reach number one.

I originally hoped to write bilingual lyrics, but that never happened. Only half the title was in Spanish. I chose the word "Loca" because, I reasoned, due to the omnipresence of El Pollo Loco's fast-food chicken chain, everyone knew "loco" meant "crazy." But CBS record exec Donnie Ienner didn't see it that way.

"You need to write an English version of the song," he said. I shot back, "It *is* in English. Every word except the title. It's all about, 'She's into superstitions, black cats and voodoo dolls.' It's all about, 'She makes you order French champagne, once you've got a taste of her, you'll never be the same.'"

"I heard Spanish," said Ienner. "Nobody's going to understand that!"

"Like I said, it's only in the title," I reiterated.

Thus, when the record was released, Ienner made certain that under "Livin' La Vida Loca," written in bold letters, were the words "Living The Crazy Life."

The record went crazy—Billboard, MTV and ASCAP awards, you name 'em. It became even more of an anthem than "The Cup Of Life." The Latin arena rock combination worked like a charm. The record was nominated for four major Grammys. I gave a "Win or Lose" party in LA that George Michael attended. He and I had met in the showers at a Koreatown spa the day before. Nothing happened. I'm glad I gave my party those positive/negative options because, much to my dismay, we lost. Carlos Santana's elegantly produced "Smooth" swept. Every time I run into Rob Thomas, the man who cowrote and sang "Smooth," I call him "Grammy Killer."

Nonetheless, Ricky's first English-language album was a sensation, selling over fifteen million copies. I produced and cowrote five of the tracks and saw it as a culmination of everything I had tried to do by coming home to Miami.

During this hectic time, Mimí placed herself in the middle of the mix. Brian Coleman, my chief of staff, who has helped keep me sane for much of my professional life, said Mimí had been slipping cassettes to Ricky Martin.

I actually busted her. During one of Ricky's sessions, I had to leave for a few minutes. That's when Mimí snuck into the studio and played Ricky "Diosa Del Mar" ("Goddess Of The Sea"), a tribute to Puerto Rico she had written when we lived there during our Daddy Lopez days. When I returned to the studio, the song was playing, and tears were running down Ricky's face.

Ricky's moment in the glaring spotlight came with challenges. The most apparent was his interview in 2000 with Barbara Walters, coming at the absolute apex of his career. Later, Walters regretted how she pushed him to say whether he was gay. Ricky's demurral was unconvincing. The interview did more damage to his self-esteem than to his career.

Ricky and I never discussed our sexuality. For a while, he supposedly had a girlfriend, a fact that was highly publicized. Having lived in various sections of closets for so much of my life, I wasn't about to criticize him for not coming out. I understood his hesitancy. His popularity was phenomenal. I thought of Luther Vandross, another friend and fabulous singer, who had also cultivated a huge following among women. Luther's female fans, like Ricky's, comprised the core of his success. To disappoint them with the reality that he was sexually attracted to men, and not to them, was a daunting proposition. Having struggled their entire lives to reach this plateau of popularity, neither Ricky nor Luther were ready to hurt their commercial standing. Too many people's livings were at stake. Internally, though, they paid a price. I say that because of my own painful past.

The world has come a long way since then. But two decades ago, coming out had real consequences. No matter how great your success, you could still lose your family. You could lose your friends. You could lose your career. You could lose everything. And tragically, in far too many places around the world, the same is still true today. In some countries, you can lose your life.

As the century came to a close, I was riding high. I had helped reignite the Latin-music explosion. I'd gone from being a songwriter/producer-for-hire and forged a new world where we did it all from soup to nuts. I supervised a team of crack programmers and engineers who worked around the clock turning out innovative music. With Winston Simone and David Simoné, I had started Deston Songs, with offices in New York, LA, Nashville, Miami Beach, and London. Forty writers were signed to me. I was hosting writing camps we called the Sand Castle to cultivate even more writers and cowrite even more hits.

All this came as a result of having made some good decisions. I hadn't tried to reinvent classic rock or chase after grunge. By embracing Latin music, I had gone a different way and found myself ahead of the game. But I was starting to feel that this complex and demanding system I had built up was bigger than me and swallowing me whole. I fed my soul into the Desmond Child Machine. That machine required I act a certain way and do certain things. I started getting caught up in a matrix of my own making. That matrix, further fueled by the expectations of others, became overwhelming.

So many people were dependent on me.

Then I met a man who, at twenty-one, was half my age and tore down the architecture of my life. I must have been having an undiagnosed nervous breakdown. Don't get me wrong. I let it happen. I felt I knew what I was doing. But I didn't.

He was a college student from a well-to-do Greek-American family and wanted to be a rock star. After I gave a lecture at the University of Miami, he approached me with a Desmond Child & Rouge album, seeking an autograph. He had long, dark hair with a dazzling smile, and in some ways his Mediterranean looks reminded me of a male Maria Vidal. Electricity ignited. He was my alter ego. He was also raw clay that I felt obsessed to sculpt, a student looking for a teacher, a musician looking for a mentor. Paradoxically, his charisma was such that he could control me. Yes, the sculptor was shaping the clay, but the clay was also shaping the sculptor. I allowed that. I no longer wanted to be the former me, the tired me, tethered to responsibility. It was as though the new me, more alive than ever, had convinced the former me to commit suicide. Maybe all this is just a fancy way of saying I was having a midlife crisis.

I never wanted Curtis to leave. I just wanted Curtis to just let me have this. Deep down, I knew it wouldn't last. But for now, I needed it.

Curtis was adamant and gave an ultimatum. He wanted him gone.

When I conveyed Curtis's reaction, the young man said, "I brought you to life. And I can't let him destroy what I created."

Yes, he thought I could make him a rock star, but I don't believe he had a master plan. He was acting out of raw instinct, the way a snake will bite you, not out of meanness, but because that's what snakes do. It was survival instinct on his part. Maybe both of our parts. He probably wasn't even bi or gay, but the circumstances of his life—his own personal rebellion against his controlling conservative parents—drove him across the line. He came after me, using adulation as a means of manipulation. It worked.

I completely compartmentalized my life with Curtis (calm, loving, intimate), and this new life (dangerous, explosive, unrelenting). And all the time, for what I was doing to Curtis, I was wracked with guilt. Curtis didn't deserve it, and he was right to leave.

Curtis moved to the Birdhouse, the home we had built together in the suburban hills of Nashville. The house was small, but the view of downtown, ten miles off in the woodsy distance, was stunning. Meanwhile, I stayed at Four Palms in Miami Beach. The Desmond Child Machine was in full gear.

Now I was free to be with my protégé. But when I brought him to a dinner party with people my age, he was bored, and I was embarrassed. The balloon burst. I saw that I was living the life of the song I had written. I was loco.

*Desmond and Curtis, Miami Beach, 1997*

# TIME OUT FOR THE KING OF POP

DRACO ROSA IS A TRUE ARTIST. His genius is exquisite. He's incapable of writing or singing anything that is not true. Most performers create their own persona. They embellish their image. But Draco is different. He had only to chisel away from the inside out to find himself—a character out of Cervantes or Picasso, a fearless and free spirit fueled by creative passion.

Since childhood, he and Ricky have been close. Ricky fought his way through the show-business wars to the top. On the other hand, Draco never really cared for fame. He'd had enough of it as a child star in Menudo. His brotherhood with Ricky was strong. Their sibling rivalry actually benefited them both. Ricky, a show boy, yearned to be a poet like Draco. No one appreciated Draco as much as Ricky. Ironically, I don't think Draco ever expected Ricky to break out as big as he did.

This was the deep dynamic I walked into. Their methodology went like this: Because Ricky was killing it on the road, Draco worked with various cowriters to mold the songs he knew would work for Ricky. He'd then sing the guide and background vocals for Ricky to learn. So, when Ricky showed up in the studio, he easily emulated Draco's swag. They became one singular sound that, combined with Ricky's explosive stage presence, took the world by storm.

A few months later, when it came time to crank out Ricky's next album, I had a problem. No Draco. The sibling rivalry had escalated. Draco felt that he was giving away too much of himself and went off to do his own music. Angelo Medina, who managed both Ricky and Draco, was a master of divide-and-conquer so he could bring everyone back together on his own terms.

*With Draco Rosa, Miami Beach, 1998*

He had convinced Draco that I was taking all the credit for Ricky's success and advised him, in speaking to the press, never to mention me. On the other hand, whenever I was interviewed, I never failed to lavish Draco with praise. Despite my efforts at reconciliation, I couldn't get Draco to work with me again.

The task I faced was daunting. The label gave us thirty days to cut and master Ricky's new album, *Sound Loaded*. I said it was impossible, but Angelo insisted. Eager to get it out ahead of the Backstreet Boys' next album, they offered Ricky a $30 million advance to deliver it on time.

Ricky's voice wasn't in great shape. The road had taken its toll. To fuel the competitive fires, Angelo had Ricky recording songs for this same album with my crosstown rival Emilio Estefan. Besides that, I was burdened by a second-rate, monotonous track the label dropped on me, written by the otherwise flawless Draco and Walter Afanasieff.

I was told not only to finish producing the track for no credit or fee, and to write all of the lyrics, and record Ricky's vocals— all for a humiliating pittance: eight percent of the copyright. If I didn't agree, the label threatened to give it to Diane Warren, who would have never agreed to that split. I caved, figuring it was better to take one for the team than lose the game . . . to Diane. The song turned out to be "She Bangs," the first single and a huge hit. I also cowrote the second single, "Nobody Wants To Be Lonely," with my Deston writers, Victoria Shaw and Gary Burr, which was sung as a duet with Christina Aguilera. By the way, I got my productions to the mastering studio twenty-four hours before anyone else did.

In the midst of this mad dash to complete Ricky's album, I learned that Michael Jackson was interested in working with me, an offer no songwriter could refuse.

I flew to New York where I was instructed to meet Michael in his rented townhouse at Four East Seventy-Fourth Street just off Central Park. It was 2000, nearly four years since his last release. Already having spent tens of millions on the production of his new album, Sony was frantic to complete it. Before I entered the picture, Michael had written dozens of songs with Cory Rooney that never went anywhere. The Michael Jackson songwriting machine had broken down, and I was called in to fix it.

I walked up the staircase of the stately townhouse and rang the bell. An assistant in his early twenties, a dark-haired Italian boy, handsome enough to be a model, greeted me. Holding a clipboard, he led me through a dark foyer in which four faceless porcelain mannequins stood. Each was dressed in 1970s brightly colored polyester church-lady outfits with matching hats and pumps. From there I was escorted into a long wood-paneled dining room dominated by a Chippendale table large enough to seat forty. I was told to take a chair and wait. I was offered nothing to drink. The wooden shades on the windows were drawn. Narrow streams of light were focused on two paintings—one the famous Raphael portrait of two winged angels often depicted on greeting cards and shopping bags. Could this be the original? The other painting was dominated by a manly Roman goddess upon a marble throne, surrounded by a dozen cherubic children. I speculated that Michael saw the androgynous woman as he saw himself: a guardian of the innocent.

Above me, I heard footsteps and mumbled voices. I waited an hour before Michael appeared, holding a three-year-old blond baby, his son, Prince. He had curly blond hair and a radiant smile. Michael kissed his forehead and handed him to his assistant, who carried him back upstairs. I was stunned by

Michael's appearance. Reed-thin, he wore a baseball cap over his stringy, shoulder-length wig, dark aviator glasses, and black-and-white striped silk pajamas that somehow made him look like a prisoner.

He sat at the end of the long table. I sat next to him. The assistant came back downstairs. Like a mischievous child, Michael, who had a dazzling smile, began tickling and poking the young man, who seemed embarrassed in front of me, but laughed to appease him. The interaction had a distinctly sexual vibe.

Finally, Michael turned his attention to me. He wanted to know all about Ricky Martin—what kind of music does he listen to, where does he go on vacation, what is his work ethic, how did I meet him, who are his favorite artists, is he as handsome in person as he is in pictures? I answered as best I could, but none of my answers satisfied Michael. He wanted to know more about Ricky. I explained that, though we were collaborators, we weren't intimate friends. My limited knowledge disappointed Michael.

I gently changed the topic to working with Michael on his music. I said how eager I was to start writing. In response, he removed his dark glasses, looked at me with big Diana Ross doe eyes and whispered, "Will you give me your all?"

"Of course," I said. "I give my all to everyone I work with."

"No, I mean, *really, really, really* your all? Will you give your all to *me*?"

"Yes."

"Then we'll start next week," he said. "We'll work at Sony Music Studios. My people will give you the dates and times."

"Great."

Except it wasn't great. I flew home to Miami and dove into finishing *Sound Loaded*, and seven days later flew back to New

York, all on my dime. I went to the Sony studio, where I found a beautifully displayed spread of sumptuous food in the adjacent lounge next to the studio. There was enough to feed an army. Inside the control room, a life-size stuffed gorilla was seated cross-legged on the couch. There was a grand piano set up in the vocal booth with a stand that held sheets of lyrics. I presumed the piano was for me. I wasn't sure how Michael liked to write, but I'd soon see.

While waiting, I picked up a lyric sheet and saw the title "Diana." Because the opening lines described the heroine living in a world that had always misunderstood her, I presumed it was about Diana Ross, who had just been detained at Heathrow Airport for assaulting a security officer. But as I read the words Michael had written, it dawned on me that it was about Princess Diana, who had died three years earlier. With his lifelong passion to befriend the most photographed women in the world—Elizabeth Taylor, Jackie O, Katharine Hepburn, Brooke Shields—Michael had yearned to be close to the Princess. But Diana, whose charitable foundation focused on children, shunned the pop star because of allegations accusing him of child molestation. The song felt like Michael's sad attempt to prove that he was, after all, connected to the princess. Or maybe it was about himself.

Meanwhile, the engineers gave every indication he was coming. An hour passed. Then two. Then three. I saw that someone had left a slip of paper on the console that showed Michael's private number at the townhouse. I called.

Michael answered, but when he heard it was me, he pretended to be his assistant.

"I'm so sorry, Mr. Child. Mr. Jackson can't come to the studio today because he's ill . . . very, very ill."

"I flew up for this session. Why didn't you call me yesterday?"

"We did, but no one answered."

I knew that was bullshit. The engineers were in place. The fresh food had been laid out. Michael was simply flaking. I was on the verge of busting him, but what would be the point? I left the studio, flew back to Miami, and never heard from Michael Jackson again. It was an age-old story: a songwriter stung by a star.

*Invincible*, his last studio album, finally came out at the end of the year, billed as the most expensive album ever made, at a total cost of $30 million.

Sales were disappointing, and Michael was so furious that he held a press conference where he called Tommy Mottola, Sony chairman, a racist devil.

After Michael, Miami seemed mild. Ricky's *Sound Loaded* had been released. Not all the critics were happy, but fortunately music fans don't heed critics. Fans loved the record. Within eighteen months, we'd turned out two Ricky Martin albums that together sold over thirty million copies.

A beautiful benefit of working with Ricky was the reclamation of the bas-relief wooden rendering that Mimí had sold to Orlando Ortís Toro for $1,200 when, thirty-three years earlier, we were flat broke and facing eviction in the slums of Miami. It turned out that Carlos Gonzalez Abella, Ricky's longtime partner, knew the Toro family in Puerto Rico. He contacted them and learned that they still had the Brazilian walnut piece in which Mimí was surrounded by three men whispering in her ear. The family was willing to sell. I was eager to buy. The price was $35,000. I didn't even try to negotiate. I wanted nothing to impede the sale. The magnificent artwork hangs in my New York apartment to this day.

*Desmond and Ricky, Four Palms, Miami Beach, 1999*

# LITTLE RED FERRARI

THE MOST LOCO CHAPTER of my *vida loca* involved a woman I met one night when I was with Ricky Martin in Miami. We were driving down to South Beach, going for a bite to eat, when I happened to ask him, "How's your girlfriend?" "What girlfriend?" he wanted to know. "Rebecca," I said, "the one you introduced us to. The one who was staying at your house." "She's not my girlfriend." "Oh," I said. Looking straight ahead and pausing several long seconds, he added, "You get to the point in your life when you know what you like and what you don't like."

Ironically, at the moment Ricky was for the first time hinting at his sexual orientation, I met a stunning woman. She was literally sitting on a street curb, holding her model's portfolio, and striking a provocative pose. She was exotic. She was Spanish. She was looking for a green card to match her eyes. Maybe it was the midlife madness that ensued when Curtis and I split. I don't know what it was, but I was smitten.

The first time I brought her to Four Palms, I did so in a leased cherry-red Ferrari that was part of my rejuvenated machismo. As soon as I pulled the car up the driveway and helped her out, we began kissing. She was a lot of woman to deal with. I'm not sure how I managed, but I did. The next day, my engineers, who were straight as John Wayne, confessed that they'd spied on us kissing. They greeted me with open arms, shouting, "Welcome home!"

I appreciated the welcome mat, which was pretty hilarious, but ran back into the arms of men. Still in a state of I'm-single-and-livin'-la-vida-loca, I met another man, this time in a steam room at the Eden Roc Hotel, where I once worked as a pool boy.

He was a dashing Italian dentist from Chicago with a dazzling smile and a charming gift of gab. He'd come to Miami to cruise and soon moved in with me. I even built him his own study. Before long, he was bossing my employees around. I took him on trips. We vacationed at Claridge's in London. It was there when the awful moment arrived.

"You know," he said, "I've been waiting for the right time to tell you."

"Tell me what?"

"I'm a singer. A great singer. A singer who, with your help, will be bigger than Ricky Martin."

*Oh, God,* I thought, *I've fucked up again.*

After that came the revelation that, without my knowledge, he had used my credit card on file at the hotel to draw out $3,000 in cash. Later, when my accountants caught this, he apologized, cried like a baby, and swore he meant to pay me back. Foolishly, I forgave him.

I had just seen *The Talented Mr. Ripley* and began wondering whether he was a complete fraud. When I called his office in Chicago, an answering service responded, giving no indication that he was actually a dentist. Who was this guy?

The final straw was still another shocker: singer-songwriter Bruce Roberts and photographer Herb Ritts happened to be seated behind the Italian on a plane when they overheard his big, booming voice tell the stranger seated next to him that I was his manager and currently producing his album. He spoke of the powerful politicians that I was close to, and the fact that I had made an ironclad commitment to take him to the top. He said we were inseparable.

I learned all this at a Diane Warren party that I was attending with the Italian in LA, when Bruce Roberts pulled me aside and said, "I need to speak with you privately." We found a quiet corner where Bruce told me the whole story. "Your boyfriend is bad news," he said. "Get rid of him."

I did.

At that same party, our California friends had conspired to make sure Curtis flew in from Nashville. Seeing him was a shock. I felt a pang in my heart. I also felt embarrassed that I was there with someone else. One thing, though, was clear. When I looked at Curtis, I saw light.

Curtis has described our time apart as his dark night of the soul. He has also said it led to a spiritual awakening. His time alone was also when he was able to connect to the universe . . . the real universe, not just the Desmo-verse. Looking up at the sky every night, his eyes inevitably landed on the constellation Orion. He found a loving spiritual teacher, the enlightened Reverend Becca Stevens, who helped him on his journey. He went to Greece with friends, a trip that turned into a personal odyssey. Sailing the Ionian coast, meditating, stargazing, awakening to a sea of startling blue, he reflected on the big questions. A man of great spirit, Curtis made peace with himself.

While he was calming his soul, my career was revving up. Through it all, I was never completely out of touch with Curtis. There was a moment when I asked him to run my Nashville office. Maybe that was my way of trying to hold on to him. Like my mother, I've always had trouble setting boundaries. Curtis, though, had the good sense to turn down the offer. If we came back together, it would have been as equal partners, not employer-employee. Finally, our close mutual friends told us they had had enough. They insisted that we belonged together.

But the way back was far from easy. I had to do a lot of work to unravel the me I thought I was. As control freaks go, I'm in a class of my own. I like calling all the shots, even when it comes to seating arrangements at casual dinners. Now, though, I saw that healing my relationship with Curtis would require a shift not only in my behavior, but in my entire view of life.

This time I'd have to take monogamy seriously. This time I'd have to consider Curtis's needs as much as my own. As Mimí and Marfy's lovechild, was I capable of that kind of change?

Curtis was patient, but also wounded. When we began seeing each other again, I feared that the wound would never heal and that I'd be taken to task for the rest of my life. I wanted to be forgiven then and there. I wanted to put the past behind us and move on. But clearly that wasn't possible.

Curtis had to work through his anger in his own time.

The fact that Curtis and I have been able to reconcile is a testimony to the power of love . . . his love. It's really that simple. It wasn't that my self-obsession went away. It was love over-riding self-obsession. Love overwhelming it. Love whispering in my ear, populating my dreams, stirring my heart, softening my fears, leading the way back to the man I adored.

I had written a thousand love songs in my life. Now I was living one.

*Desmond and Curtis, Four Palms, Miami Beach, 1997*

*Curtis, Desmond, and Angela Whittaker,*
*Four Palms, Miami Beach, 2002*

# TWO

MY LONGING FOR A REAL FAMILY would not be fulfilled until Curtis and I created a family of our own. We're both crazy about kids, and our commitment to have children put us on the ride of a lifetime.

We looked into adoption. That's when we got a quick reality check about how—at least in 2000—society viewed gay couples. No gay adoption allowed in Florida. Fuck Florida.

We decided to look into surrogacy. We also decided to take off a week and relax at a health resort in San Diego we dubbed Camp Wheatgrass. It was New Age-ish but cool. Each morning when we formed a prayer circle, we were given the word of the day. The first word was "joy." Curtis and I liked that because we had just bought an essential oil called Joy. That same day we met a Native American shaman we fondly called Harry the Healer. He asked me to reach into a bag filled with smooth river rocks. Each stone was engraved with a word. Without looking, I fished around and pulled one out. When I looked at it, I had to smile. The word was "joy."

That same week, between colonics, massages, and yoga, we met a wonderful woman from Ashland, Oregon. She was especially interested in our story—two gay men seeking to have a child—and offered to give us one of her eggs. We were stunned, even more so when she told us her name: Joy.

The spiritual joyride continued when we accepted an invitation from Deepak Chopra to a retreat in India built around his recent book *How To Know God*. When we checked into our hotel, the first person we encountered was Angela Whittaker. This was remarkable because Curtis had met Angela through Mike, a man he had dated while we were apart . . . but let's not go there. Angela co-owned a yoga studio in Nashville where she also taught Deepak Chopra's meditation method.

From that moment on, through the ten-day seminar, the three of us were inseparable. I felt as though I'd known Angela my entire life. It was more than the typical bonding of tourists meeting in a foreign land.

Something deeper was stirring. In one of his talks, Deepak said, "Love is more than a sentiment. Love is the ultimate truth at the heart of the universe." Whatever that meant, we were there and flying high.

On the last night, there was an extravagant celebration. The moon was full, the air perfumed with frankincense. Torches lit an expansive lawn where we sat listening to the mystical sounds of holy mantras and chants.

At one point Angela caught me staring at her.

"Why are you looking at me like that?" she asked.

"Because you're going to have our baby."

Laughing, she said, "Ewww . . . get away!"

A month passed. We were back in Nashville, and Angela asked me to meet her for breakfast at a New York-style deli called Noshville. We were chitchatting when she happened to ask whether we were still going forward with surrogacy. I said we were.

She asked, "Who's going to carry your baby?"

I looked in her eyes and said, "You are."

After a long pause, Angela took a deep breath and told me,

"I have something to confess. In India, after you and Curtis told me about your plans to have a child, I had a dream. It was like a vision. I dreamt that I was pregnant with your baby. I was dressed all in white and I kept saying over and again, 'I'll carry your baby, I'll carry your baby.' I awoke in a cold sweat and frantically reached for my stomach to see if there was a swell. I was certain I was pregnant."

"So, does that mean yes?"

"The idea is scary but beautiful. I'm not saying it's not confusing. It is.

"But I think I'm supposed to do this."

Later, Deepak described Angela's prophetic dream as biblical.

Millions of parents think the story of the birth of their children is so special it demands detail-by-detail recounting. That's understandable. In that regard, Curtis and I are breathtakingly ordinary. Looking back, though, we now realize that we *were* pioneers. As two men seeking to have our own biological children, we were charting new territory, an experience unlike anything we could have imagined.

Back to Joy, the original egg donor. We were told that at her age, forty, the quality of the eggs sharply declines, thus lessening the chance for pregnancy. Then a physician rejected Angela because this would be her first child. He insisted that surrogates who have had their own child are better able to navigate the ups and downs of pregnancy. A woman who had previously given birth has proved her ability to do so. Additionally, having had her own child, she's less likely to become attached to the new baby.

We had a long and thoughtful talk with Angela, explaining that the process might take a different turn and that it might not work out. Our hopes, once high, were now dashed.

Those hopes, though, were soon raised again when we learned about Growing Generations, a wonderful organization that facilitates surrogacy. They found a doctor willing to work with Angela. They also connected us to a woman who served as our "egg broker." She brought us the files and pictures of twenty-four women. Realizing we were considering the female who would supply half the DNA of our child, Curtis and I were profoundly moved.

Despite the cut-and-dried business-like transaction, something magical happened. Magic was present, in fact, at every juncture. On the table before us, a stack of manila folders was placed, each tabbed with the first name of a potential anonymous egg donor. One name in the middle of the stack caught my eye. I asked if we could start there. The name was Joy. Curtis and I opened the folder and carefully read through the profile. She candidly explained that she was an actor trying to make ends meet and also pay for acting lessons. As an actor himself, Curtis felt a strong affinity. Studying her picture, we got goose bumps. She was perfect. She looked like a combination of my mother and Curtis. Yes, yes, yes, it was still all about joy.

Our first attempt, because Joy was sensitive to the hormonal medication, she developed too many eggs. If the doctor had attempted to harvest more than a couple, she would have become very ill. We ended up with only one embryo that didn't take. Our dream remained unrealized. That was a tough moment for everyone. A major setback, but not enough to crush our spirit.

Donor Joy agreed to go through another cycle with us. This time we took a different approach. No frozen sperm. We did what's called a live cycle. Joy, whom we never met, was in a private room on one side of the Los Angeles clinic. In another private room, no thanks to the dog-eared seventies hetero porn provided, I produced fresh live sperm. Then the doctor microscopically took fifteen sperms and married them to fifteen eggs. Three were highly viable. The doctor advised us to implant at least two. Curtis and I loved the idea of twins, but Angela had to be part of the decision. Courageous soldier that she is, she agreed that two embryos could be implanted, but not three. Once again, we were of the same mind. The rest were frozen for future siblings.

Three days later, on September 7, 2001, it was time for the transfer of the two embryos.

Curtis and I were there to support Angela. We all went into a procedure room. We lit a candle and prayerfully invited the spirit of our children to come forth. When the doctor entered, though, he said, "What's that smell?" He saw the candle and explained, "No, you can't do that. We don't know the effect the fumes might have on the embryos." So much for our New Age mumbo jumbo.

Wearing surgical masks, we followed the doctor into another procedure room. Carrying the golden eggs on a gleaming tray, the lab technician arrived like an attendant angel. We held our breath as the doctor transferred the precious gifts into Angela's womb. Now it was a matter of waiting ten days to see if she would become pregnant. Ten long days.

Curtis and I said goodbye to Angela where, for an extended time, she stayed in bed at the Elan Hotel in West Hollywood, her legs raised to maximize our chances of success. Curtis returned to Miami and I flew off to Paris, where Pascal Obispo, a French superstar, asked me to write a song for his AIDS charities. The composition—"Live For Love United"—came together quickly, but we had problems finding a recording facility. I suggested we fly to Stockholm, where my friend and collaborator Andreas Carlsson, the brilliant Swedish song-writer, could easily accommodate us in his studio with a top-notch programmer.

Twenty years my junior, Andreas saw me as I had seen Bob Crewe. In part, he originally had come to Four Palms because of his KISS obsession. He had to meet the cowriter of "I Was Made For Lovin' You" and "Heaven's On Fire." He showed up in a pink button-down shirt with a white tennis sweater over his shoulders, as if he had just raided Burt Bacharach's closet. With dolphins frolicking and manatees meandering by, we lunched on the dock when Andreas spoke about Cheiron Studios, the Stockholm songwriter/production operation from which he had emerged along with other hit-makers like Max Martin. Cheiron had turned out smashes for *NSYNC, Backstreet Boys, and Britney Spears.

Back in the house, Andreas studied me. He saw how I positioned myself behind an enormous Art Deco desk while he, cradling a guitar in his arms, sat in a big leather club chair across from me. He noticed a huge globe on a shelf behind me. The globe, he was certain, represented our ambition for world domination. It was an Austin Powers kind of thing. I called Andreas my "mini-me." Because he too was the product of a broken home and had a frustrated musician parent—in his case, a father—who had never found fame, we related. We both grew up poor and bore the weight of financial insecurity, no matter how great our income. We were both driven beyond reason, like two rats scratching into the air on the tip of the masthead of a sinking ship. Having made it, we both needed to make it again—and again, and still again. We both understood the daily do-or-die challenge of a hit songwriter: staying ahead of the relentlessly changing trends.

It was during that same initial lunch in Miami that Andreas mentioned his working with Lou Pearlman, the Svengali behind the Orlando boy band explosion who would eventually become the subject of one of our most important creative projects, a feature film, twenty years in the making, called *TRANSCON*.

One of the first songs we wrote together was with Howie D. of Backstreet Boys: "Put Your Money Where Your Mouth Is." The label rejected it, but Andreas and I used the line later in a Number 1 hit we wrote with Katy Perry, "Waking Up In Vegas."

In France in the summer of 2001, anxiously awaiting news about Angela—was she or was she not pregnant?—I tried to concentrate on the AIDS benefit song "Live For Love United." Figuring the record date in Sweden wouldn't take more than a day, I never bothered checking out of my Paris hotel. Once in Stockholm, Pascal Obispo and I went to work. A few hours later, Andreas raced into the studio, screaming, "Come with me! Come with me!" We ran down the street to the Sony offices, where a crowd had gathered in the lobby around a huge television screen. We stood there and watched in disbelief. The first tower had already been hit. Now it was the second.

The post-9/11 days were insane.

My plans were in shambles. I needed to meet Curtis in Paris so we could head to Crete where we had scheduled a work vacation for me to write with Sakis Rouvas, the Adonis-looking "Greek Ricky Martin." Pascal was petrified to fly, and I practically had to shove him onto the plane. When we arrived in Paris, in the middle of the night, the airport floors looked like a refugee camp, a sea of stranded humanity. At the hotel, I was told I had to vacate my room. I refused. All planes were grounded, and I had nowhere to go. The management was insistent. I threatened to call CNN with the story of being kicked out of a hotel while my country was being attacked. They backed off. Later I realized, because of the tight security, perhaps they were trying to empty the hotel to receive Saudi VIP members of the Bin Laden family who were flying in from all parts of the globe. After a few more days in Paris, it became clear that Curtis couldn't get there, so I took off for Crete. Sakis put me up at a superluxurious hotel where each town-house suite had its own swimming pool. But all I could think of was one thing: Did the pregnancy take?

My dream that night was startling. That very day, someone had told me the story of King Aegeus, namesake of the very sea that lulled me to sleep.

The king sent his son to war. The ship bore black sails. If the son was victorious, he was told to replace the black sails with white ones. The son *was* victorious, but in his excitement to return home he forgot to switch sails.

When the king saw the black-flagged ship on the horizon, he presumed his son was dead, and, in despair, leaped from a high cliff to his death into the sea below.

In my dream, I was the king staring up at a purple sky, standing between two tall marble columns. In the distance were bolts of lightning that illuminated great castles floating above the water. I was the emperor, the ruler, the producer, the father who was still not certain he had a son. Like most dreams, the overlapping maze of images was confusing, but one thing was clear: in each hand I held a large gold coin bearing the face of a king.

Since 9/11, there'd been no cell phone service. That meant Angela and Curtis couldn't reach me. I tried to calm myself by writing with Sakis, but my mind was on Angela. When would I hear? That night, September 14, Sakis took me to a fishing village on the other side of the bay. We went to a bare-bones tavern owned by fishermen who caught their own fish, cooked it, served it, and played music while we ate. On their bouzoukis and ouds, they serenaded us with traditional songs of the sea.

It was a beautiful moment. The world seemed at peace. Yet I knew it wasn't. I studied the moon. I studied the stars. I studied my watch. I studied my useless cell phone. The night, for all its beauty, was closing in on me.

I closed my eyes. I breathed deeply. I silently prayed.

And then the phone rang. From across the world, I heard the distant but distinct voices of Curtis and Angela.

"We're preggers," said Angela. "With twins!"

I jumped, screamed and cried. Sakis and the fishermen all went crazy. They jumped on the tabletops. They danced and threw plates on the floor. They kissed and hugged me. It had happened. It had really happened.

By now the moon had gone, as we floated serenely back across the bay to our hotel, looking up at a crystal-clear Milky Way soaring high above me. I thought about the mad world into which we were bringing our children. Frightening, dangerous, uncertain, and yet, with this news, an altogether different world than I had ever known. A world where Curtis and I would assume the responsibility of parenthood. Would I be a dad? Would I be the mom? Having known so many fathers in my lifetime and been so emotionally entangled with such a supremely eccentric mother, parenthood was daunting. At the same time, I was thrilled. What my own parents got wrong, I would get right. The universe, for all the doom and gloom of this post-9/11 period, was opening its arms to new creation. My world was suddenly and gloriously new.

Two gold coins, one for each child.

Curtis had seen signs of his own. He was swimming in our pool in Miami when a cloud of dragonflies formed above him. They stayed for a good twenty minutes. Two single flies swooped down at various intervals, only to rejoin the cloud. When he got out of the pool, Angela called with the blessed news, which was when they called me.

Angela spent the first six months of her pregnancy in our Nashville Birdhouse. Curtis helped her navigate the ups and downs. We assured her that she'd always be in our lives. We were also eager to include her parents, Ruby and Ken. We'd met Ruby at the Deepak Chopra seminar in India. She supported her daughter's decision, but understandably had to face her own doubts. "You go through all this discomfort and then hand these two guys the prize," she said. "Where does that leave you? Where does that leave me?" Ken remained aloof.

Weeks passed. Curtis and I were at Four Palms while Angela stayed in Nashville. From her doctor's office came another monumental call.

"You guys ready for more good news?" she asked.

"Don't keep us waiting."

"It's two boys!"

"Hallelujah!" I shouted. "One we will name Roman and the other Rivero."

"No Rivero," Curtis insisted.

"You're just prejudiced against Hispanics."

"I'm just telling you . . . no Rivero."

Didn't take us long to find a name we both liked. Nyro, after my muse Laura.

Roman and Nyro.

Perfect.

At one point, Angela broke down. It's one thing to talk about carrying two children for nine months; it's another to do it. We heard her out. We didn't argue, we didn't cajole, we listened, we reinforced our love for her, and we watched as she bravely walked through her fears.

From the very beginning, we had decided that Angela would move in with us and live at Four Palms for the final trimester. It was a beautiful time, though intensely emotional. The pregnancy stirred up all sorts of old and new feelings within Angela's soul. There was crying and laughter and, strangely enough, the continual presence of two dragonflies hovering over our pool.

The day arrived. May 8, 2002. Angela decided to have a caesarean. Ruby met us at Miami's Mt. Sinai Hospital. We were all in the operating room, all in gowns, all in face masks, all in awe.

I watched as the first little head emerged. Roman. I went over and helped clean his tiny body. The doctor handed me the scissors to cut the cord. Roman didn't cry. He simply stared into my eyes. I knew he was an old soul. A minute later came Nyro, a ball of pinkness trembling and mewing like a kitten. As I cut this second cord, I sensed he was a first-timer fresh off the comet.

All the while, Ruby was comforting Angela. Then, as she walked over to marvel at the newborns, she burst into tears. Curtis sat with Angela, wiping her brow, and holding her hand. The boys were cleaned and swaddled into fresh blankets. Curtis called them little tamales. He and I followed as they were carried to the nursery, where they were footprinted and weighed, their first encounter with bureaucracy. Roman had to be placed in an incubator for several hours, where I could sit, reach in, and lay my hands on his little body, feeding him his first food from a tiny bottle. Over the loudspeakers in the hallway, Abba's "Dancing Queen" was playing. Perfect for the moment.

Curtis and I stood there before the glass and looked, and looked, and looked. Our sons.

When it was time to bring the boys home, I had to sign as the biological dad. Bigoted Florida state law still forbade Curtis to be included. He was not even allowed to adopt the children as any nonbiological stepfather would.

We all came home to a room that Curtis had spent months preparing in a treasure-map pirate theme. The matching cribs, the bassinets, the diapers—we were well prepared. We cherished the privilege of changing and bathing our babies. The smallest tasks felt like sacred rituals.

Among the many gifts, arrived a small package from Deepak Chopra, two gold coins, just like in my dream. Deepak's note explained the Hindu custom of gifting a gold coin at the birth of a child.

The birth of Roman and Nyro became the defining moment of my humanity. It was as though I stepped from one room into another and never looked back. Now my principal role in the world was not that of an artist but a parent. The shift was profound.

My devoted manager Winston Simone and his wife, Carleen, invited us to Lyford Cay in Nassau, Bahamas, a private compound of fancy villas anchored by a colonial clubhouse painted pastel pink with stately white columns. We had vacationed there before, and when the babies were three months old, we naturally brought them along. This was our first trip with the kids. I insisted that we travel by sea. An overly protective dad, I was afraid that plane pressure would damage our infants' ears. I booked the presidential suite on an overnight cruise ship from Miami to Nassau. Big mistake. Our rooms were right above a twenty-four-hour nonstop disco. The stink of booze and cigarettes permeated the walls. Curtis was not happy. He was even less happy when we docked in the Bahamas with two hot crying babies, sixteen pieces of luggage, portable cribs, baby carriages, baby wipes, and diapers to last a year. The taxi stand was at the end of a pier at least five city blocks long. The schlepping was epic. It took three cabs to get us all to the secured gates of the ultraexclusive Lyford Cay.

Winston and Carleen introduced us to Vivian and Franki Carrera. Vivian was a Pedroso, one of the most powerful and wealthy families of pre-Castro Cuba. Franki was a Bacardi through his mother's side and had become the rum corporation's global chairman. They were warm and wonderful people, and loved life, laughter, and music. Vivian was enchanted by Roman and Nyro. Our family was a revelation to her, and she became passionately sympathetic to the idea of a two-father family. Being accepted and taken in by the owners of Bacardi Rum felt like a profound homecoming for me. Underneath it all . . . I was still looking to win back the family status lost long ago in Cuba.

"I PRAY TO LA CARIDAD DEL COBRE
REDEEMER OF SHIPWRECKS LOST AT SEA
TO GRANT US THE STRENGTH TO FACE TOMORROW.

"AS WE HOLD ON
TO THE FRAGMENTS OF OUR MEMORIES
LIKE AN ORPHAN COUNTS THE SUNSETS
TILL THE MORNING COMES AND WE CAN START AGAIN
CUBA LIBRE . . . MI CUBA LIBRE . . . CUBA LIBRE"

Spending time in Lyford Cay ignited my determination to make Four Palms the premier destination for Miami Beach high society. I went for it. I was on the cover of Miami Business magazine in a pinstripe Turnbull & Asser suit and Charvet French silk tie. We joined the Mount Sinai Founder's Club and became active in the United Way. Donning a white linen suit and brandishing a

Cohiba cigar, I hosted a fundraiser, honoring the dazzling Eartha Kitt, who, at seventy-three, looked forty. I also became increasingly active in ASCAP, the performance-rights organization that I'd joined back in the seventies.

I planned an elaborate ASCAP party that promised to be the event of the season. Invitations called for a 6:00 p.m. arrival. At 6:30, the sky exploded. Thunderstorms deluged the city. The streets were flooded, cars overturned, electricity lost. And yet, despite the monsoon, the mood of our party never dampened. We lit candles. The musicians played their instruments acoustically. Our guests flung off their shoes and danced the storm away.

Merriment prevailed, and the party became the stuff of legend.

The most memorable Four Palms event focused on our sons. It happened when they turned six months. We went all-out, wanting the ceremony to reflect our time in India when Curtis, Angela and I were brought together. Our mission was to create the festive feeling of Deepak Chopra's *How To Know God* celebration. The Indian Dance Society at the University of Miami sent a troupe of fifteen beautiful girls and boys whirling in free-flowing multicolored saris. The procession began. Our Nashville minister, Rev. Becca Stevens, entered first. Then came the children's godparents: Maria Vidal, Jon Bon Jovi, and Winston and Carleen Simone. Suddenly the dancers stopped whirling and bowed down for Angela's grand entrance. She was our queen for the day. Seated on a golden Indian doli, adorned with a luminous tiara, Angela was carried aloft by four shirtless musclemen in turbans.

Then a pause. A few moments of silence. And the ringing of sacred bells.

Heads turned with the arrival of the blessed honorees themselves. Curtis and I carried in Roman and Nyro, each wearing a bejeweled and feathered green-gold turban with matching booties. Everyone burst into laughter and applause. The babies were sprinkled with water from the River Jordan and blessed by Becca: "We thank you, God, for the gift of water."

Curtis's mom, Mary Ann, read from Isaiah: "For you shall go out in joy and be led forth in peace. The mountains and hills before you shall break forth into singing and all the trees shall clap their hands."

Davitt Sigerson read a love sonnet by Pablo Neruda: "I love you in this way because I know of no other way of loving you but this, in which there is no I or you, so intimate that your hand upon my chest is my hand, so intimate that when I fall asleep it is your eyes that close."

Jon Bon Jovi wrote a poem for his godsons, titled "Two": "In a world that needs love, you have love in twos. Two loving parents. Two godmothers. You'll always have the two of you and two godfathers as well, so there's no waiting. When you're going to need a shoulder to lean on, I've got two. When you need a hand to hold, know that I've got two."

In spite of the fact that our marriage was still outlawed, Curtis and I exchanged vows:

His: "You are my partner, my lover, my brother, and my teacher."

Mine: "You are my life and my love. Forever."

We both blessed the boys:

Curtis: "You've traveled far to reach these arms of mine . . . riding down a rainbow of love onto the wings of a dragonfly into my heart."

Me: "As my father, who is here today, told me, 'When you are lonely, I will find you. After I am no longer here, look for me in your heart. Nothing will break this invisible thread.'"

Maria Vidal and her Rouge sister Diana Grasselli sang "Looking In The Eyes Of Love."

The party flowed into the wee small hours. I relished seeing so many strands of my life: my mother; my father's former wife Valeria; my father's new wife, Kati; many of my aunts, uncles and cousins; Angela's mom, Ruby; my sister Esther, my brother Fred and his wife, Nancy, and daughter, Natalya; Mary Ann and Bob Shaw, Curtis' parents and two of his four brothers, Steve and Stuart—more than one-hundred-fifty guests, all unified in joyous celebration of our new family.

In bed that night, with the babies asleep between us, Curtis and I thought about the past two years that had led up to this remarkable day. The stark and improbable truth was this: this seemingly random yet inextricably woven chain of events came about only as a result of the fact that Curtis and I had once separated. Had we not, Curtis wouldn't have gone to Nashville to find his spiritual bearings as his own man. And if Curtis hadn't gone to Nashville, he wouldn't have dated Mike. If he hadn't dated Mike, he wouldn't have met Angela. And without Angela, who gave our children life, this miracle would never have happened.

*Proud daddy and papa with Roman and Nyro,*
*Four Palms, Miami Beach, 2002*

# GHETTO FABULOUS

IT HAPPENED ON THE WAY to the Isle of Capri. Andreas Carlsson and I were sailing across the Tyrrhenian Sea to meet Jon Bon Jovi and Richie Sambora to write songs for their next album. The setting was idyllic. The water was smooth as glass, the afternoon sun warm, the soft breeze intoxicating. Sculpted out of the side of a mountain, Capri loomed ahead like a dream.

Andreas and I were considering the future. In addition to being Andreas's collaborator, I had also become, along with Winston Simone and David Simoné, his manager.

"I need to change my life," Andreas said, looking out in the distance.

"In what way?"

"I need to be in LA. I think you need to be there, too."

I had been thinking the same thing. Though I certainly had a hand in creating the Latin Music Explosion, Emilio Estefan rose to become its godfather. The next big movement in music was happening in Los Angeles, home of *American Idol*, which in 2003, was the most popular show on television. In unprecedented fashion, *Idol* was creating stars and selling songs. Rock was dead. Big sentimental ballads were on the rise, and big sentimental ballads were my specialty . . . or at least they could be. From our Birdhouse in Nashville, I had tried to break into mainstream country but remained an outsider.

Adding to the attraction of Southern California was the state law allowing gay adoption. That meant Curtis could officially become the boys' legal father. That prospect excited Curtis, who never felt completely at home in Miami Beach.

"We'll take over LA," said Andreas. "We'll conquer it."

Those words hit hard, triggering my insatiable ambition.

The clincher was a gated five-acre estate surrounded by the Santa Monica Mountains in Monte Nido, an enclave of Calabasas, thirty miles west of LA. There was a guardhouse and two small bridges that led to the Santa Barbara/Tuscan-style 10,000-square-foot mansion.

It happened in a hurry. We sold all the Four Palms properties at a profit. We hired five huge trucks to haul our belongings from one coast to the other. We bought Mimí a beautiful two-bedroom apartment at the King Cole Building on Miami Beach, with our promise to visit often.

We christened our new California home Dragonfly, for obvious reasons, and it was there that Roman and Nyro had a dreamy year, running around the property and learning to swim in our pool. I rented a studio in nearby Woodland Hills. Life in the San Fernando Valley was good. During the boys' tender toddler years, it was great being close to Angela and godmother Maria Vidal.

Back in Florida, though, Mimí's health was failing. She had a serious lung disease and was forbidden to smoke. So, we moved her to California to live with us. On our property, she had her own little house and a full-time Filipino caregiver, Edna. We once arrived home to find Mimí and Edna sitting on the porch smoking their heads off.

On October 28, 2003, I celebrated my fiftieth birthday with a blowout party. Mojitos in the main house before moving upstairs to the deck, where we had a sit-down dinner for seventy. We hired four, vinyl-clad, muscled mermen that swam in formation and frolicked in the pool as we dined. The heated pool wasn't heating so well that night, and the poor mermen froze their fins off.

On a more poignant note, Marfy arrived, but, due to recent treatment for pancreatic cancer, he was fragile. As I drove him into our Monte Nido neighborhood, which is high enough above sea level that it actually has four seasons and the leaves had already turned brown and fallen off the trees, he looked out the window of the car and said, "Vat is this place? It looks terrible." I replied that it was very beautiful and lush during the summer, when we bought it. Shaking his head, he wearily replied, "So that is how they deceived you."

When he got out of the car, he fell to the ground. I picked up my dad and saw that he wasn't long for this world. "Don't worry," he said. "I'm stronger than you think."

If you had asked me, I would have said that I had long forgiven my mother for lying to me about my father's identity; similarly, I would have said that I had overcome my resentment over Marfy's refusal to override her wishes and declare his fatherhood for the first eighteen years of my life. But had I really forgiven my parents? On the surface, yes. I treated Mimí like a queen and Marfy like a king. Mom was living in our home. Dad was invited to every major event in our lives. I wanted to show them that I had not only turned out OK but was a brilliant and extraordinary person on every level. I accepted his Hungarian heritage as my own. I was proud to call myself a Cuban Hungarian American. I had redeemed the fallen glory of my mother's family. I had embraced the European culture of my father. In my mind, Havana and Budapest had been brought together. Reconciliation realized. Yet if all that were true, why, in the midnight hour, did I still feel a gnawing desperation to prove myself? Why did I feel the need to continue to reinforce my identity as a success? Why did I need the grand houses, the grand parties, the grand adulation that served to quiet my desperation, but only temporarily?

I thought about Mimí, whom I introduced during my induction speech at the Songwriters Hall of Fame. It was my moment but turned into hers.

There she stood, bathing in the glory and waving to the roaring crowd as if she, not I, had been inducted. I also thought how Mimí continued to call me Johnny, pronounced "Yonnie," for thirty-three years after I changed my name. I only became "Desmond" when "Livin' La Vida Loca" became an international hit.

I thought about Marfy when I first told him that Curtis and I were having twins through Angela. I explained the surrogacy process and told him that the sperm was mine.

"Impossible," he said.

"What are you talking about? It's happening. Angela is pregnant."

"Homosexuals don't have enough testosterone to fertilize a female egg."

For all my father's intelligence, he lived with the illusion that his queer son was incapable of fathering children.

On the day of my fiftieth birthday party, after regaining his strength with a couple of strong drinks, he took me aside and, waving his arms around our palatial grounds, said, "Look what you've gotten yourself into now."

"What do you mean?"

"You've overspent like crazy. You've chewed off more than you can swallow."

It was tough for me to swallow that comment, especially because Marfy proved to be right. After nine months in the dream house, the dream began to fade when the maintenance and utility bills proved too much. We had to cut down. The compromise, though, was sweet because of a stately 1930s Spanish Revival home we found in Santa Monica on Twenty-Fourth Street and Georgina. Only half the square footage of Dragonfly, our new home, Casa de Cuba, nonetheless had six bedrooms, six bathrooms, guest quarters, maid's quarters,

private terraces, a pool, a gym, and a step-down living room
with the wooden-beam-and-fireplace feeling of the golden age of
Hollywood. Yes, we were downsizing but the omnipresent
hand-printed tiles and wrought iron detailing made it more than
palatable. Roman and Nyro were enrolled in the Little Dolphins
by the Sea preschool. We organized another festive party to celebrate Curtis's official adoption of the boys. The extended families attended and recognized the beauty of the moment.
Adoption rules required that Curtis have home visits from a
social worker for four months to determine his fitness as a parent. Unsurprisingly, he passed the tests with rainbow colors.

Mimí required more intensive care. Her private nurse—
Edna's replacement, Mary Villaseñor—after a fight with her,
suffered a heart attack. My mother could give anyone a heart
attack. We had no choice but to move Mimí to a nearby
assisted-living home, the Ocean House. That didn't last long.
She insisted on smoking in bed and was caught stealing dough-
nuts at teatime from other residents. Soon after, she moved into
the guesthouse of our Santa Monica property.

I rented an office for Deston Songs near Sunset Plaza in West
Hollywood. Andreas's notion of conquering LA was still on my
mind. I was ready to roll, but I didn't see the rocks in the way.

In his final years, Marfy continued to impress me mightily. He
was a survivor. He had survived the Russian massacres in
Budapest. He had survived the rise and fall of a dozen different
business ventures the world over without losing his fiscal stability. He had survived countless affairs. By convincing Kati to
become a nurse, he had survived old age by having his own
handpicked lover-caretaker. He had even survived the emotional
fallout of his scattered family, who had been confused, angered,
and injured by a life centered on himself. His survival was due to
more than his remarkable tenacity. He was a man who had

simply learned to deal with the world and found ways to bend the curve of events his way. In short, I saw him as a success.

His death at age eighty-four didn't come as a surprise, but the loss cut deep, opening the old wound. The omission of truth on his part and Mimí's was patently foolish. In so many ways, my childhood was a charade. But Marfy had mastered the art of the charade. He did so with great aplomb. No matter how long it took, he did embrace me fully.

I used the money he left me to buy a Bentley. Curtis was right to call it self-indulgent, but I justified it because it wasn't "our" money.

It happened when Paul Stanley asked me to go car shopping with him in Beverly Hills. He was looking to buy a Bentley.

"Great," I said. "You buy a Bentley and I'll buy your tricked-out Benz."

"Deal."

When we arrived at the showroom, there it was: the most beautiful object I'd ever seen. The Bentley's styling was out-landishly deco. The interior was accented in burled walnut and made to look like the dashboard of a vintage speedboat. The lines were sleek and breathtakingly elegant. I saw it as an ageless, perfect piece of sculpture.

The more I studied it, the deeper my love.

Paul liked it but was hesitant.

I wasn't.

"If you don't," I said, "I will."

And I did. I signed the papers on the spot. Paul got the thrill of buying a brand-new Bentley without having to pay for it. To this day, the Bentley remains one of my prized possessions.

My friend Davitt was right to say, "The Bentley is merely the latest manifestation of Desmond's aesthetic. At all times he has to be ghetto fabulous."

*Baron Joseph S. Marfy, Casa Paloma, Santa Monica, 1993*

*With Meat Loaf and Todd Rundgren*, Bat Out Of Hell III, *2006*

*Nyro, Desmond, Roman, Meat Loaf, and Brian May at*
*Village Recorder Studio, Santa Monica, 2006*

# LEFTOVER MEAT LOAF

MEAT LOAF WAS A SINGER with big chops. He could belt it out with the best of them. Heavyweight Todd Rundgren produced the mega album *Bat Out Of Hell*, and Jim Steinman wrote all of the songs. The record sold over forty million copies. That was 1977. Steinman and Meat Loaf fell out after that. I wasn't privy to why. They finally reunited in 1991 and took two years to do *Bat Out Of Hell II: Bat Into Hell*. It sold over fourteen million. By the time I was invited into the third circle of hell, it was 2006. Jim and Meat Loaf had suffered another estrangement and were in the midst of a nasty lawsuit over who owned the brand *Bat Out Of Hell*. Jim had been writing a Broadway musical titled *Bat Out Of Hell*. I was brought in to save the day. It felt like a calling. I believed that the final rung of this classic rock trilogy could be one of the major achievements of my career.

Everybody thought I was crazy, and everybody was right.

The album was aptly titled, *Bat Out Of Hell III: The Monster Is Loose*.

The monster was undoubtedly Meat Loaf himself, as he often joked. But I would later suspect that he made the record with me out of spite, to show Steinman that he could carry on with *Bat Out Of Hell* without him, to prove his point that he and he alone owned and controlled the *Bat Out Of Hell* franchise.

By then, I had developed a reputation as a tough-minded producer able to work with difficult people. I seemed to specialize in superstar rock acts that weren't as super as they used to be.

Meat Loaf needed to get back, as the Beatles said, to where he once belonged. I encouraged him to start voice lessons. He refused. But still, I kept inviting my dear friend Eric Vetro, known as the "voice coach to the stars," to hang out at our sessions, hoping Meat Loaf would warm up to him. Eventually, more than halfway through the album, he did, and it made a world of difference. So much so, that we had to begin rerecording all the lead vocals again from scratch, which delayed the album another three months.

We butted heads so often that my dismissal seemed inevitable. In fact, I was in the studio one afternoon when I was told Meat Loaf was on his way to fire me. The thought was alarming—not that I wanted to work with him forever, but by then I had put in thousands of hours of grueling work and put my career on hold with crushing overhead costs. The songs were there. So were the arrangements. All he had to do was take care of his voice and sing.

He burst through the door, got right up in my face, and screamed, "I'm *not* going to fire you! So there!"

My reaction was strange. I felt nauseous. I felt so sick that I ran to the bathroom and vomited. What a response to supposedly good news! I had to go home and get in bed and wound up in the hospital. The doctor told me that if I had thrown up any harder, I would have busted my aorta and died. Meat Loaf's verbal abuse was so vicious that my dear friend Diane Warren dragged me to my first Al-Anon meeting, where people find strength and hope in sharing their experience in dealing with what they call "qualifiers"—people who are emotionally challenging to them in their lives.

Armed with my newfound insight and life skills, I finally made it back to the studio, vowing that I would never subject myself to this kind of treatment again. It was a turning point in my producer-artist relationships. Meat Loaf sensed my new attitude and chilled considerably. Or, at least, I thought. He never did stop barking "Fuck you and the horse you rode in on," whenever I asked him to try singing another take.

The work went on. His manager persuaded Todd Rundgren to arrange and sing background vocals on a few songs, as he had done on the previous Meat Loaf albums. A lifetime earlier, when Nightchild was recording our demos in Woodstock, Todd had been a less-than-welcoming presence. At that time, I was a nobody and couldn't complain. I saw Rundgren as a pop maestro who had crafted a sonic landscape all his own. Like Phil Spector, he didn't simply work in the studio, he played the studio like an instrument. This time, under my supervision, I was looking for him to see me not necessarily as an equal, but certainly a peer. But he hardly saw me at all. He did the background vocals flawlessly, treating me as if I wasn't there. His only comment was to argue about the title of a song I'd written with Marti Frederiksen, "If God Could Talk."

Todd insisted it should be "If God *Would* Talk," adding, "Everyone knows God can talk."

"Since Moses and the burning bush," I shot back, "we haven't heard a peep from him."

He scowled, but the original title remained. Rundgren and I were not fated to be friends.

Meanwhile, Meat Loaf's resentments mushroomed. Things took a particularly ugly turn when, after a long night in the studio, he left before me. An hour later, I walked to the parking lot where his Mercedes had been parked in the number-one slot marked "Mr. Loaf," while my Bentley had the number-two spot, "Mr. Child." I had the feeling he might have subconsciously resented my longer and fancier car.

Those feelings were confirmed when I saw that someone had deeply gouged the right side of my Bentley from one end to the other, a $5,000 repair job.

I asked him about it the next day.

"Given the single-piece construction of the Bentley," I said, "my whole car has to be repainted. You don't know who scratched it, do you?"

"No," he said, his eyes averting mine.

The next day, I asked him a second time. "Sure you don't know anything about my car?"

"Not a damn thing."

On the third day, I took another approach.

"Turns out that there's a security camera out in the parking lot," I said over the talk-back when Meat Loaf was in the recording booth. "They're reviewing it right now to see who hit my car."

After a few seconds, he whispered into the mic so quietly I could barely make out his words.

"I did it."

I pushed the talk-back button and said, "Excuse me, did you say something?"

A little louder, he repeated, "I did it."

Finally, with full force, he screamed out, *"I DID IT! I CRASHED YOUR FUCKIN' CAR!"*

There was no security camera.

I'm not sure how, but we kept on working. Over the course of nine months, every song required between 100 and 350 lead-vocal takes. Every syllable, consonant, and breath were painstakingly edited. My mania for completing the project overwhelmed all obstacles. This motherfucker had to sound great.

We held a wrap party at our home for everyone who had worked on the project. Over a hundred people attended. The theme was medieval Gothic. Meat Loaf was seated at the center of a long banquet table on a velvet throne. Before him was an apple-in-its-mouth pig worthy of Henry VIII. I paid for the party, not realizing that he'd stiff me for the $65,000 backend portion of my production fee. He even managed to insult the luminous Jennifer Hudson, whom I'd convinced to sing a duet on the record. This was after Jennifer had done the still-unreleased film *Dreamgirls* and was on her way to Oscar glory. I knew Jennifer was destined for superstardom. At the party, though, Meat Loaf, sitting across from her, completely blanked her.

After nine grueling months, *Bat Out Of Hell III: The Monster Is Loose* was finally completed. But the bat never got out of hell, and the monster never got loose. For reasons I never understood, Meat Loaf refused to do promotion. Even worse, he canceled many make-it-or-break-it gigs on the tour to sell the record, including the biggest TV shows in Europe. The monster retreated, never thanking me for pulling off the minor miracle of crafting a record that, thanks to my hardworking team, restored his voice to all its former glory.

Adding insult to injury, in huge letters on the credits were the words DEDICATED TO JIM STEINMAN, despite the fact that Jim and Meat were still feuding. The label wanted fans to think this was another Meat Loaf/Steinman production. You had to look hard to see my credit, which was buried in illegible small print. After Jim Steinman passed away, I realized why Meat Loaf was so hostile toward me. He could never forgive me for not being Jim Steinman, even though he was the one who pushed him away.

I truly regret that I never got a chance to tell Meat that I had been in constant contact with Jim, behind the scenes, to get his feedback and blessing on the seven Steinman "covers" that Meat

Loaf and his management insisted I record. Because of the litigation, Jim wouldn't share the songs he had been saving for a future *Bat Out Of Hell III* that was never meant to be. They were too embroiled in their dispute. Perhaps those were the songs that eventually got recorded on Meat Loaf's final album, before his death—on which Jim Steinman participated in the majority of the songwriting—titled "Braver Than We Are," whose album cover depicts the image of Meat Loaf and Steinman facing an apocalypse of demons in a dust storm. This probably should have been *Bat Out Of Hell IV*, but that would have meant acknowledging there actually was a *Bat Out Of Hell III*.

In a 2016 *Rolling Stone* interview, Meat Loaf is quoted, "I wanted to strangle somebody, but not Jimmy, trust me. There is no *Bat Out Of Hell III*. That should have never happened. To me, the record is nonexistent. It doesn't exist."

Well, the album certainly does exist, and it is a fucking masterpiece forged with the talent, sweat, and tears of my fantastic team. Yet Meat Loaf has seen to it that fans can't stream the album on Spotify, Apple Music, or any other digital streaming service. They can find the CD on Amazon if they really look for it. As I've said many times, the music business is a business of credits, so please see my acknowledgments, where I've listed every last soul who was invaluable in the making of this record. Now that he's gone on the bat he flew in on, I look back at my work with Meat Loaf as a great adventure, even an honor, because, in the final analysis, the man was a powerful musical force. Despite everything he put me through . . . and with a deep low bow to my artist, colleague, and teacher, I salute the proud, larger than life, irrepressible Texan Michael Lee Aday, whom the world would come to know as . . . Meat Loaf.

*With Meat Loaf, Village Recorder Studio, Santa Monica, 2006*

*With Scorpions, Santa Monica, 2007*

# HUMANITY HOUR I

AT THAT SAME *Bat Out Of Hell III* wrap party, Scorpions, the German heavy metal band, showed up looking like Poison circa 1986: cowboy hats, leopard-skin shirts, ripped jeans, and gold chains. When I was asked to produce them, I accepted, knowing I might be in for another rough ride. To prepare for the album we called *Humanity: Hour I*, I put together a songwriting intensive in Nashville with some of my favorite collaborators, to explore new musical styles and themes. We left room for the band to complete them, thus bolstering our camaraderie and my ability to take them in a radically different direction.

I developed the album's intellectual theme with futurist Liam Carl, who brilliantly photographed and designed the project. We sought to dramatize the nuanced dynamic between humanity and robotics. We acknowledged that with the evolution of the species, robots are the next step in our biological development. Born of humans, they contain our essence, yet could go far beyond us to control our world . . . and eventually, our galaxy.

I envisioned transforming Scorpions from being a legacy rock band on the oldies circuit to reinventing them as important cutting-edge artists with an urgent message. They had a unique place as German rock artists in the pop world. Thus, the concept was particularly prescient: a warning against the global slide toward authoritarianism (which is exactly what's happening today). I was obsessed with the challenge. It was a tall order. I dived in and took over the task of re-imaging them. No more dated rock gear. I wanted a sophisticated European art vibe. We achieved it. One reviewer wrote, "It's obvious that radio needs the Scorpions more than the Scorpions need radio."

Jumping genres, I worked with Joss Stone, the precociously talented English soul singer. Her early demos were given to me by Steve Greenberg, the man behind Hanson and owner of S-Curve Records. Joss blew me away.

When I asked her age, I was blown away even more: fifteen.

"She's a stone soul singer in the Etta James–Gladys Knight– Patti LaBelle tradition," I told Greenberg. "She needs soul songs and a soul-singing mentor."

I immediately thought of Betty Wright, with whom I'd gone to Edison Junior High School in Miami. Betty was a stone soul singer herself, an African American diva who exploded on the R&B charts in 1971 with her radio hit "Clean Up Woman." I was close to Betty because we both served on the board of the Florida chapter of the National Academy of Recording Arts and Sciences.

When Betty and I met with Greenberg about the process of writing with Joss, Betty said, "Well, the girl's got a right to be wrong." "That's a song," I said, and Betty and I ran off to write it with Joss. It was very Aretha. Betty called it a "monster hit." Just like that, we wrote another, "Don't Cha Wanna Ride," that Betty was dead certain was another smash.

As good as those songs were, it would take some time to create an album's worth of them, and, I argued, that to introduce her to the world, Joss would do better covering obscure soul songs. We'd put her in the studio with seasoned soul musicians and give her that old-school sound. Steve agreed, and the understanding with my manager Winston was that I would be the producer.

The music business, like the film business, blows hot and cold. Over-the-top enthusiasm one day, silence the next. A long silence from Steve Greenberg. My calls went unanswered. One day, Betty called and asked, "What ever happened to that little blond girl we were writing with?" "Trying to find that out myself," I said.

When I did find out, the truth stung. Despite Betty's query, she knew damn well what had happened to that little blond girl. Betty had gone to New York and already cut a deal for her and Steve to coproduce Joss singing old soul songs. I was completely cut out of my own concept. Betty sang all the vocal demos, and Joss copied her, riff for riff. The resulting record, *The Soul Sessions*, made Joss a star. No one could understand how a sixteen-year-old schoolgirl from England could sing like a fifty-year-old, life-weathered soul singer from the seventies. That's how.

On the next Joss album, they included "Right To Be Wrong" and "Don't Cha Wanna Ride," but Betty claimed I had nothing to do with writing them, and Joss, being under the influence of her maker, Betty Wright, didn't stick up for me either.

Even though he was there when we wrote them, Greenberg demanded I send him the multiple tapes of our long writing sessions across several days that, of course, proved that I was an equal composer. Rightfully, I got credit for "Right," but six other writers I never met were also listed as collaborators on "Don't Cha Wanna Ride." It would have been nice to have been included in the decision to bring the others on.

The Betty Wright saga took an even more bizarre turn. She and I were at a Florida NARAS board of governors meeting led by then-president Mike Green. Tom Dowd, the legendary Atlantic Records engineer and producer, was also on the board. I had met Tom, one of my original mentors, through Lisa Wexler and her dad, Jerry, Tom's boss. Since then, Tom had become king of Criteria Recording Studios in Miami and renowned for his productions for, among others, Eric Clapton, Rod Stewart, and Lynyrd Skynyrd. These were, though, his last years. He had become a frail white-haired, wise man wheeling an oxygen tank.

One day, he took me aside and, still my mentor, said, "Desmond, I see the powerful way you conduct yourself in these meetings. Did you ever think that you could become the next Clive Davis or David Geffen?" "I'm an artist and musician," I said, "not a mogul." Tom's next words haunt me to this day: "Can't you be both?"

At one of the board meetings, we learned about the creation of the Latin Grammys. I was thrilled. Latin music had been woefully neglected by the Academy. Betty's reaction shocked us all. She exploded. She lost it. "If you're gonna make a Latin Grammys, why isn't there a BLACK GRAMMYS!" Mike Green screamed back at her, arguing that, given how many Grammy winners had been Black, the Grammys *already were* the Black Grammys. The verbal fighting grew fierce. Tom Dowd, the sweetest of men, tried to calm Betty, only to incur more of her wrath. Green literally threw her out of the room and off the board. She wouldn't let it go and engaged Mike in a blood feud, trying to rile up Aretha Franklin, Gladys Knight, and Patti LaBelle to join her cause to stop the plan. Fortunately, she failed, and the Latin Grammys were born.

Feuds also characterized much of the backstory behind *American Idol*. There were two prime Svengalis, Clive Davis and Simon Fuller, pulling all the strings, and if a songwriter wasn't careful, he or she could easily get entangled. I was staunchly in the Clive camp, but decided to be smart and collaborate with one of Simon's favorites, who had written the *American Idol* theme, Cathy Dennis. She, Gary Burr, and I wrote "Before Your Love" for Kelly Clarkson. I thought I was entanglement-free until Simon demanded that I coproduce Kelly along with Cathy, an imperious, no-nonsense English woman who spoke like Queen Elizabeth and ruled the studio like Margaret Thatcher.

Already exhausted, Kelly clashed with Cathy. The tension was almost unbearable. I felt sorry for Kelly, but given our tight deadline, there was nothing I could do to comfort her. She even snapped at me when I was trying to adjust her mic. Despite all this, the song did become the best-selling single of 2002. Ironically, that was because it was the flip double-A-side of the *real* hit: "A Moment Like This," a Swedish import championed by Simon Fuller.

The second year of *Idol* was all about Ruben Studdard and Clay Aiken. I put together a songwriter camp called the Sand Castle, where four teams of three writers composed night and day. These were among the most talented writers in the world. As a result, we came up with three songs on Clay's debut album, *Measure Of A Man*. The first, "Invisible," written by Andreas Carlsson, Chris Braide, and myself, became Clay's signature hit. The subject was voyeurism—"I wish I could be a fly on your wall . . . I could just watch you in your room." Andreas gave the song a strongly Swedish flavor, and the story fit Clay's enigmatic personality. He was still in the closet and appealed to a mass audience of older women. Two other songs from Deston Songs, my publishing group, made it on the album—"Run To Me" and "This Is The Night"—selling millions of copies.

*Measure of a Man* turned out to be one of the big records of the young new century. It felt good to be in step with the times . . . but was I?

*Katy Perry and Nyro, Casa de Cuba, Santa Monica, 2005*

*Katy and Nyro reunited in Las Vegas, 2022*

# WAKING UP IN VEGAS

BACK IN THE LATE NINETIES, when Curtis and I bought the Birdhouse, our small, rustic cabin in the hills overlooking Nashville, I had a good feeling for the city.

Despite my insurmountable optimism, I had not been able to move the vitality of my Miami operation to LA. Just as Emilio Estefan had been outgunning me in Florida, Max Martin, another powerhouse Swedish writer-producer, was outgunning me in California. Case in point: Miss Katy Perry.

Katy had initially been one of the two lead singers in a new project being created by a production team called the Matrix, responsible for Avril Lavigne's first album. After leaving the Matrix and being signed to Columbia by Steve Greenberg, Katy turned up for a writing session with me and Andreas. At the time, Alanis Morissette was a strong inspiration for Katy. That drew us to compose a dark and brooding ballad, "Last Cry." Katy, though, was anything but dark and brooding. She was lighthearted and high-spirited. In the most loving sense, I saw her as the ultimate fag hag.

"Why are we writing all this angry shit?" I asked her. "You aren't angry. You're fun. You should be singing like how you are. Let's write a song about you and your gay best friend hitting Vegas and losing all your money."

We did just that. Andreas, Katy, and I wrote "Waking Up In Vegas," convinced it was a hit. But before Katy could record it, Columbia Records dropped her. Columbia also fired Steve Greenberg's other young artist signings, Fountains of Wayne and the Jonas Brothers. The song, though, helped Katy get another deal, and we were sure it would be the first single on her debut

Capitol album, *One Of The Boys*. But Max Martin cockblocked us. At the time we were pissed and didn't see the eventual benefit. The label put out Max's "I Kissed A Girl" first, a huge smash.

Two other Max Martin hits followed, building up tremendous momentum for Katy. Even though "Waking Up In Vegas" was her fourth and final single, it still reached Number 1.

I wanted to extend the reach of the song further by doing it as a country duet between Katy and Dolly Parton. Katy was all in, but that year Dolly was only interested in duetting with Kenny Rogers. Then came the Academy of Country Music Awards when Katy and Dolly sang a medley. I sat on the edge of my seat, hoping to hear "Waking Up In Vegas," but, alas, the sparkling duo sang only Dolly songs.

Though Nashville was the seat of country music, in the past quarter century it had become much more. It was becoming a mecca for premier songwriters in virtually all genres. As an urban center, it has grown in sophistication. And its green suburbs were every bit as beautiful as Beverly Hills or the Hamptons. More importantly, with Roman and Nyro turning five, it was an appealing place to raise children. Though conservative, the private schools were excellent. Our kids might have a better chance of finding stability, something I never had, in mid-America than in hyped-up Hollywood.

Curtis was the chief advocate for Nashville. During the eighteen months of our separation, he had planted roots and forged strong friendships. He argued that he and our boys would be happy there. With three against one, I didn't have a chance. Besides, we had bought a lavish three-bedroom apartment on Fifth Avenue, so an escape to the big city was always available. The renovation took two years, but the ultra-Art Deco results were worth the wait. I could see Jean Harlow, cigarette in hand, slouched in our rust-colored matching mohair couches as she watched the autumn leaves gently falling on Central Park. I could also see my ten-year-old self with Mimí at a Miami furniture store, ordering beautiful furniture that would never arrive. At long last, the furniture had arrived.

We kept the small Birdhouse in Nashville, but it wasn't large enough to house the four of us. And then there was Mimí. She wanted to be with us. So, with Mimí in mind, we bought a stately, newly built McMansion, complete with an elevator, in the suburbs of West Meade, not far from the Birdhouse. We named it Draycott, after the elegant Draycott Hotel in London. Once settled in, my mother did not improve. She antagonized the private caretakers we hired and became even harder to handle.

Draycott didn't sparkle with the ocean-blue opulence of Miami or the seaside glitter of Santa Monica, but it offered us solidity. And also apprehension. Would, for instance, this tiny suburb of "Old South" Nashville, where streets were named after Robert E. Lee, welcome a gay couple with twin boys? Would we be criticized or ostracized? Would our kids be shunned?

The answer was no. Much of the credit for our acceptance goes to Curtis, whose warm charm and parental skills made a positive impression on everyone. His great affability helped integrate our family into Nashville society. Not high society, but a society of other parents with young children. Though we were among the very few same-sex couples in sight, surprisingly we experienced little prejudice. We were seen as representatives of a brave new world. For the first time, straight families were witnessing the incontrovertible truth that two queer men were raising their young children with the values we all hold dear: kindness, compassion, honesty, responsibility, and grace. We realized that here we could change hearts and minds.

Another element that added to our life in Nashville: the presence of Valeria Marfy and her daughter, my sister Esther. Despite her long-ago divorce from my father, Valeria looked to Curtis, myself, and our boys as family and became a loving part of our lives.

After a year of living with Mimí in Nashville, things got out of hand.

Although smoking was killing her, she couldn't stop. I tried, Curtis tried, the doctors tried, but she listened to no one. Behind our backs, she paid the gardeners twenty bucks for a single cigarette. She kept pleading with us to send her back to Miami, so we bought her a two-bedroom apartment there at Belle Towers. My dear cousin Ana and her husband agreed to look after her. But Mimí was incorrigible. Eventually, Ana couldn't handle her. We moved her to an assisted-living home in Aventura, Florida, where her dementia deepened. On more than one occasion, she tried to escape. Her last years were heartbreaking and left me feeling powerless to do anything about it.

Ricky Martin offered a welcome respite. He asked me to produce his new album, a mixture of songs in Spanish and English. He was so intent on a close collaboration that he insisted that I bring my whole family—Curtis, Roman and Nyro—to live in his waterfront Miami mansion on Golden Beach while we wrote and recorded. I had my Bentley shipped down from Nashville and had the surreal pleasure of chauffeuring my husband and sons through the down-and-out Miami projects where Mimí had raised me and my younger brother, Fred, in government housing that cost forty-eight dollars a month. After the three of them giving me shit for years about how the car was an extravagant gas-guzzling mistake, we slowly drove the glistening black Bentley through the rough and dirty neighborhood. Curtis and the boys fell silent . . . the car never to be mentioned again.

The recording process was hectic but exhilarating. Ricky's manager constantly pressured us to complete the album because of a looming tour deadline. In addition to the studio in his main house, a few miles away, we set up four more studios at the beach house with programmers. I brought in a cadre of composers, including Claudia Brandt, Jodi Marr, Andreas Carlsson, Eric Bazilian, Ferras AlQaisi, and Fernando Osorio, and, together with Ricky, we wrote and recorded dozens of songs before whittling the selection down to thirteen.

Ricky and I had our first talk about the heretofore unspoken subject of our sexual orientation. Since we had first met, though, our circumstances had drastically changed.

Curtis and I had our twin sons in 2002, and Ricky, who was single, had his twin sons, Matteo and Valentino, through a surrogate in 2008. In that same period, he went underground, grew spiritually, and put all his energy into caring for his children. The Barbara Walters encounter had traumatized him to the point that he shut down, refusing all interviews. But now it was 2010.

One late afternoon, he asked to speak to me. He led me to a quiet corner of his estate overlooking the bay. The sun was setting, turning the billowing clouds into purple-colored lanterns.

"How should I come out?" he suddenly asked.

I thought about it for a few seconds and then said, "Oprah. She's our national therapist."

Ricky was so excited about his decision to declare that he couldn't wait.

The next day on his website, he announced that he was gay. *Saturday Night Live's* "Weekend Update" response was that

Ricky Martin has come out and it's also been announced that the sky is blue.

Ricky wanted to call his album *Musica + Alma + Sexo* (Music, Soul And Sex), giving us the idea of shortening it to *MAS*. He gave me the freedom to produce him the way I heard him: a restless, creative and ebullient spirit. It was important for Ricky to cowrite every song, encouraging me to invite in other luminous collaborators, including Wisin & Yandel and Residente from Calle 13. Letting bygones be bygones, I also brought in Joss Stone for a duet in English, "The Best Thing About Me Is You," and Ricky brought in Natalia Jiménez in Spanish, "Lo Mejor De Mi Vida Eres Tú." The Spanish version hit Number 1 and the record was nominated for four Latin Grammys, including a nod to me as producer of the year.

Before the album's release, I was privileged to experience a precious and intimate moment. We were completing the mixes when Ricky walked his mom into the studio to play her "Basta Ya," the centerpiece of the record, a song that said *enough*: enough hiding his true self from the world. While listening, tears streamed from his mother's eyes. "Mi hijo, como has sufrido" (My son, how you have suffered), she whispered. They embraced. Words were no longer necessary.

In late summer 2010, I headed back to Nashville with Curtis, Roman, and Nyro. I was not happy. I needed more creative stimulation. I needed New York—New York energy, New York studios, New York singers and songwriters. I convinced Curtis, who always preferred Nashville, to indulge me. So, we moved into our Fifth Avenue apartment and enrolled the boys, then in third grade, at the Cathedral School at St. John the Divine, where they flourished. We also tried moving Mimí from Miami to a Manhattan independent living facility a few blocks away from us. She was dressed exquisitely. Her hair was coiffed and her makeup immaculate; she blew the interview when she asked the doctor if he had any interest in dating her and, with some strange looks, gave hints to the staff that I was somehow holding her captive.

During the New York trip, though, there was the great blessing of showing Mimí the beautiful bas-relief of herself rendered in Brazilian walnut, sculpted so long ago in the far recesses of my childhood and hung in a place of honor in our many apartments. In a moment of clarity upon seeing it again after so many years, she tearfully whispered, "It was very important that this came back to us." The return of this artwork represented our triumph over everything she had lost and all the failures she had endured.

After a year in Manhattan, restlessness got the best of me. I was ready to move back to Los Angeles, where the action was, but Curtis put his foot down.

"We'll keep the New York apartment," he said, "but we are not under any circumstances going back to La-La Land. These boys need stability. Our home is in Nashville. It's time to go home."

That's just what we did—the four of us moving into the 1,800-square-foot Birdhouse. It was tight but sweet. I saw us as the Swiss Family Robinson—or, better yet, the Swish Family Robinson—two gay dads, a female English bulldog named Frank, and two sons excelling at school and in love with sports. Curtis and I became what we vowed never to become: soccer dads standing on the sidelines, jumping up and down as our sons scored goals. We went to teacher conferences, where, bursting with pride, we were told that Roman and Nyro possessed great social skills, beautiful manners, and strong study habits. Much credit to Curtis, who supervised their homework with diligence and patience.

Where Desmond goes, so goes Mimí. As soon as we returned
to Nashville, for her own comfort and safety we moved my
mother to Barton House, a secured, memory-care facility, spe-
cializing in Alzheimer's disease and dementia, only a few minutes from the Birdhouse. Curtis and the boys would visit her
after school several days a week . . . and Juan Galano, our longtime chef, would bring her delicious Cuban food. We had a private beautician come to do her hair, nails, and makeup, so she
was always well dressed and looked like a queen. I would go
often and sit with her and watch Spanish-language television or
listen to her boleros, read her poems, many still unfinished,
which she would continue to add to as we went along. This would
bring the real Mimí suddenly back in a rush of poignant, sometimes rewritten, memories and unsettled feelings. It would
break my heart to hear her say, "Get me out of here . . . take me
home to Pinar del Rio."

For Mimí, the end was near.

*Mimí at Akwenasa, Ghent, New York, 1986*

*"La Musa" Elena Casals, Miami, 1967*

*Mimí, South Pointe Towers, Miami Beach, 1992*

# MIMI OF MIAMI

Elena Casals passed into eternity on March 17, 2012. She was eighty-five.

Despite all the conflicts and contradictory feelings, despite the raging ambivalence I felt for my mother, I was committed to honoring her. I made her Miami funeral a two-day extravaganza. Her powerful spirit relished all the attention.

She loved yellow roses, so I found every yellow rose in Florida and on the invitation wrote, "In lieu of a charitable donation, please send flowers." Nine truckloads showed up. I hired the city's premier embalmer, who fashioned her to look like Elizabeth Taylor. An all-female string quartet played old-time Cuban music. The *coup de grace* was employing a Catholic priest who looked like Walter Mercado, the Puerto Rican tele-psychic. With his plucked eyebrows and bouffant hairdo, El Padre resembled Leona Helmsley. During our initial interview, I mentioned that I worked with Ricky Martin. "Oh my God, that boy has such a beautiful body!" he exclaimed. That's when I knew he was our man. In his long, gold-trimmed black vestments and manicured black coif, the priest looked like a pharaoh, lending the occasion the high-campy touch Mimí would have appreciated. Everyone showed up, from Jon Bon Jovi to KC of the Sunshine Band.

After services at the Coral Gables Church of the Little Flower, the procession followed the path of Calle Ocho, the famous Cuban street in Miami where Mimí roamed. At the mausoleum, I hired seven trumpeters in white *guayaberas* to play the Cuban national anthem—twice. Her stone read:

*Elena Casals*
*MIMÍ*
*Enero 28, 1927—Marzo 17 2012*
*Poetisa Compositora Inventora*
*Visionaria Patriota Callejera*

She was a poet, a composer, an inventor, a visionary, a patriot, and a "callejera," the Cuban term for "streetwalker." I meant it both literally and figuratively. She was a woman who wandered the streets of the world looking for life.

From the mausoleum, it was off to Versailles Restaurant in Little Havana, Mimí's favorite Cuban restaurant, where over a stupendous *paella* dinner we celebrated her extraordinary spirit and shared hilarious stories about her incorrigible and unrepentant life.

Why such extravagance? Why not? It felt right, it felt necessary to arrange an outrageously outsized farewell for a woman whose hopes and dreams for her own success were so outrageously outsized. It was the last thing I could do for her.

ELENA CASALS
MIMÍ
ENERO 28. 1927 - MARZO 17. 2012
POETISA COMPOSITORA INVENTORA
VISIONARIA PATRIOTA CALLEJERA
MIS CAJAS DE CARTÓN. TODO LO DICEN.
MIS CAJAS DE CARTÓN. TODO LO CALLAN.
MADRE AMADA DE DESMOND CHILD Y FRED BARRETT

*Best men, Roman and Nyro, on our wedding day, Conservatory Gardens,
Central Park, New York City, 2013*

# CHAPEL OF LOVE

THE RITUAL OF MARRIAGE, and its legal protection for our children, became of paramount importance. With all this in mind, Curtis and I drove to San Francisco with Roman and Nyro to take advantage of the state's brief same-sex matrimony provision, only to be told, after arrival, that all such marriages had suddenly been stopped that very day. We were heartbroken. We accepted Mayor Gavin Newsom's kind invitation to his office, where he comforted us. He told us in confidence that President George W. Bush had called Gov. Arnold Schwarzenegger, threatening to cut off billions in federal funds to California if San Francisco didn't cut it out. The governor, who was personally not against same-sex marriage, and the mayor agreed to let it go through a legal process. The unfortunate result was the passage of Proposition 8, a law forbidding same-sex marriage. But history would soon right the wrong.

On October 4, 2013, Curtis and I were granted the right of a legal marriage, this time in New York's Central Park. On a glorious sunlit morning, we arranged a symmetrical procession into the six-acre Italianate formal Conservatory Garden. From one side came Curtis with friends and family; from the other, I arrived with my loved ones. With everyone singing Ellie Greenwich's joyful "Chapel Of Love," groom and groom walked up the steps of the wisteria pergola, where our best men, Roman and Nyro, then eleven, stood beside us.

The day after our wedding, we released the documentary film that Curtis and I had been producing since we first considered surrogacy. We called it *TWO: The Story of Roman and Nyro*, after the poem Jon Bon Jovi wrote for the boys' blessing ceremony. Directed by Heather Winters, the film follows the story of our sons' birth and the first ten years of their lives.

Because we knew we were breaking new ground, we conscientiously filmed all the critical events as they happened. Heather also interviewed the major characters, including Angela, Roman, and Nyro, and Curtis' mother, Mary Ann, whose deep compassion touched the heart of every viewer.

We traveled to eighteen film festivals from Honolulu to Havana, winning three separate audience-favorite awards. The boys themselves took the lead. They walked the red carpet and stood onstage with astounding confidence, handling the Q&A like pros. Their precocious wit won over the most skeptical of crowds. And all this at age eleven! We addressed the biggest fear of many heterosexual parents of LGBTQ people: not having grandchildren in their lives. Roman, Nyro, and the success of our family became living examples of what is possible. *TWO* is a testament to the universal power and ultimate triumph of love—that it is love that makes a family, affirming modern families like ours may be modern in their making, but timelessly human at their core.

*"Lady Liberty" recording session, Malibu, 2018*

# BARBRALAND

I'VE SAVED MY BEST Barbra Streisand moment for last. The truth, though, is that the natural course of events set up this chronology. It took a lifetime to realize one of my deepest dreams.

The key was Jay Landers, Barbra's exec producer for over three decades. Every song presented to Streisand goes through Jay, her ultimate gatekeeper. One can only imagine the staggering volume of songs he must evaluate. Achieving a Streisand cut is the hardest-earned accomplishment in the industry. Realizing that goal would require both a circuitous route and a flawless song.

The path began when, after decades, I recently decided to appear on stage as a singer of my own songs and the songs of other writers close to my heart. Going full circle was life-affirming. It all came together during a sold-out three-day engagement at Manhattan's chic Feinstein's/54 Below. My show, directed by Richard Jay-Alexander, included a much-heralded reunion of Desmond Child & Rouge.

A lifelong friend, Richard also has directed dozens of Streisand's concerts and TV specials. Determined to lead me into Barbraland, he invited Jay Landers to one of my show rehearsals. I was struggling with the sound in a cramped rehearsal room in Chelsea. When Jay appeared, I grew nervous. After all, he has worked with some of the greatest voices of all time. But gentleman that he is, he sat quietly, smiled, listened, and, when the rehearsal was over, approached me warmly. Would I be interested in writing a song for Barbra's new concept album? *Would I!*

The assignment, though, was strict. There were to be no "me and you" love songs. The original album title was *What's On My*

*Mind (*then later changed to *Walls).* She was looking for songs that mirrored her reflection on the state of the world.

I had submitted countless songs to Jay for Barbra before but had always struck out. She had long forgotten about that time I had performed in her Beverly Hills home the song Diane Warren and I had written for her.

That incident, though, hadn't stopped me from continuing to study her music. I did, in fact, know her music, but I didn't know her. I wasn't on the inside of her world enough to get it right. But this time I was ushered in by Jay and invited to his Beverly Hills home, where he graciously spent the entire day guiding me through Barbra's sonic landscapes.

I had always longed to write in the rich harmonic styles of my composer idols Michel Legrand, Burt Bacharach, and Stephen Sondheim. But in my rock-Latin-pop world that was never the challenge. Suddenly, that changed. With Streisand's soaring voice and intellectual depth, I could finally let my musical imagination fly . . . in *her* sky.

As Jay went over Barbra's oeuvre, I realized she had created a musical genre all her own. We listened to classics like "What Are You Doing The Rest Of Your Life?," "How Do You Keep The Music Playing?," and "Papa, Can You Hear Me?," all three composed by maestro Michel Legrand, to the profound lyrics of Marilyn and Alan Bergman.

As my magical day with Jay unfolded, my mind went back to those first images of Barbra in *Funny Girl* singing "Don't Rain On My Parade" on the weather-beaten tugboat with the Statue of Liberty looming in the distance.

At the same time I was remembering twenty-six-year-old Barbra and fifteen-year-old me, Jay played me the quintessential Streisand: "I Remember," written by Stephen Sondheim in

1967 for the *Twilight Zone*-like television musical *Evening Primrose*. The haunting song is sung by a beautiful young woman who has lived in deep seclusion, hidden away since childhood in a department store. Barbra made the composition her own. Her interpretation is definitive.

As I reflected on writing an original composition for Barbra, I kept hearing "I Remember." A second Sondheim song, one that Streisand never recorded, also played inside my imagination: "I Wish I Could Forget You." No doubt, Sondheim had set the bar extremely high—perhaps, I feared, even out of reach.

Nonetheless, as I plucked away at Jay's piano, a title came to mind.

"What about 'Lady Liberty?'" I asked him.

He nodded, smiled, and replied, "I like it."

That was my green light.

On the plane home to Nashville, I decided to do something I've rarely done: write the song alone. Music and lyrics. In bits and pieces, melodies and words kept flying past me like fragments of parchment of an ancient sacred text. All I had to do was grab them. At the same time, I felt fear—fear of not being good enough to write on the same sublime level as the great masters.

The climb seemed daunting, but my determination was strong. I had to eliminate distractions from my *vida loca*. I had to sit down and just write the damn song.

Two weeks went by. Ideas kept swirling through my mind, but I couldn't quite mold them into shape. Jay kept calling me. Timing was urgent. There was only one remaining slot left on Barbra's album. I needed to fill it. Jay needed the song.

Enough procrastination. Face the fear. Walk through the fear. Get to work. Get to my Deston headquarters in Nashville, ignore the comings and goings of my energetic interns, writers, staff assistants, and engineers. Demand that I not be disturbed. Turn my attention to my arranger, Clay Perry, who, with his gear cranked up and ready to go, patiently waited in the corner of my office for me to give him something—*anything*—to arrange.

The busy-beaver interns brought me my chilled water and my PG Tips tea in my special Wedgewood cup. Not only was I starting to think like Barbra, but I was taking on her high-tea hijinks. Finally, I sat down at my lucky autographed grand piano (signed by Laura Nyro and Burt Bacharach) and focused, focused, focused. Disparate fragments began coalescing. A cohesive story began to unfold. Melodies married words, words inspired new melodies, countermelodies wound their way through the verses, chorus, and bridge.

The bridge from my heart to Barbra's took form. The bridge felt sturdy, strong, and right. I was ready to produce the demo.

Clay's arrangement was perfect. So was Vanessa Campagna's vocal. Old pros had told me that the demo vocalist should not imitate Barbra, who might find the similarity offensive. But I had no choice with this song. The pronunciation of every lyric and nuance of every leaping melody, with its contrasting alchemy of vibratos and straight tones, had to be phrased as a perfect blueprint for Barbra.

*Lady Liberty*
*Lift your lamp of hope a little higher*
*Burn that flame of freedom*
*Just a little brighter, please*
*For all the world to see*
*And still believe*

*Lady Liberty*
*Show us how to stand, and feel a little prouder*
*As the anthem plays, let's sing*
*And raise our voices even louder*
*Since the real danger lies in the sound of silence*

*Lady Liberty*
*I see you rise above the crashing waves*
*Bearing witness to our darkest days*
*Like that terrible September*
*When we stopped and cried together . . . remember*

*Lady Liberty*
*Give me your tired and your poor*
*Your huddled masses yearning to breathe free*
*The wretched refuse of your teeming shore*
*Send these the homeless*
*The tempest-tossed, to me . . . to me*

*So lift your lamp and lead us through the golden door*
*Tell the whole damn universe*
*There's room for all of us and more . . . forever*

*Lady Liberty*
*My country 'tis of thee*
*Lady Liberty*
*For all the world to see . . . please*
*Lady Liberty.*

With the demo done, I played it for colleagues before sending it to Jay. The reaction was overwhelmingly positive to where a few friends burst into tears. I then gathered up my courage and sent it to Jay, expecting nothing less than a ticker tape parade. Instead, Jay flatly replied, "I think there's a great song in there." Before he would play it for her, he insisted, much to my relief, on what I considered minor lyric changes.

Jay's suggestions were smart. I quickly made the fixes and, after redoing the demo, sent the second version back to Jay to play for Barbra. The wait was excruciating. I was sure she'd love it. It was written from my soul to hers. But if I was really so certain, why was I so nervous? Sometimes singers don't like songs for reasons unknown even to themselves. There's no guarantee. My mind kept chattering, my nervous system on the brink. How many times could I check my phone for an email or text from Jay? How obsessed could I be over one song? I've written thousands of songs. This was just another one.

Except it wasn't. This was *the* song. Barbra, please like it. Barbra, please love it. Jay, please call me.

The email arrived a few days later.

"I like the song" was in the subject box.

I thought it came from Jay. But wait . . . on second glance I saw that the message wasn't from Jay. It was from Barbra! *I was in!*

A week later, my heart aflutter, arranger Clay Perry and I nervously drove up to the iron gates of Sea Cliff, the stunning high-walled estate compound in Malibu where Barbra lives with her movie star husband, James Brolin. Before I rang the buzzer on the talk box, I looked up at the sky, where a mass of clouds took the shape of a hundred winged angels. Angels were sending me to Barbra.

But not yet. A proper British voice over the talk box said that Barbra was running late. We'd be told when to return. Feeling like Dumb and Dumber, Clay and I killed time at a local bar. I was Dorothy being turned away at the entrance to Oz.

The call finally came. This time the big iron gates slowly opened to reveal a spectacular storybook setting. The grounds were immaculately groomed, with giant shade trees lining the driveway that led to the majestic main house. I couldn't wait to be ushered inside to see the famous Streisand art collection. We were greeted by Jay Landers and the elegant English personal assistant, cast right out of *Downton Abbey*, whose regal voice had shooed us away earlier. Instead of bringing us in to meet Barbra, though, they led us down a narrow path through a wooden gate that opened up to an enormous sunlit rose garden. Set around this sea of fragrant blossoms of every shape and color was a large manor house and various small guest cottages. We were escorted into a cottage called Grandma's House. I felt like I'd stepped into a 1940s Bette Davis movie set in New England. The interior was exquisitely decorated with whimsical retro antique market treasures, vintage lamps, and floral chintz.

Grandma's House is where Barbra rehearses her music. On the small dining room table was a spread of luscious chocolate-dipped strawberries, grapes, cheeses, and crackers. I wasn't sure if those were for us or for her, so I cautiously restrained myself. In the far corner by a bank of windows with a panoramic view of the Pacific, sat an ivory baby grand piano with the rare and famous long-legged Second Hand Rose Fanny Brice doll seated above the keyboard. The piano was exactly like the one I had bought for Mimí when I moved her from the ghetto to Miami Beach. I took this as a sign of being in the right place at the right time . . . so I started to relax.

Jay showed us the lay of the land. "This is where she sits to chat. Then she moves to the high stool next to the piano with the antique wood music stand. There's the microphone she uses to be able to hear herself better over the music."

I paced back and forth as Clay got into position at the piano. We were ready to go.

And then I suddenly saw her. It was only a glimpse of her approaching the cottage, but it was her. She wore a hip all-black ensemble, black top, black leggings, black sneakers. But then, in a flash, she inexplicably disappeared. What had happened? Several minutes passed. I was bewildered. Had she changed her mind at the last minute? I started to hyperventilate. I started to lose it. But just when I thought I could no longer take the waiting, the door swung open.

Barbra.

She began by saying she had been distracted by a butterfly that had landed on a rose and felt compelled to photograph it. Jay made the introductions. When her deep-set blue eyes looked right into mine, I felt an electric charge.

Jay had already coached me beforehand on the proper decorum, explaining, "Barbra's not a hugger. Don't try to make her kiss you hello or goodbye. Don't ask her to pose for a photo. And especially don't ask her for an autograph for your Jewish grandmother." So I kept to the script and asked her if I could "fawn a little." Laughing, she sat down in her cozy armchair and said, "Fawn away."

So, like Luca Brasi's rehearsed and halting speech to Don Corleone from *The Godfather*, I began as Jay had advised . . . "Barbra [pause] . . . after having had dozens of #1 hits for over five decades [pause] . . . working with you [pause] . . . is the pinnacle of my career." I looked around the room. Jay was nodding his approval.

I went on to say, "Barbra, you've created more than a style of singing. You are a genre of music all your own."

Her reaction was so warm and personable that I decided to just let it all hang out. I started talking at a faster clip. "When I was fifteen and first saw you in *Funny Girl,* you instantly turned me gay!" Barbra jumped in to say, "People tell me that all the time!" Then I turned serious. "Seeing you on that tugboat in front of the Statue of Liberty fifty years ago made a deep impression on me. That's what inspired me to write 'Lady Liberty' for you." At this point, I could tell she was definitely swooning. I had won her over.

The conversation drifted to the topic of women unsupportive of other women. She spoke of the time she had trusted a female author interviewing her for a serious biography. This journalist had been given full access to Barbra's life. Then she betrayed her and published a tabloid tell-all book of vicious false stories about how she was cruel to her musicians and would dismiss one half of a sixty-piece orchestra, to the left or the right, if she was displeased with the sound coming from either side. "I'd never do such a thing," Barbra said. "Can you imagine that? Who would ever do that?"

The intimacy of this story demonstrated her trust in me. I was flattered and even more excited about working with Barbra.

The room felt electric, and after a few more laughs Jay moved us toward the piano as we began to slowly go through "Lady Liberty." Barbra quietly went over phrases under her breath for the longest time, never unleashing any of her big notes. I could barely hear what she was singing. As she grew more confident in the lyrics and melodies, she started singing entire verses straight through. At times I sang along with her in octaves. It was a duet! "FUCK! I'M SINGING WITH BARBRA STREISAND!" I silently screamed. I grew so intense that I began hovering over her and conducting. Realizing I'd gone too far, I pulled back. Barbra jokingly said that I should go outside and conduct from the other side of the garden window.

We discussed the key and decided that the body of the song would sound best a half step down from the demo. At the same time, a challenging D flat above high C in full voice was required on the last syllable of the word "remember." When she expressed concern, I said that singing at the top of her range would give the song the dramatic angst it needed. I reminded her that in her "People" she had sung the high notes in full voice two half steps higher. She laughed and said, "Yes, but I was twenty years old!"

She added, "Now it all depends on the vowel sound and the note that comes before it."

We worked for two hours straight. No break. Barbra was tireless, meticulous, ever so slightly increasing her volume each time she sang. Then came the first time she belted out the glorious note on the word "brighter." Shivers shot up my spine. I started jumping around the room singing "I'M GONNA BE RICH AGAIN!" to the tune of "Ta-ra-ra Boom-de-ay." Barbra thought that was hilarious.

Rehearsal was over. As I stood by the door to say goodbye, Barbra surprised me by giving me a big hug and a beautiful compliment. "Thank you for writing me such a great song."

After Barbra returned to the big house, Jay gave us a quick tour of the Barn, the manor built to perfection with detailed Art Nouveau and Craftsman woodwork. The basement level was built as a series of quaint English storefronts to house Barbra's antique-doll collection, movie costumes, and other priceless treasures. There's even a working ice cream shop.

All this was familiar to me—at least in my imagination—because I had seen Jonathan Tolins's hilarious one-man play *Buyer & Cellar* about a struggling gay actor who lands a job curating this very basement. It's the gayest open love letter to Barbra ever written. I had wondered if it was really as wonderful as the play made it out to be. The answer is yes.

There were shelves upon shelves of exquisite dolls, some of them centuries old. I was overcome with an eerie feeling that they were breathing, just waiting for their owner to come and play with them. She put this fairyland in the safest possible place, underground, a private reserve where new treasures could be added and time would be forever suspended.

A few weeks later I flew back for my first official recording session with Barbra at the home studio of her personal recording engineer, Jochem van der Saag, located a short drive from Sea Cliff. Jay Landers was already there. I had brought a gorgeous arrangement of white and mauve flowers and attached a note: "To my Lady Liberty . . . let freedom sing!" and placed them in her vocal booth.

Barbra also arrived bearing gifts for me and Jay, hand-crafted bracelets featuring a tiny piece of original copper from the Statue of Liberty. They were crafted in the shape of the flames from the torch, salvaged during the 1984 centennial restoration.

Back to work. She immediately sang through the entire song a few times. She had it down. She then decided to concentrate on perfecting each section at a time. She did so in no more than four takes. With anyone else, I'd require dozens of takes and be forced to spend endless mind-boggling days piecing those takes together into a reconstituted vocal. Not with Barbra. In these high-tech days of unlimited electronic trickery, it's amazing how much of her first run-through ended up as the final vocal. Hers is the sound of pure truth; truth is her art form. I recalled Bob Crewe telling me how Barbra had sung the original "People," one time from beginning to end, grabbed her fur coat, and simply walked out of the studio to a standing ovation from the orchestra.

At the same time, producing her required intense energy and focus. How far to push her? How to suggest that she lay back? How to allow her to find her own way through the song? Fortunately, we found a good balance. She trusted my feedback. She came in to hear several playbacks. She asked me about a certain phrase I knew was imperfect. I swallowed hard and said I heard a flaw. Then I held my breath. She placed her hand on her heart and indignantly asked, "Did you say . . . a FLAW?" Before I could answer, she broke out laughing. It was just a test. She was pleased I had the confidence to speak my mind.

That moment let us relax. More laughs, more fun. More willingness on my part to encourage her to redo passages I knew she could improve upon. "You're a taskmastah! And a slavedrivah!" was her response before going back to the mic and blowing us all away.

The session turned into a musical lovefest. Between singing, she hurried off into another room where she was re-editing "A Star Is Born." She'd decide to reinsert a scene that she had cut from her 1976 film with Kris Kristofferson where she's playing acoustic guitar and humming the melody of "Evergreen," the song for which she won an Academy Award with her collaborator, Paul Williams.

While Barbra was editing her movie, Jochem and I crafted together a final vocal version of "Lady Liberty" that, a few days later, she listened to with intense concentration. During that playback, I found the courage to hold out my fist for her to gently bump. Then I couldn't help myself. For a brief, breathless moment, I held her hand in mine. Time stood still. Then, with the flair of a Spanish dancer playing a castanet, Barbra slowly closed her hand, one finger at a time, and gently pulled away.

It was now getting late. I had only one other wish. Jay voiced it for me: "Let's have Barbra go for the barn-burner ending, the triumphant high note in full voice." I seconded his suggestion, and Barbra, fearless artist that she is, hit it dead on. Perfect!

Not long after, her husband, James Brolin, appeared. He sat on the couch behind us with Jay, fiddling with his iPad. "Put that away," she said. "I want you to hear my work . . . *our* work." Her sly smile was aimed in my direction.

James listened attentively and loved what he heard, especially the heart-gripping a cappella finale.

A few silent seconds passed before The Great Streisand, on her way out, gave me a tight hug, looked up at me and said, "You're a pain in the ass . . . and I commend you."

*With engineer Jochem van der Saag*

# HITMAKER TO THE STARS

| LIVE ON STAGE | PERFORMING THE SONGS |
|---|---|
| DESMOND CHILD | LIVIN' ON A PRAYER |
| ALICE COOPER | POISON · BED OF NAILS |
| BONNIE TYLER | IF YOU WERE A WOMAN |
| RITA WILSON | ANGEL · CRAZY |
| SAKIS ROUVAS | OLA KALA · THE LIGHT |
| THE RASMUS | LIVIN' IN A WORLD WITHOUT YOU |
| LEO DANTE | I HATE MYSELF FOR LOVING YOU |
| KIP WINGER | LIVIN' LA VIDA LOCA |
| CHRIS WILLIS | DUDE LOOKS LIKE A LADY |
| TABITHA FAIR | KINGS & QUEENS |
| GEORGE LEMBESIS | BORN TO BE MY BABY |
| JUSTIN BENLOLO | YOU GIVE LOVE A BAD NAME |
| ANDREAS CARLSSON | I WAS MADE FOR LOVIN' YOU |
| ATHENS PHILHARMONIA | ARTISTIC DIRECTOR: FOIVOS |
| POP ORCHESTRA | DIRECTOR: FOKAS EVANGELINOS |

# DESMOND CHILD
## ROCKS THE PARTHENON
### ODEON OF HERODES ATTICUS
#### ATHENS · GREECE
27·6·22

# ROCKING THE PARTHENON

"The Parthenon is a prayer wrapped in marble. This
prayer cannot be fully answered until all the pieces have
been returned to their rightful birthplace . . . this place."

—DESMOND CHILD, JUNE 27, 2022
*Odeon of Herodes Atticus in Athens, Greece*

ALTHOUGH WORKING INTIMATELY with Barbra Streisand was the
fulfillment of a dream I had dreamed for decades, only recently
did I realize that another dream burned just as brightly:

I had never headlined a really big, full-length show of just my
songs. I've regularly performed a few songs at a time over the
years at various songwriter events, cabarets, and more recently
at the Appel Room at Lincoln Center in New York, but I had
never performed a show highlighting my songs for more than
four hundred people. This dream of mine would be sculpted to
reveal not simply a part of me, but all of me. I've always believed
I could pull it off, but I'd never really had the opportunity.

Through a circuitous set of circumstances, the opportunity
arose, and my big dream was realized. Even now, as I think
through the details of the event, I still can't quite believe that it
all really happened!

Call it my Big Fat Greek Rock Concert.

A seed was planted fifteen years ago when Curtis and I, along
with our young sons, discovered the Aegean Island of
Folegandros in the Greek Cyclades. It became an annual devotion. Each summer we've reunited with the same friends, our
group ever expanding to include fun and fascinating people

from all over the world, many of whom we met when we first arrived. Running up and down the ancient cobblestone streets, our kids have grown up together with the local children, all of us forging friendships to last a lifetime. We sit for hours on end, eating and drinking at Nico's Taverna, seated in the center of the enchanted village. Worries vanish. Time stops. Our only evening agenda is to watch the sun melt behind the tip of the island and into the sea as the cloudless sky turns from radiant blue to blazing orange to faded gold.

In 2005, the first year we arrived, we stopped over in Athens to meet up with our dear friends Melanie and Albhy Galuten, who had originally introduced us to Folegandros and Greece. That's when Melanie phoned me at my hotel to say that Ana Vissi, "the Cher of Greece," was nearby in the city and eager to meet me.

In flip-flops and shorts, I ran down to a café. Ana could not have been more charming. Within minutes of our meeting, we were joined by pop rocker George Lembesis who, much to my delight, was a fan of my music. Thus began an unbreakable bond with George and his beautiful wife Sofia.

Unexpectedly, the bond planted the seed and birthed the dream.

In the summer of 2021, George and megaproducer Phoebus Tassopoulos suggested an evening of my songs at the two-thousand-year-old Odeon of Herodes Atticus. This outdoor venue is unrivaled, situated at the base of the southwestern slope of the Acropolis, below the Parthenon, which sits at the summit of the Sacred Rock of the Acropolis.

The concept was simple: I invite my favorite collaborators and artists to perform our biggest hits together. Then, for reasons I can't explain, the concept expanded. A light bulb went off inside my head. Why do just a concert? Why not turn it into a benefit, under the auspices of the Acropolis Museum, where proceeds would be used to bring the global spotlight on the just return and reunification of the Parthenon sculptures that have been housed at the British Museum for the past two hundred years?

The back story is well known. In the early nineteenth century, marble statues and ornamentations were removed from the Parthenon and shipped to Britain by the kingdom's ambassador to the Ottoman Empire, Thomas Bruce, better known as Lord Elgin. The circumstances of his acquisitions were, to say the least, shady. The great English poet Lord Byron condemned him as a vandal. According to historians, Elgin's original intention was to use the art to decorate his palatial home. But then his fortunes changed. He went bust and sold them to the British Museum.

These timeless works of art were an integral part of the Parthenon, the temple that stands at the summit of the Acropolis in Athens. Built in the fifth century BCE, the Parthenon remains an unparalleled achievement, a glorious fusion of engineering, architecture, and art.

The mission was clear: use music to bring attention to the issue. Bring back the marbles. Use music as the bridge connecting all languages and cultures. Along with still another George—Phoebus's production partner, George Stampolis—we took on what quickly became an international event.

Preparations were arduous. I struggled my way through a series of serious health issues—a debilitating knee injury, a kidney stone, tachycardia followed by a successful heart ablation procedure . . . and then I caught COVID—all the while, along with my devoted partners, on weekly Zoom calls planning what would come to be called "DESMOND CHILD ROCKS THE PARTHENON!"

We arrived in Athens a month before the show itself. The preparations were mighty, the rehearsals strenuous, the logistics mind-blowing. But somehow, some way, it came off. The dream was no longer a dream. It was real.

The setting was stunning.

To highlight the majesty of the Odeon of Herodes Atticus, built in 161 CE by Roman citizen Herodes Atticus, our brilliant director, Fokas Evangelinos, along with Renos Papapaschos, head of production, meticulously built a round, mirrored stage and wrapped a nine-foot grand Steinway piano in blue metallic vinyl. To add to the spectacle, my Venezuelan Sicilian cousin, Ionee Waterhouse, programmed the video-mapping, animated projections onto the ancient three-story stone walls of the historic amphitheater.

Musically and sartorially, homage was paid to Greece's national colors of blue and white, symbolizing the sky and the sea.

I opened the concert wearing a fantastic, sparkling, over-the-top, high-collared Elvis-inspired blue-satin ensemble and kicked things off with an explosive medley of my global hits cowritten with Draco Rosa for Ricky Martin, including "Livin' La Vida Loca," "The Cup Of Life," "Shake Your Bon Bon," and "She Bangs."

The enthusiastic sold-out audience of 4,400, many wearing T-shirts of the artists closely associated with my career—KISS, Bon Jovi, Aerosmith, Alice Cooper, Joan Jett, Scorpions, The Rasmus, and others—responded with the first of many standing ovations.

As the show progressed, I was joined onstage by a cavalcade of American, Greek, and international stars, including Alice

Cooper, Bonnie Tyler, Rita Wilson, Sakis Rouvas, The Rasmus, George Lembesis, Kip Winger, Chris Willis, Tabitha Fair, Andreas Carlsson, Justin Benlolo, and extraordinary debut artist Leo Dante. The all-star rock band was led by US/Greek music directors Clay Perry and Kostas Platanias, accompanied by the Athens Pop Philharmonia Orchestra. In a thrilling moment, a sixty-voice children's choir came down the aisles holding glowing orbs surrounding the circular stage.

We performed my most famous collaborations: Bon Jovi's "Livin' On A Prayer" and "You Give Love A Bad Name," Aerosmith's "Dude Looks Like A Lady," "Angel," and "Crazy."

Additional megahits included KISS's "I Was Made For Lovin' You," Joan Jett's "I Hate Myself For Loving You," Alice Cooper's "Poison" and "Bed Of Nails," Katy Perry's "Waking Up In Vegas," and a trio of my most recent global smashes, "Beautiful Now," by Zedd; "Jezebel," by the powerhouse Finnish band The Rasmus; and Ava Max's multiplatinum dance-floor anthem, "Kings & Queens."

For the finale, I, along with the entire cast, donned elegant white outfits for a Bon Jovi-styled, fists-in-the-air version of "Livin' On A Prayer."

As an encore, I sat at the piano of the empty stage and sang "You Wanna Make A Memory," a song I had composed with Jon Bon Jovi and Richie Sambora, dedicating it to Curtis, Roman, and Nyro.

In that moment, a lone soul beneath the Grecian sky, I felt a blessing that defies description. The stars were aligned. Peace prevailed. I felt transported. Transcended. Overjoyed with the knowledge that music—and music's mystical power—had brought me to this remarkable place. And nothing felt more welcome or beautifully gratifying than looking up to see my twenty-year-old sons' tear-stained faces as they found me back-stage in my dressing room after the concert had concluded. I'm just so grateful for so many blessings in my life.

The aftermath had an additional excitement all its own.

Before leaving Greece, Phoebus and I visited Prime Minister Kyriakos Mitsotakis at the Maximos Mansion, the official residence and seat of government in Greece. He greeted us with genuine warmth and enthusiasm. In fact, he raised the possibility of bringing the show to London.

The profound distance between growing up dirt-poor in the projects of Miami's Liberty City and sitting in the office of a prime minister was not lost on me.

The next day, flying back to New York, I still hadn't caught up with myself. My mind was swirling when a heavy realization washed over me. I finally understood the great subtext of this enormous project and why it felt so personal and mattered so much to me.

The crusade to bring lost artwork back home mirrored the long journey of the carved Roman-Greco-inspired bas-relief, carved by sculptress Lee Burnham in 1954, of my mother, Mimí—the same artwork that had been missing for forty-five years. I flashed back to that remarkable moment when Mimí was able to view that image of herself a final time before she died. I remembered how she gently ran her hand over the thick carved Brazilian walnut masterpiece. I remembered the tears running down her cheeks.

"It was so important that this came back to us," she whispered. "Never let it go again."

I never will, I silently said to my mother as the plane landed at JFK.

A few hours later, we arrived in our New York apartment, where I stood and stared at that magnificent carving of Mimí that, thanks to gods of good fortune, found its way back to us.

That night, jet-lagged yet unable to sleep, I thought of the director general of the Acropolis Museum, Professor Nikolaos Stampolidis, who gave us a private tour of the Parthenon Sculptures the night before the show. He stood before the chalk-white casts of the missing original marbles and, like Mimí, was emotional and teary-eyed.

"Thank you for your beautiful contribution," he said. "Thank you for helping to bring the sculptures back home."

A museum director in Greece seeking a home for his country's precious marbles.

A woman in Florida seeking a home for her Cuban poetry and songs, a home for her restless soul.

Art that is missing. Art that is found. Art that is eternal. Art that is healing.

With Mimí's haunting bolero "Muchisimo" floating through my exhausted mind, I finally fell into peaceful sleep.

*With Bonnie Tyler (above) and with (left to right) Lauri Ylönen, Alice Cooper, Sakis Rouvas, Rita Wilson, Bonnie Tyler, and George Lembesis (below)*

*Mimí, Pinar del Rio, Cuba, 1943*

WRITING "LADY LIBERTY" was one of the most profound creative acts of my life. If I never write another song, I'll feel complete. I don't need another hit to prove that I'm somebody.

Except that I do. The truth is that the hustle continues. I don't know any other way to live. My wish is to keep writing songs that touch hearts and change minds. I'll never stop wanting hits. Hits mean millions of people are loving something emanating from my soul.

I was conceived in the heat of the jungles of Venezuela by two people never meant to be together. To avoid scandal, my Cuban mother found refuge on a dairy farm in Florida with a man she did not love so I could be born in America. I guess that makes me in today's terms . . . a dreamer.

I'm fortunate and proud to be an American, where I was taught to believe all things are possible if you dream big enough, want it bad enough, and work hard to attain it. I know that isn't true for everybody. Dark skin and poverty are a deadly combination, yet I still lived to see a distinguished black president serve our country with dignity, giving hope to billions around the world.

Even though I hit my head up against the white hetero glass ceiling many times and experienced the discrimination and rejection of being Latin, poor, and gay during the course of my life, I stubbornly carved out my own lane.

Looking back, I see that the facts of the story of my life had already been written in my mother's daydreams. As a teenager, she composed a poem, using the pseudonym Demian, in which she speaks to her alter ego. I hadn't read the poem when I changed my name from Johnny and almost chose Demian, the name of a Hermann Hesse novel I loved. Desmond Child won out because it sounded more like Elton John, the biggest singer-songwriter of the era. Sometimes I feel like I'm an extension of one of Mimí's poems or songs.

Her dream became my war map, her fantasy my driving force. One of the reasons I've toiled so arduously is to make sure that her memory will not die in shadows. Her vow to join the threads of her story has become my vow. Case in point:

When I was inducted into the Songwriters Hall of Fame, I was surprised to learn that in the half century of its existence, the institution had admitted only two Latino composers before me: Antonio Carlos Jobim and the Cuban composer, Ernesto Lecuona. Where were giants like Agustín Lara, Violeta Parra, Armando Mansanero, and Carlos Gardel, the man who invented the tango?

With the blessing of Linda Moran, the CEO and president of the Songwriters Hall Of Fame, with Rudy Pérez, a legendary Latin songwriter and music producer, who, like Mimí, was born in Pinar del Rio, I cofounded the Latin Songwriters Hall of Fame.

We've worked tirelessly to honor writers who would otherwise go unacknowledged. Mimí was my motivation. To honor her, we named the statuette award "La Musa," a miniature version of the sculpture of my mother made by Lee Burnham in 1954 when we were still living on John Barrett's dairy farm.

Today a silver Musa is given to songwriter and composer inductees and a bronze one to performers, producers, and industry executives. A further award, Premio La Musa Elena Casals, is presented to promising young female songwriters. In a multitude of ways, my mother has achieved the fame that eluded her in life.

Coming to terms with my father and my Hungarian heritage took on special urgency when our sons were born. I had lived for eighteen years before I even knew about it. And when I did learn, I was overwhelmed with anger. Adding to the emotional complexity was the fact that, in society's view, I was illegitimate. My very existence caused my mother lifelong shame. Now, though, I was determined that our children feel none of that illegitimacy or shame. That's why it was so vital for this country to grant legitimacy to my marriage to Curtis—and for our boys to know their paternal lineage.

Fate intervened. Out of the blue, in 2016, David Singer, Hungary's cultural attaché in Washington, DC, reached out to the diaspora, drawing prominent Hungarians the world over to Budapest to work in their respective fields. I was included, but before I was given dual citizenship, I had to jump through hoops to prove that Joe Marfy was my biological father. I did so, and the prime minister himself welcomed me with a special medal of honor. That led to several trips to Budapest, where Curtis and I, along with our sons, washed down and placed fresh flowers at the Marfy family tomb. The Hungarian ambassador to the United States, Dr. Rèka Szemerkenyi, also hosted us at the official residence in Washington, DC, granting Roman and Nyro dual citizenship as well. I was later asked to write an anthem celebrating the sixtieth anniversary of the Hungarian Revolution. The result was "Egy Szabad Országért,"/"Steps Of Champions," cowritten with Andreas Carlsson and Hungarian lyricist, Tamás Orbán, and sung by the top Hungarian superstars in a "We Are The World"-style video.

My life began as a lie. I was thrown into chaos and uncertainty. All I knew and felt was abandonment and soul-crushing worthlessness. I took an inordinate number of wrong turns. But some right ones too. Altogether, though, my life was inexorably guided towards illuminated spirits who exemplified a deep humanity that shaped my destiny. I'm talking about Violeta Drouet, Marie Louise Mansfield Leeds, Sandra Seacat, and Bob

Crewe. With my decision to commit myself to my husband, Curtis, and our sons, Roman and Nyro, I chose life.

As I retrace the seemingly random twists and turns of my big life, the enduring footprints I leave in the sands of time are my songs. This is why I will keep writing them . . . till my very last note.

As expected, though, the final words belong to my beloved Mimí. Of all the poems my mother wrote, the most poignant is one she kept revising until her final days on earth. She began it when she was only twenty years old. She named it "Mis Cajas de Carton," ("My Cardboard Boxes").

## MIS CAJAS DE CARTÓN

Yo guardo en mi desván atesoradas
a través y a lo largo de mi vida,
"mi razón de vivir" yo las llamara;
son unas viejas cajas carcomidas.

Esperando por mí, porque las abra,
ponerme a revisar su contenido,
me han de traer recuerdos y resaca
que hasta el día de hoy, he detenido.

Pudieron escuchar junto conmigo
los ruidos de velorios y
mudanzas y de herencias perdidas,
sin sentido, las fotos de familia en esas cajas.

Cajas llenas de amor, fueron testigos
de los muchos proyectos en enjambre,

*viajaron, se mojaron, se han herido,*
*pero guardan las trenzas de mi madre.*
*Ha llegado el momento cuando miro,*
*y no quiero ésta vez perder la calma,*
*los libros de mi padre y gran amigo*
*y unos versos . . . antiguos como el alma.*

*La muerte es una amiga cumplidora,*
*mis cajas de cartón ya están afuera,*
*cuidado si al pasar la moledora*
*un error familiar, las destruyera.*

*En un final, Rodaje de mi vida,*
*la cita que tenemos nunca falla;*
*mis cajas de cartón, todo lo dicen,*
*mis cajas de cartón, todo lo callan.*

—ELENA CASALS (1927–2012)

La Musa, *sculpted by Lee Burnham, 1954*

## MY CARDBOARD BOXES

*I have saved in my attic*
*as if a treasure*
*across the width and breadth of my life,*
*"my reason for living," I could call them;*
*some old crumbling cardboard boxes.*

*Waiting for me to open,*
*and rummage through their contents,*
*they are sure to bring back memories and undertows*
*that to this day I have avoided.*

*They heard along with me*
*the commotion of wakes and the many moves,*
*and family fortunes that were lost, senselessly,*
*all the family photographs are in those boxes.*

*Boxes filled with love that were witness*
*to all the many projects hanging in the air,*
*they traveled, they got soaked, they were wounded,*
*but they guarded the braids of my mother.*

*The moment has come for me to look,*
*this time I don't want to lose my calm,*
*through the books written by my father, my great friend*
*and some verses . . . ancient as the soul.*

*Death is a dutiful friend,*
*my cardboard boxes are already outside,*

*lest the shredder passing by*
*due to a familial blunder . . . destroys them.*

*In one final Sojourn of my life,*
*the appointment we have made is never canceled;*
*my cardboard boxes tell everything,*
*my cardboard boxes silence everything.*

# CODA: THE HUSTLE

THIS BOOK IS THE RECKONING of the jumbled details of my life. I've tried to make sense of it all . . . but this is unfinished business, because the hustle doesn't stop.

The hustle is deep. It's more than a steely-strong work ethic; it's more than connecting to people who can make things happen; it's more than pushing through seven or eight or nine projects at the same time; it's more than staying current with pop culture; more than getting ahead of the musical curve; more than writing new songs; more than discovering new singers; more than working with new bands, new producers, new record executives, and new technology.

It's the joy of the creative process itself. The joy of the journey. It's the hustle of driving myself to be truly great. The hustle for real, earned glory.

At almost seventy years old, I continue to throw myself at life. I see the creative hustle as the heartbeat, the impetus that makes us want to improve the world and give back to others. At ASCAP, on whose board I serve, I've extended my hustle to become a songwriters' activist and advocate. When I was put on the legislative committee, I walked the halls of Congress with my colleagues—legendary figures like Paul Williams, Jimmy Webb, Valerie Simpson, Jimmy Jam, Terry Lewis, Jerry Leiber, Mike Stoller, Dean Kay, Linda Perry, Nile Rodgers, Patti Austin, Kelly Clarkson, Aloe Black—and legendary music publishers such as Irwin Robinson, Evan Lamberg, John Titta, Marty Bandier, Jody Gerson, Jon Platt, and Carolyn Beinstock, spending time with representatives and senators to discuss the dire situation of working songwriters no longer able to survive.

Seven decades ago, each radio play of a recorded song might bring the writer two cents. Today, that amount, instead of increasing with the cost of living, has—incredible as it sounds—decreased dramatically. The culprit is a technology that financially squeezes composers while disregarding authorship. Physical albums listed writers, producers, and musicians.

Streaming music simply streams. Along with help from other concerned songwriters, Michelle Lewis and Alex Shapiro, together with the Spotify music-creator advocate, Adam Parness, we were able to push the streaming services Spotify and Pandora to initiate digital liner notes that will provide information of who made the music.

It's also part of the hustle. We're hustling for the heirs of deceased composers. That's why I initiated ASCAP Legacy. Our watchwords are "honoring the music that has elevated the repertory and ensuring an impact for generations to come." The first priority is to protect the monetary value of the estates. I grow sad when I think of how families of so many deceased writers have been robbed of royalties. There's also the mandate to pay ongoing respect for writers neglected by history. Beyond respect, ASCAP Legacy—through performances, publicity, and blogs—works to keep that music alive.

Then there's my Nashville hustle—Nashville where songwriters have been hustling ever since Boudleaux and Felice Bryant pulled their trailer into town with their two kids in tow, twenty-five cents in their pockets and an unstoppable drive to pitch their songs, some of which wound up as huge hits for the Everly Brothers. No wonder I'm hard at work cowriting a musical with Carolyn Smith-Bryant and Sharon Vaughn about the Bryants, who've earned their high, venerated place in the Country Music Hall of Fame.

That brings me to my Broadway hustle. With my long-time collaborator Davitt Sigerson, we've written *Cuba Libre,* a musical dramatizing the stories of my mother's two beautiful sisters who came to Havana, one Batista's mistress and the other Castro's lover. There are scores of other projects that get my creative juices flowing, including *Transcon: The Making Of Lou Pearlman & the Boyband Revolution,* the feature film I've been creating with Andreas Carlsson about the rise and fall of Orlando entrepreneur Lou Pearlman, whose $500 million Ponzi scheme bankrolled the making of the Backstreet Boys and *NSYNC.

And then there's this book, which has been a labor of love, pain, sadness, and renewal over the last seven years. My good friend, Helene Cooper, Pulitzer Prize-winning correspondent for the *New York Times,* keeps telling me that in reality, my book will never be finished . . . until I am . . . and then some. So, like mother, like son, I'm a compulsive schemer, songwriter, poet, inventor, visionary, patriot, and streetwalker . . . the hustle that is my life continues . . .

# ACKNOWLEDGMENTS

I thank all of you so much for believing in me,
my dreams, my words and my music.

X Alfonso & Sandra Lopez

Heather Aman

April Anderson

John Angelos &
 Margaret Valentine

Michael Anthony &
 Tom Massman

Polly Anthony

Antonina Armato &
 Tim James

Burt Bacharach

Martin Bandier

Ciro Barbaro

Freddy Barrett

Fred, Nancy, &
 Natalya Barrett

Eric Bazilian

Justin Benlolo

Skip Bishop

Diane Blagman

Jon & Dorothea Bon Jovi

Chris & Olivia Braide

Nancy Brennan

Tony Brown

Sampson Brueher

Carolyn & Del Bryant

Gary Burr

Vanessa Campagna

David Campbell

Adrienne Campbell-Holt

Randy Cantor

Claribel Caraballo

Dr. Patricia Carey

Andreas Carlsson

Dario Carnevale

Michael Cava & Rip Parker

Denise & Luby Chambul

Kristin Chenoweth

Cher

Deepak Chopra

Chick Ciccarelli

David Codikow

Tracy Cole

Brian & Lisa Coleman

Helene Cooper

Sheryl & Alice Cooper

Bob Crewe

Fran Curtis

Barbara Daane

Whitney Daane

Michael David &
 Lauren Mitchell

Carol Davidson & Jody Silver

Clive Davis

Doug Davis

Susan Dechovitz-Musto

Ron Delsener

Violeta Drouet

# ACKNOWLEDGMENTS

Stelios Droumalias
Stacey Dutton
Jeffrey & Elaine
    Hastings Edell
Linda Edell Howard
Chad & Kerri Edwards
Kári Egilsson
Brian Elliott
Erika Ender
Adam Epstein
Roy Ericson &
    Matthew Mark
Ed Ewing
Jan & Bob Ezrin
Suzee Factor
Tabitha Fair
Carol Fenster
Ana Fernandez
Esther & Wayne Fink
Fletcher Foster &
    Dennis Johnson
Kelly Ford
Gina Franano
Alan Franklin
Marti Frederiksen &
    Kari Smith
Carol Free
Mark Fretz
Celia Froehlig
Juan Galano &
    Gerson Germano
Phil Galdston
Melanie & Albhy Galuten
Susan Garia
Martha Gehman
Iggy & Claudia Gelabert
Lola Gelabert

Jody Gerson
Jules & Liberty Gondar
Leslie Gonzalez
Joan, Frankie &
    Ariana Grande
Diana Grasselli
Steve Greenberg
Holly Greene
Ellie Greenwich
Sue Gregory
Leslie & Diane Greif
Matt Gruber
Michael Guido
Alejandra Guzmán
Gyan
Landon Hall
Lena Hall
Greg Harvey
Jeffrey Hatcher
Alex Heiche
Egill Helgason
Jonas Herbsman
Dr. Thom Holter
Eliot Hubbard
Laurent Hubert
Jennifer Hudson
Levi Hummon
Marcus Hummon &
    Becca Stevens
David Hurst and
    Dr. Keith Meritz
Donny Ienner
Joanna Ifrah
Lauren Iossa
Jimmy Iovine
David Israelite
Matthias Jabs

Turner Jalomo

Richard Jay-Alexander

Jay Jensen

Joan Jett & Kenny Laguna

Jill Kahn

Lucia Kaiser

John Kalodner

Helen Kalognomos

Sigurveig Karadottir

Joel Katz

Zach Katz

Danny Keaton

Maria Keeling

Carole King

Jean & Jyl Klein-Riendeau

Dr. Ted Klontz

David Kokakis

Charles Koppelman

Christina Kounelias &
    Richard Brous

Evan Lamberg

Despina & Jay Landers

Jennifer Lane

Bob Lange

Dina LaPolt

Cyndi Lauper

Mrs. Marie Louise
    Mansfeld Leeds

Bob Lefsetz

Sofia & George Lembesis

Dr. Catherine Linn

Melanie London

Craig Lozowick

Maia Luna

Jeff Mahl

Marsha Malamet

Nathan Malki

Betty & Raul Malo

Arif Mardin

Valeria Marfy

Kati Marfy

John, Kim, Joey, Spencer
    & Gia Marfy

Jodi Marr & Eamara Dillon

Carianne Marshall

Michael & Amy Martin

Ricky Martin

Elizabeth Matthews

Ava Max

Angelo Medina

John Meglen

Klaus Meine

Damian Miano

Nicolas Michailidis

Sam Miller

Drake Milligan

Jimmy & Angela Milligan

Joni Mitchell

Joey Monda

J. C. Monterrosa

Linda Moran

Ellen Moraskie

Amy Morrison

Deborah Mulvihill

Loretta Muñoz

Nancy Muñoz

Billie Myers

Virgil Night

Rick Nowels

Annelise Nutt Carey

Laura Nyro

Obie & Denise O'Brien

Rosie O'Donnell

Deirdre O'Hara

# ACKNOWLEDGMENTS

Geoff O'Leary

Peter Oakmund Madsen

Debbie Ohanian

Mike & Sonia Ohanian

Orianthi

Jorge Palmer Real &
  Ionee Waterhouse

Panos Panay

Wendy Parr

Cristina Parvu

Cornelia & Dimitris Pateli

Danai Pateli &
  Dimitris Voulgaris

Mary Megan Peer

Emma Perez

Rudy & Betsy Perez

Clay Perry

Joe Perry

Katy Perry

Evan Phail

Chynna Phillips &
  William Baldwin

Barbara Pritchett

Ilias Psinakis

Monica Quinones

Ana & Prisco Radcliff

Zsuzsanna Rahói

Tarik Ramusovic &
  Dr. Maja Skikic

Shahrokh Rezai

Frankie Ricigliano

Camilo Ricordi

David Ritz

Lisa Roberts

Irwin Robinson

Gisela Rodríguez

Jesus Romero

Draco Rosa

Howard Rosenman

Sakis Rouvas & Katia Zygouli

Jennifer Rush

Lindsay Rush

Dr. Vicken Sahakian

Juaretsi Saizarbitoria

Totty and Juanito
  Saizarbitoria

Ira Sallen

Richie Sambora

Margot Sande

Amy Sapp

Steven Jay Savitt

Josefina Scaglione

Rudolf Schenker

Stephen Schwartz

Steve Schwarzberg

Greta Seacat

Sandra Seacat &
  Thurn Hoffman

Ruta Sepetys

Lizzy Shaw

Mary Ann Shaw

Rob & Jeannie Shaw

Steve & Debi Shaw

Stuart & Julie Shaw

Victoria Shaw

Karen Sherry

Tomi Shirota & Evelyn Tan

Dinky & Davitt Sigerson

Gene Simmons

C. Winston, Carleen, &
  Winston C. Simone

David Simoné & Shelley Ross

Isabelle Simone &
  Jack Eriksson

364

# ACKNOWLEDGMENTS

Valerie Simpson
David Singer
Barbara Skydel
Craig Sneiderman
Ronnie Spector
John Stamos
George Stampolis
Paul Stanley
Joanna Staudinger
Billy Steinberg
Barbra Streisand
Armando Suárez Cobián
Bette Sussman
Dr. Rèka Szemerkenyi
Amalia & Phoebus Tassopoulos
Marylou, Mark, Sam,
    Wesley, & Jack Tawney
John Titta
Kent & Susan Tobiska
Olga Guillót
Olga Maria Touzet Guillót
Dr. Rosario Trifiletti
Carolyn Truscott
Bonnie Tyler &
    Robert Sullivan
Steven Tyler
Steve Vai
Myriam Valle
Marlene Vasilic

Csaba Vastag
Sharon Vaughn
Jose Vega
Nora Velasquez
Jon Vella
Eric Vetro
Maria Vidal
Diane Warren
Scott Waxman
Jimmy Webb & Laura Savini
Bruce Weber & Nan Bush
Shelby Weimer
Greg Wells
Rob Wells
Angela Whittaker
Ruby & Ken Whittaker
Paul Williams
Robbie Williams
Allee Willis
Chris Willis
Howard Wills
Michael Wilson
Rita Wilson & Tom Hanks
Heather Winters
George C. Wolfe
Linda Wortman
Mark Wylie
Lauri Ylönen
Don Paul Yowell

A very special thanks to my creative team who put this book together:

Brian Coleman, Heather Winters, Curtis Shaw Child, Jorge Rodríguez, Ionee Waterhouse, Turner Jalomo, and Don Taylor Atkinson. I couldn't have faced the story of my life without you.

—DESMOND

## ACKNOWLEDGMENTS

# *BAT OUT OF HELL III*

I'D LIKE TO TAKE THIS OPPORTUNITY to again thank all the song-writers who contributed to *Bat Out Of Hell III*: Jim Steinman, Diane Warren, John 5, Nikki Sixx, James Michael, Holly Knight, Andrea Remanda, Marti Fredriksen, John Gregory, Russ Irwin, and, of course, my mother, Elena Casals, who wrote the Spanish lyrics to "Monstro."

I'd like to thank the wonderful featured artists: Jennifer Hudson and Marion Raven, Brian May and Steve Vai for their dramatic performances, and the hauntingly inspired string arrangements by David Campbell.

Musical talents of: Kenny Aronoff, Brett Cullen, Todd Rundgren, Eric Troyer, Mark Alexander, Carolyn "C. C." Colletti-Jablonski, Paul Crook, Randy Flowers, John Miceli, Patti Russo, Kasim Sulton, Eric Bazilian, John Shanks, Rusty Anderson, Stephanie Bennett, Victor Indrizzo, Corky James, Lee Levin, David Levita, Don Marchese, Graham Phillips, Eric Rigler, Matt Rollings, Bettie Ross, Eric Sardinas, Tom Saviano, Clint Walsh, Dan Warner, Jeanette Olsson, Jason Paige, Keely Pressly, Camile Saviola, Maria Vidal, Diana Grasselli, Storm Lee, Becky Baeling, Andreas Carlsson, John Gregory.

Arrangements by: Randy Cantor, Doug Emery, Harry Sommerdahl, Chris Vrenna.

And props to all the other talented session musicians who were part of the team that helped create this Monster Masterpiece.

Dedicated in memory of Michael Lee Aday . . .

MEAT LOAF
(1947–2022)

*Day 1 recording of* Bat Out Of Hell III, *O'Henry Sound Studios, Burbank, California, 2005*

# PHOTOGRAPHY

I wish to acknowledge each photographer and provide the year of each photograph appearing in the book.

Cover—Stephen Danelian (1991)
Sleeve—Desmond Child Archives (1971)
Page *ii*—Ros Raia (1975)
Page *vi*—R. J. Capak (1992)
Page *x*—Curtis Shaw Child (2019). With Paul Stanley, Nashville Bridgestone Arena
Page 4—Curtis Shaw Child (2016)
Page 6—Andrew Melick (1998)
Page 12—Desmond Child Archives (1943)
Page 16—Desmond Child Archives (1955)
Page 19—Desmond Child Archives (1951)
Page 20—Desmond Child Archives (1954)
Page 22—Joe Marfy (1954)
Page 28—John Marfy (1954)
Page 29—John Marfy (1954)
Page 34—John Barrett (1955)
Page 43—Desmond Child Archives (1960)
Page 44—Desmond Child Archives (1961)
Page 55—Harry Paul (1994)
Page 56—Desmond Child Archives (1962)
Page 59—Desmond Child Archives (1961)
Page 60—Desmond Child Archives (1971)
Page 73—Desmond Child Archives (1958)
Page 74—Desmond Child Archives (1964)
Page 76—Desmond Child Archives (1964)
Page 77—Desmond Child Archives (1967)
Page 78—Ciro Barbaro (1976)
Page 80—Idaz Greenberg (1972)
Page 83—Desmond Child Archives (1986)
Page 84—Idaz Greenberg (1972)
Page 90—Elena Casals (1954)
Page 101—Charles Roberts (1972)
Page 102—Greg Gorman (1987)
Page 107—Desmond Child Archives (1979)
Page 109—Desmond Child Archives (1981)
Page 115—Desmond Child Archives (1976)

# PHOTOGRAPHY

Page 116—Ciro Barbaro (1978)
Page 123—Greg Heisler (1979)
Page 124—Ciro Barbaro (1978)
Page 125—Ciro Barbaro (1979)
Page 126—Greg Heisler (1979)
Page 131—Gene Bognato (1977)
Page 132—Ciro Barbaro (1977)
Page 133—Ciro Barbaro (1979/1978)
Page 134—Ciro Barbaro (1980)
Page 146—Desmond Child Archives (1982)
Page 147—Ciro Barbaro (1983)
Page 148—Bob Crewe Archives (1970)
Page 149—Ray Nugent (1996)
Page 150—Idaz Greenberg (1972)
Page 152—Benjamin (1970)
Page 161—Ciro Barbaro (1978)
Page 169—Obie O'Brien (1988)
Page 170—Top photo by Ciro Barbaro (1992);
    bottom photo by Curtis Shaw Child (2012)
Page 171—Curtis Shaw Child (2012)
Page 172—Curtis Shaw Child (1997)
Page 180—Desmond Child Archives (1991)
Page 181—Top photo by Desmond Child Archives (1990);
    bottom photo by Curtis Shaw Child (1996)
Page 182—Merzan/Marc Blake (1988)
Page 190—Desmond Child Archives (1988)
Page 191—George Hurrell (1989)
Page 192—Amy Womack Dodson (1990)
Page 194—Desmond Child Archives (1989)
Page 202—Kristen Dahline (1991)
Page 212—Michel Comte (1991)
Page 213—Desmond Child Archives (1991)
Page 214—Gary Gershoff (1992)
Page 225—Ciro Barbaro (1993)
Page 226—Stephen Danelian (1991)
Page 228—Michael Kolasa (1993)
Page 239—Salvador Ochoa (2018)
Page 240—Jill Kahn (1999)
Page 248—David Fields (1997)
Page 250—Curtis Shaw Child (1998)
Page 256—Jill Kahn (1999)
Page 261—David Fields (1997)
Page 262—Dee Nichols (2002)

# PHOTOGRAPHY

Page 279–Stefan Würth (2002)

Page 280–David Vance (2000)

Page 287–Curtis Shaw Child (1993)

Page 288–Top photo by Desmond Child Archives (2006); bottom photo by Curtis Shaw Child (2006)

Page 295–Jay Rustin (2006)

Page 296–Liam Carl (2007)

Page 302–Curtis Shaw Child (2005/2022)

Page 310–Desmond Child Archives (1986)

Page 311–Desmond Child Archives (1961)

Page 312–Desmond Child (1992)

Page 315–Desmond Child Archives (1944)

Page 316–Daniel D'Ottavio (2013)

Page 319–Daniel D'Ottavio (2013)

Page 320–Jay Landers (2018)

Page 334–Jay Landers (2018)

Page 335–Jay Landers (2018)

Page 336–Stephen Danelian (1991)

Page 343–Clay Perry (2022)

Page 344–Thomas Daskalakis (2022)

Page 345–Top photo by Andreas Nikolareas (2022); bottom photo by Noah Winters Morley (2022)

Page 346–Andreas Nikolareas (2022)

Page 347–Top photo by Andreas Nikolareas (2022); bottom photo by Curtis Shaw Child (2022)

Page 348–Desmond Child Archives (1943)

Page 353–Sculpture by Lee Burnham (1953)

Page 355–John Barrett (1954)

Page 356–Garrett Mills (2020)

Page 360–Nadine Joy (2018)

Page 367–Desmond Child Archives (2005)

Page 368–David Vance (2000)

Page 372–Desmond Child Archives (1979)

Page 374–John Parra/Getty Images (2022)

Page 376–Desmond Child Archives (1992)

Page 385–Desmond Child Archives (2021)

Page 386–George Hurrell (1989)

Page 388–Stefan Würth (2012)

Page 389–Desmond Child (2016)

Page 390–Ciro Barbaro (1992)

Back Sleeve–Garrett Mills (2019)

Back Cover–Stephen Danelian (1991)

371

*Desmond and Maria*

WITH PROFOUND GRATITUDE AND RESPECT,
*I want to sincerely thank all of my
songwriting soulmates, singers, musicians,
coproducers, and recording engineers
who helped me fill the pages of this book.*

*Latin Songwriters Hall of Fame LA MUSA Awards,*
*Hollywood, Florida, 2022*

For Desmond Child's full songwriting and
producing discographies, merchandise,
upcoming events and new releases, please visit:
**www.DesmondChild.com**
or scan the QR code below.

# INDEX

For clarity, locators within index entries that reference photographs are indicated with an italicized "*p*" following the page number.

*The Shaw Child family, Folegandros, Greece, 2021*

*Desmond Child portrait by George Hurrell, 1989*

# ABOUT THE AUTHOR

GRAMMY-WINNING AND EMMY-NOMINATED songwriter Desmond Child is one of music's most prolific and accomplished hitmakers. From Aerosmith to Zedd, his genre-defying collaborations include KISS, Bon Jovi, Cher, Barbra Streisand, Dolly Parton, Garth Brooks, Ricky Martin, Alice Cooper, Joan Jett, Michael Bolton, Katy Perry, Kelly Clarkson, Carrie Underwood, Cyndi Lauper, Christina Aguilera, Ava Max, Mickey Mouse, and Kermit the Frog, writing and producing more than eighty *Billboard* Top 40 singles, selling more than five hundred million records worldwide with downloads, YouTube views, and streaming plays in the billions.

Desmond Child was inducted into the Songwriters Hall of Fame in 2008 and serves on its board of directors, as well as the Board of ASCAP. In 2018, he received ASCAP's prestigious Founders Award celebrating forty years in the music industry. In 2012, he also cofounded the Latin Songwriters Hall of Fame, where he serves as chairman emeritus. In 2022, "Livin' La Vida Loca" was inducted into the National Archives of the Library of Congress for its global impact and cultural significance to America. In 2023, "Livin' On A Prayer" was certified to have reached one billion streams on Spotify.

*Clive presenting me with the Clive Davis Legend
in Songwriting Award, 2012*

# ABOUT THE COLLABORATOR

DAVID RITZ, cocomposer of "Sexual Healing," has collaborated on the life stories of, among others, Aretha Franklin, Ray Charles, Willie Nelson, Marvin Gaye, Janet Jackson, Lenny Kravitz, B. B. King, and Smokey Robinson.

*David Ritz, New York City, 2016*

"Blood on blood . . ."

*Desmond Child, Richie Sambora, and Jon Bon Jovi*